Human Rights and Private Wrongs

Other titles in the *Global Horizons* series, edited by Richard Falk, Lester Ruiz, and R.B.J. Walker

International Relations and the Problem of Difference
Naeem Inayatullah and David L. Blaney

Methods and Nations: Cultural Governance and the Indigenous Subject
Michael J. Shapiro

Bait and Switch: Human Rights and U.S. Foreign Policy
Julie A. Mertus

The Declining World Order: America's Imperial Geopolitics
Richard A. Falk

Human Rights and Private Wrongs
Constructing Global Civil Society

Alison Brysk

ROUTLEDGE
NEW YORK AND LONDON

Published in 2005 by
Routledge
270 Madison Avenue
New York, NY 10016
www.routledge-ny.com

Published in Great Britain by
Routledge
2 Park Square
Milton Park, Abingdon
Oxon OX14 4RN
www.routledge.co.uk

10 9 8 7 6 5 4 3 2 1

Library of Congress Cataloging-in-Publication Data

Brysk, Alison, 1960–
    Human rights and private wrongs : constructing global civil society/
Alison Brysk.
        p. cm.—(Global horizons)
Includes bibliographical references and index.
    ISBN 0-415-94476-7 (hb : alk. paper)—ISBN 0-415-94477-5 (pb : alk. paper)
    1. Human rights. 2. Globalization. 3. International agencies. 4. Civil society. I. Title. II. Series.
JC571.B756 2004
    323—dc22

                                                                    2004011027

*To Ana, who has taught me
boundless compassion and to think outside the box*

Contents

Preface   ix
Acknowledgments   xi

Chapter 1 Introduction: Globalization and Private Wrongs   1

Chapter 2 Norm Change in Global Civil Society   15

Chapter 3 Children Across Borders: New Subjects   29

Chapter 4 New Strategies: "Follow the Money"   61

Chapter 5 New Rights: "Our Bodies, Ourselves"   89

Chapter 6 Conclusion: Private Authority and Global
           Governance   117
Notes   129
References   133
Index   149

Preface

I wrote this book because I was puzzled and disturbed by daily reports of abuses that seemed to add up to a new genre I could not name or analyze. My first project on human rights reform in Argentina had acquainted me with the "classic" pattern of state-sponsored violations and (largely) national response, still all too common—but increasingly understood and theoretically manageable through the "international human rights regime." My subsequent work on indigenous peoples expanded my knowledge of global sources of both abuse and response, but the baseline for rights and reforms was still the national government, and a transnational version of the human rights repertoire still seemed to be (somewhat) effective.

By the turn of the millennium, globalization seemed to permeate every issue I researched, taught, or read about, and the human rights impact of globalization had become a focus of worldwide debate and protest. Seeking to map the contours of this tectonic shift, I called on the collective wisdom of colleagues, through a series of conferences that resulted in edited volumes. The issues that haunted me at these conferences, such as trafficking in children, seemed to affect the most vulnerable groups and clearly violated the victims, yet they were issues we could barely discuss with the scholarly, legal, and policy vocabulary of human rights developed to restrain states from abusing their citizens. My colleague Jack Donnelly adumbrated the agenda for this project at the January 2000 conference on Globalization and Human Rights; commenting on my persistent concern with accountability for nonstate actors, he said the question I kept asking was—"who ya gonna call?"

As I began to research this question, I felt like an epidemiologist trying to tease a pattern from widely scattered reports of similar symptoms from "primary care" activists, journalists, and case studies. I consulted the work of specialists in the well-known pathologies of repression, as well as more fundamental anatomies and physiologies of civil society and globalization, seeking to contribute to a deeper understanding of contemporary suffering.

Like the scholars of our era's medical plagues, I have found a mix of chronic infirmities and new pathogens, new routes of transmission for both, clusters of co-occurring maladies, and the promise of new treatments blunted by the emergence of conditions resistant to governance. And just as many analysts of public health problems come to advocate similar structural changes to ameliorate a wide spectrum of disorders, my study of global private wrongs suggests that a world order that supports human dignity at all levels will be mutually reinforcing.

The bad news is that poverty, repression, failed states, and distorted globalization all go along with private wrongs—and in many cases, progress on private wrongs will depend on difficult changes in these parameters. But the good news is that under more mixed conditions, changes in one area can support progress in others. For example, international programs to improve children's education can help struggling but willing states to decrease trafficking, improve family incomes and access to health services, and attract more constructive forms of foreign investment. Across the spectrum of private wrongs, greater monitoring of abuses, accountability for violators, and empowerment of victims can make a difference—and transnationalism can contribute positively to all of these aspects of change.

My research, teaching, study, and personal experience have taught me a template for personal and political change that frames the message of this study. Change begins with awareness. Awareness must be followed by compassion. But effective compassion must be matched by judgment. This book tries to supply awareness and analysis. The compassion of the reader can take the next step—turning knowledge into wisdom through action.

Acknowledgments

This study would not be possible without a wide range of intellectual, academic, personal, and even financial support. I am immensely grateful for the contributions of the following persons and institutions—they share in the project's merits and are absolved of its defects.

An earlier version of Chapter 2 was presented at the 2002 Conference on "Transnational Dynamics and the Emerging Architectures of Governance" hosted by the John Kennedy School of Government, Harvard University and benefited from the comments of participants. A prior draft of Chapter 3 appears in my volume coedited with Gershon Shafir, *People Out of Place* (Routledge 2004), and was stimulated to further development by the suggestions of my coeditor. Chapter 4, "Follow the Money," also appeared in an earlier incarnation as an eponymous Working Paper of the Global Peace and Conflict Center at the University of California, Irvine. Timely support for research on financial accountability was provided by the Global Peace and Conflict Center. "Our Bodies, Ourselves" was presented at the 2004 International Studies Association, Montreal, at a very useful panel on "Rights on the Rise: How and Why New Human Rights Issues Emerge"—discussions during and following helped to refine that chapter.

My understanding of the private wrongs chronicled in this book was constructed with the help of a series of research assistants at UC Irvine. Celine Jacquemin assembled prodigious resources on socially responsible investment. Tanaz Korami, Rebecca Griffin, Michael Struett, and Jaime Carrillo assisted with "Children Across Borders." At a deeper level, Professor Henry Greely of Stanford Law School very generously shared his time and research to improve my understanding of the complex field of genetic research.

Once the manuscript was completed, several colleagues contributed comprehensive, analytical readings and critiques. Sanjeev Khagram of Harvard University helped me to stay connected to the big picture of transnationalism as well as rooted in the real world of policy. My colleague Wayne

Sandholtz vastly improved the theoretical clarity and consistency of the book. Bill Maurer, also at UC Irvine, has been a generous ongoing source of education and supportive critic on questions of financial accountability, critical and postmodern theory, and social science reflexivity.

Routledge and the editors of the series have also helped to shape as well as host this book. Eric Nelson, the original editor, encouraged and guided the project from its inception. Richard Falk thoughtfully invited me to join the series' dialogue and set the agenda for our contributions, and Rob Walker provided useful critique from a different perspective. Julie Mertus (American University) went beyond a detailed and rigorous peer review to work with me directly to develop the manuscript and refine its message. Rob Tempio, Angela Chnapko, and the editing team have worked hard to bring it to fruition.

My husband, Mark Freeman, connected the dots of my disparate concerns to frame the subject of this book. My daughter Miriam has contributed through her patience with my absences, as well as her passionate advocacy for children's rights. I also wish to honor the influence of my uncle Peter Tauber, whose literary career was tragically cut short this year—our last conversation was about this book. Miriam asked the big question that underlies this study, "Isn't that the government's job?"

1

Introduction: Globalization and Private Wrongs

When abuse crosses borders, it does not always wear a uniform. From sweatshop smugglers to Swiss bankers, private actors are an increasingly influential source of human rights violations in a globalized world. At the various trials for the genocide of half a million Rwandans, the defendants included prominent members of "civil society": journalists, businessmen, and nuns—most with transnational ties and some later sheltered in exile communities in the United States and Europe (Simons 2002). As the judge at the United Nations (UN) tribunal stated to Rwandan journalists convicted of genocide, "Without a firearm, machete or any physical weapon, you caused the deaths of innocent civilians" (LaFraniere 2003). U.S. multinational corporations in Colombia—such as Drummond, Coca-Cola, and Occidental—are being sued for conspiring with local death squads to assassinate unionists (Forero 2003). Even official war is increasingly privatized—outsourced to private contractors and unaccountable security services (Forero 2004, Singer 2003), creating the specter of private war crimes.[1]

The human rights tradition, a necessary and continuing struggle to limit state repression, grapples with a world in which some violators cannot be picketed at the presidential palace or sanctioned by the UN. These newly visible abusers are more than simple criminals wielding brute coercion because they often exercise delegated authority through legitimate social institutions—such as families, businesses, religions, and professions. The dark side of the private power of civil society and its alternative to government authority is the ability to harm. And global civil society's private wrongs fall hardest on the world's most vulnerable populations, who

1

tend to lack full access to state citizenship, public protection, and even visibility: women, children, the poor, the sick, refugees, and victims of state terror.

How can human rights, established to limit state power, defend the individual from private but powerful social institutions? How does globalization change the politics of private authority? And what does this new kind of struggle for rights tell us about how norms and principles are crafted and gain influence?[2]

This book begins to map an emerging politics of human rights for private wrongs: how rights norms are constructed and adapted for new claimants, new targets, and new practices in global civil society. It chronicles one normative response to the global reach of private power, through expanding the human rights agenda. At the same time, this study shows how struggles over authority *in* global civil society contribute to new sectors and strategies *of* global civil society: new social movements, networks, and coalitions; expanded "international regimes" linking global institutions and transnational communities; enhanced repertoires of contention (such as transnational litigation). In the end, some of the responses to these norms help pave the way for global governance of private wrongs.

What do Swiss bankers, Romanian orphans, and Brazilian scientists have in common? All are participants in global struggles over the governance of transnational social institutions, whose policies affect the ability of millions to secure their fundamental rights. The issues profiled in this book are flash points on the human rights frontier: children's migration, financial social responsibility, and transnational medical markets. These are areas of pathbreaking debate that affect large numbers of people worldwide. Although these issue areas are not necessarily the sites of the worst violations, they are pilot cases that represent key patterns of globalization.

This book shows how these challenges have affected global governance in the areas of migration, finance, and health care. As children cross borders, nascent norms of children's rights disrupt the embedded authority of the family and make children visible as individual *persons*, legitimate claimants for human rights. This has begun to shift receiving states' policies toward increased receptivity for child refugees and increased regulation of transnational adoption. In parallel fashion, the *process* of international finance becomes a new target for human rights accountability. Transnational litigation of Holocaust-era financial intermediaries has resulted in significant settlements, while capital controls are turned on the ill-gotten gains of dictators. Socially responsible investment expands human rights conditionality from official aid to billions in private flows. In another realm, the conventionally neutral realm of science and medicine has been subject to *new normative claims*, responding to new practices in global health care. Patients with the acquired immunodeficiency syndrome (AIDS) and advocates demand life-saving access to privately controlled pharmaceutical research as a health right, and indigenous peoples assert privacy and cultural self-determination against the expansion of genetic mapping. As advances in organ transplants have created transnational trafficking, doctors struggle to define the rights of donors and recipients and their own responsibilities across borders.

As a result, international agendas and standards shift to incorporate principled boundaries to previously ungoverned activities. Children move from parental property and national patrimony to rights-bearing individuals. The opaque and anarchic activities of transnational finance are loosely bounded by an "invisible handcuff" of legal and market pressures that sanction profits visibly derived from gross abuses. Even the imperative to seek new knowledge and apply new technology freely and universally, one of the core norms of Western progress, is checked by human rights challenges that redefine the boundaries of the "body politic."

The struggle for human rights for global civil society thus provides an important lesson in how new norms are constructed and applied. First, victims of private authority and their advocates articulate new claims. Such claims must usually expand the human rights agenda in one of three ways: by identifying new bearers or subjects of existing rights, establishing new causal mechanisms for accountability, or proposing normative standards for some new practice or changing social condition. To articulate a new message, activists must use the recognizable grammar of norm change—introducing a new subject, new predicate/process, or new object. The constructivist analysis of the political process of communicative action applies readily to these campaigns against private as well as public wrongs, including similar dynamics of symbolic politics, information politics, leverage and legitimacy challenge, and institutionalization of new norms. Such analysis tells us that norm innovation will be relatively more effective if it builds on existing standards and frameworks—such as equal access for a new group to an established right. Similarly, new coalitions and strategies often supplement or transform long-standing organizations and activities. But human rights for global civil society carry a critical new content, questioning and sometimes reconstructing deeply embedded boundaries between public and private social arenas.

The construction and content of these norms have significant implications for the future of global governance. The story of private wrongs shows how liberal globalist visions have concealed important arenas of private power and conflict that must be addressed to secure universal rights. Furthermore, the process of constructing new norms reveals a shifting role for the globalized state, which is called upon to regulate and mediate among *transnational* private forces at the very moment when many states have lost the capacity or mandate to regulate domestic private forces. In this vacuum, the response of human rights networks and campaigns matters more than ever. Activists' ability to frame new subjects, identify new strategies, and articulate new rights that expand the core values of human dignity across public-private as well as national borders is the key to comprehensive, sustainable and ethical global governance.

Private Wrongs: Roots and Responses

In the search to overcome the horrors of the twentieth century, some defenders of human dignity have concluded that the problem is state power—and therefore the solution is civil society. States have certainly sponsored the most and bloodiest abuses; because governments hold the "monopoly of legitimate force" (Weber 1964), they maintain the ability to do the most damage. It is on this basis that states are the privileged subject of international law and human rights treaties, incurring ultimate responsibility for the protection of citizens. However, a narrow focus on government repression misses its civic underpinnings, as well as nongovernmental social abuses such as coercion by religious communities. Furthermore, private actors may cause serious harm for self-seeking motives. When such violations are committed sporadically by unorganized individuals, they are best understood as crime, but when private abuses are more systematic and institutional they must be seen as part of a social order.[3] Both local and global social orders must be evaluated for civil society's capacity to violate human rights and appropriate responses.

The Holocaust is ground zero for our understanding of human rights abuse, and the evolution of an international human rights regime catalyzed by the need to address the enormity of state terror (Ignatieff 2001). The Nazi regime also forms the template for totalitarianism—a system of total social control characterized by the systematic violation of human dignity on the basis of ideology and state domination of the private sphere (Arendt 1958). Yet the Nazi murder, torture, enslavement, and displacement of tens of millions were not simply Big Brother run amok. Private citizens, civic organizations, and entire social sectors collaborated actively in the genocide (Berman 1997, Goldhagen 1997). Moreover, the victims' neighbors, employers, doctors, banks, and other private persons in positions of trust and authority sometimes committed independent abuses.

There are precedents for each genre of private abuse profiled in this book in the Holocaust experience: migration, finance, and medicine. The Nuremberg trials revealed more than the machinery of state terror—they also showed the participation of businesses and physicians as pillars of persecution. German industrialists were convicted of using slave labor, looting assets of occupied countries, and manufacturing "weapons of mass destruction"—the Zyklon B gas used in the gas chambers of the concentration camps. Millions of prisoners and captured civilians from occupied countries were forced to work under horrendous and often deadly conditions; IG Farben's facility at Auschwitz alone enslaved an estimated 83,000 people. The United States indicted 43 German industrialists for war crimes and crimes against humanity. Alfred Krupp, who used slave labor to manufacture munitions for Hitler, was imprisoned for 12 years and subsequently paid $2.38 million in restitution to Jewish slave laborers. Karl Rasche, then chairman of Dresdner Bank, was convicted of plunder in acquiring Jewish and occupied country properties but acquitted of making loans for slave labor. On the other hand, corporate officers of IG Farben were convicted of both slave labor and looting. And Emil Puhl, who directed the German state bank program transferring stolen property to Switzerland, was sentenced to five years imprisonment by the international tribunal. These precedents in international law provide a foundation for historical and contemporary questions of business's social responsibility, from Swiss banks' acceptance of Nazi gold to shareholder campaigns against Unocal for use of slave labor in Burma (Ramasastry 1998, Borkin 1978, Dubois 1953).

In a further violation of civic trust, the perversion of medicine during the Holocaust was especially horrifying. Doctors played a special role in Nazi ideology because of the emphasis on "ethnic cleansing" and the practice of eugenics. About half of German doctors joined the Nazi party, and Nazi physicians selected victims for execution in hospitals, mental institutions, and concentration camps. In addition, a number of doctors engaged in atrocious medical experiments in the concentration camps, during which more than 100,000 inmates were killed. Many of the experiments themselves were torture, such as subjection to extremes of heat and cold, surgery without anesthesia, infection with deadly diseases, and removal of body parts. Prominent Nazi doctors were put on trial at Nuremberg—15 were convicted, and a universal code of medical ethics was drafted that was later widely referenced by international organizations (Lifton 1986, Nazi Medicine 1986). At least some of these crimes were inspired by private professional agendas as much as state ideology. One of the doctors convicted of atrocious experimentation had been on the faculty at Harvard Medical School (Claude 2002: 85). "Although we are not accustomed to thinking of the Nazi doctors in the mundane terms of careerism, part of their motivation was typical academic ambition. These scientists wanted to be among the first to make the medical breakthroughs that would advance the military goals of the Third Reich and make them heroes of racial medicine" ("The Dilemmas of Experimenting on People" 1997). Some Nazi doctors continued practicing after the war, and the Allies drew on the research results and sometimes the direct expertise of the broader spectrum of Nazi scientists.

Finally, the Holocaust adumbrated current patterns of global migration as it generated enormous numbers of refugees and eventually the international organizations that administer refugee flows. Deprived of nationality, security, family, property, livelihood, and often health and education, refugees disrupted national systems of citizenship and social authority. Among their number were 10,000 Jewish children sent alone into exile in

1939—the *Kindertransport*. Their plight was collateral damage from Nazi denial of emigration to their parents, with transnational adoption in Britain under a special humanitarian program that superceded wider denial of immigration rights to Jewish refugees by most of the Allied countries. Ninety percent of these children were orphaned by the Holocaust (Harris and Oppenheimer 2002, Fox and Abraham-Podietz 1998, Drucker 1992). The Kindertransport was one of the largest movements to date of children across borders, and the parallel situation of postwar orphans laid the foundations for contemporary transnational adoption.

International response to the Holocaust established key elements of the contemporary human rights regime: global standards through UN treaties, international legal accountability at the Nuremberg trials, monitoring commissions at all levels, and new understandings of transnational accountability for issues that transcend state sovereignty (Henkin 1999). It was these types of institutions that permitted the United Nations International Tribunal for Rwanda to convict the journalists cited previously of fomenting and directing genocide (LaFraniere 2003). Civic powers are increasingly subject to standards and strategies of accountability promoted by the international human rights regime. But the "first generation" of civil and political rights and their concomitant international institutions left much unfinished business in both theory and practice.

A generation later, international debate focused on a broader spectrum of economic and social rights and the connections among economic and political abuses (Felice 2002). Decolonizing developing nations and the socialist bloc introduced economic requisites of human dignity such as the right to food to the global agenda. Such rights were slow to institutionalize for a range of pragmatic and philosophical reasons. Social rights were too collective and positive to fit the emerging legal architecture, and they were politically tainted for the dominant West by association with socialism during the Cold War. Liberal welfare states did incorporate some social and economic rights in their citizenship package, but only within national membership—not as a universal entitlement. Globalization has had a contradictory effect on social and economic rights norms and their availability to respond to private wrongs. On the one hand, globalization has displaced citizens from the site of social rights and deflated citizenship and states' capacities to provide social entitlements. But globalization and the backlash it has generated have also advanced the normative recognition and theoretical accountability for social rights, by showing the social roots of security violations, and global determinants of local social conditions that some argue mandate universal standards —such as labor rights (Brysk and Shafir 2004). Very recently, there has been a partial convergence responding to globalization of rights claims by development movements, increasing recognition of social rights by mainstream human rights nongovernmental organizations (NGOs), new organizations that blend political and social rights agendas, and growing coalitions of human rights, development, and environmental groups (Dorsey and Nelson 2004).

Finally, contemporary human rights discourse has wrestled with collective rights. Collective and cultural rights may be necessary to counter challenges such as environmental devastation and defend identities such as indigenous peoples', in ways not contemplated by individual civil liberties or even state-sponsored social rights (Kiss 1993). Death and destruction by the degradation of a physical or social environment may be just as harmful as political persecution, and such threats may emanate from private actors as well as governments. Private violations of collective rights are at issue in many financial campaigns and some of the medical concerns discussed subsequently.

Alongside this normative evolution, an international human rights movement began to campaign across borders, using increasingly accessible information and media (Korey 1998). As with expanding norms of social rights, globalization fostered new forms of transnationalism that eventually facilitated a contemporary response to private wrongs. Along with the general globalization of information, human rights monitoring has been increased by the preparation of annual reports on countries and situations by dozens of NGOs, aid-giving governments, some regional organizations, UN treaty bodies, and some national human rights secretariats.

Several streams of human rights transnationalism have flowed into a widening—albeit increasingly muddy—river, carving canyons through world politics. The oldest tradition of humanitarian advocacy speaks for victims who cannot speak for themselves, such as slaves or children. This has been especially important for introducing new claimants who lack agency or recognition to the human rights agenda.

A second kind of internationalism unites people with elements of a common identity or function—coreligionists, for example, or women, or workers—around mutual defense by the members with sufficient resources and security to lobby their own states and international organizations. Groups as diverse as Holocaust survivors, Burmese exiles, and Christians seeking religious freedom have played parallel roles in demanding financial accountability through these types of organizations.

Direct mobilization by those affected by violations is increasingly possible in a globalized world, especially where private violations occur in a formally democratic regime. The participation of grassroots organizations of people with AIDS in South Africa and Thailand, for example, was an essential element in the relative success of the transnational campaign for access to essential medicines. Another growing form of internationalism consists of regional or sectoral coalitions of human rights organizations for victims/survivors.

There are also "transnational issue-networks" (Keck and Sikkink 1998) and more informal human rights partnerships between northern NGOs and grassroots groups. Such issue-networks responding to private wrongs are not necessarily composed of traditional human rights organizations and often combine labor, religious, and perhaps professional or environmental groups. Children's rights have evoked a particularly vigorous and flexible cluster of international organizations, NGOs, grassroots groups, and even parts of some states to promote the dignity and welfare of the young.

Lawyers founded the human rights movement, but they have now been joined by other professionals acting to project their estate's norms into the global arena, notably *Doctors Without Borders*. Such movements of professionals play an important role as internationally recognized expert gatekeepers in monitoring, research, certification of the status of groups and violations, as well as presentation of policy alternatives—from social investment metrics to pharmaceutical formulas. As we shall see, each of these genres of human rights activism has contributed to the ability to contest private wrongs.

Another important development has been the establishment of advocacy groups for almost every sector and sphere of human activity—and the adoption of a rights framework by many of these independent organizations. The Human Rights Watch rubric of monitoring for accountability has diffused to Corporate Watch, Sweatshop Watch, Organs Watch, Global Trade Watch, Judicial Watch, World Watch (environment), Women Watch (UN)—and even NGO Watch. Diverse sectors have mobilized against private as well as government abuses on the basis of *rights*: the Human Rights Campaign (gay and lesbian), Campaign for Disability Rights, and Campaign for Labor Rights are examples of mobilizations formerly based on identity, compassion, or equality that now draw on rights rubrics. Even organizations assisting children—which were conventionally the most apolitical and humanitarian—have been supplemented or transformed into a worldwide network of children's rights activists, mobilized around the UN's most widely subscribed treaty. All of this means that when private abuses occur, they are more likely to be noticed, publicized, and linked to a human rights campaign with global reach.

Private Wrongs: Branches

Private wrongs have taken new shape in a globalized, liberal world order. Sometimes private actors violate rights in partnership with dictatorships or even "illiberal democracies" (Zakaria 2003). Doctors participate in torture in jails, or multinationals draw on forced labor extracted by the state. In some cases, states may even "outsource" violations to private actors to evade nascent accountability for abuse (Gordon 2003). Other violations reflect local and global power vacuums: neighborhood lynchings in urban shantytowns, trafficking of migrants, or warlord/guerrilla/terrorist domination of "failed states" or ungoverned regions.

But many violations are the unregulated behavior of legitimate social institutions authorized by the state to exercise power within their domain.

Throughout the Americas and Europe, pedophile priests raped children and were protected by the institutional autonomy and transnational domain of the Catholic Church (Goodstein 2002). Corporate sweatshops, or women imprisoned by family or religious "customary law," violate human rights but do not violate the social order. They are part of a social contract hitherto hidden and unbounded, which has become the site of struggle for this generation (Jochnik 1999). In a recent issue of Amnesty International's magazine, three of the six featured articles concerned private wrongs: community ethnic riots, experimental drug trials by multinationals, and "honor killings" of women by their own families (Amnesty International 2003).

The Universal Declaration of Human Rights not only is addressed to "all peoples and all nations" but also states that "all individuals and every organ of society, keeping this Declaration in mind, shall strive . . . to secure their universal and effective recognition and observance. . . ." The core documents of the International Bill of Human Rights—the Universal Declaration plus the International Covenants of Civil and Political and Economic and Social Rights—recognize a number of rights that may be violated by private actors with delegated power. Families or religious authorities may contravene freedom of movement, the right to marry, freedoms of religion and expression, privacy, adequate food, housing, and medical care—and may even participate in slavery, inhumane punishment, or murder of their members. Businesses may also violate liberty, adequate living conditions, freedoms of expression and assembly, the right to rest, and nondiscrimination. Licensed professionals such as physicians may have a particular impact on privacy, the right to health care and social services, education, and the right to "recognition before the law." The UN 1993 Vienna Conference on Human Rights affirmed a broad post–Cold War consensus that these rights are "universal, indivisible, and interdependent." More specific international accords on the rights of women (Convention on the Elimination of All Forms of Discrimination Against Women [CEDAW]), children (Rights of the Child Convention), labor (International Labor Organization [ILO] Conventions), and indigenous peoples (Declaration on the Rights of Indigenous Peoples) discuss a range of such rights located in the home, workplace, and other private sphere activities.

Human rights organizations first approached private abuse through violations of international humanitarian law by armed opposition groups (Rodley 1993). The major human rights groups and emerging international law now hold nongovernmental insurgents fully responsible for respecting human rights and laws of war in their areas and operations, regardless of their legal status (Schabas 2003). Private sector accountability also began to expand through campaigns for vulnerable groups. In addition to country reports, Human Rights Watch has divisions on Women's Rights and Children's Rights—and both have grappled with nongovernmental issues of trafficking, labor exploitation, and domestic violence, in addition to state-sponsored repression and discrimination. Amnesty International also has a Women's Human Rights Program, which has published reports on private abuses including "Domestic violence as torture," "Economic, social, and cultural rights," and "Female genital mutilation" (Amnesty International, *InterACT*). The human rights regime has grown to encompass recognition of a variety of private threats to human dignity—from guerrilla abuses to domestic violence to transnational business practices (Symonides 1998, Steiner and Alston 1986: 945–961).

Private Wrongs in Global Perspective

The issues I discuss in this book have unique characteristics, but each is representative of one of the main arenas and sources of private wrongs in an era of globalization. Migration may be the single greatest behavioral risk factor for human rights abuse in the contemporary world. Detached from the potential protections of family, community, and citizenship, migrants are subject to violations by traffickers, employers, host country governments, and host country societies. Immigrants may also have been pushed across borders by repressive states, exploitive families, or neglectful communities. Traffickers and bosses may be neighbors, kin, or coethnics. Host governments' detention, deportation, and mistreatment of refugees compound the home government persecution that impelled their flight. When Chinese voyagers to the United States suffocate in shipping containers, Haitians die in Dominican cane fields, or Burmese girls are infected with AIDS in Thai brothels, states, families, and commercial enterprises are all at fault (Kyle and Koslowski 2001).

Children's migration highlights two additional broader phenomena: the problematic role of the family as source of both protection and abuse and the addition of new groups as subjects of international norms. The family's ambivalent role is even more apparent in a series of internationally contested issues related to women's rights: female infanticide, forced marriage, genital mutilation, and "honor killing." These abuses are often enacted on girl children, so they may also be children's rights issues.[4] In addition, family functions have now been transnationalized, with women from poor countries providing domestic, reproductive, and sexual services to northern families. Unregulated domestic labor overseas, transnational adoption, sex trafficking, and sex tourism often violate the rights and dignity of the world's surrogate "wives" (Anderson 2000, Bertone 2000, Pyne 1995).

But—at least in theory—children are now special subjects of human rights protection, like women, the disabled, indigenous peoples, and members of ethnic minorities. The children of the *kindertransport* were sent "into the arms of strangers" as an act of charity; the custody of Elian Gonzalez was played out in the courts. The international system sets standards for the rights and needs of groups previously embedded in social authority systems. International law grants married women an independent right to nationality, and indigenous peoples can appeal to international human rights courts for the preservation of culture and language (Spiro 2004, Anaya 1996). Not only are new groups included under the human rights umbrella, recognized as legal individuals, but some groups are assigned special rights deemed appropriate to their unique identity or condition. And these are the very groups most subject to private wrongs in practice.

Beyond migration, global markets have the capacity to violate human rights in a wide variety of ways, and the commodification of all types of global flows generally poses new threats to the rights of their participants. Although Chapter 3 concentrates on finance, global business commits private wrongs as a producer, seller, and source of capital. The most widely publicized type of abuse is exploitative production by multinational enterprises (or for export markets, as local capitalists try to squeeze local labor for competitive advantage in trade). Sweatshops in Asia and Latin America usually combine abusive labor conditions, harmful health and safety practices, denial of the rights to assemble and organize, breach of privacy, and often discrimination against women or ethnically distinct workers (Fung, O'Rourke, and Sabel 2001). Multinationals may also collude with repressive governments to repress labor disputes, as in Colombia or Nigeria—where Shell was condemned for complicity in the death of Ogoni community activist Ken Saro-wiwa. A classic case has been revealed in a lawsuit against Ford by an Argentine survivor of state terror who was marked for "disappearance" by his employer because of his union activities (Rohter 2002). Coerced or bonded labor is often tantamount to modern slavery, usually private but often state tolerated, occasionally state sponsored, and often producing for global markets.[5]

Another aspect of business' impact on rights is responsibility for the products and services provided. Business may be culpable for providing or promoting unsafe products, or unsafe uses, such as when Nestle's marketed infant formula in the Third World under unsafe conditions and was subject to a worldwide boycott (Sikkink 1986). Discrimination in marketing may also violate rights: Bayer knowingly marketed the human immunodeficiency virus (HIV)-contaminated blood serum to Asian hemophiliacs during the mid-1980s, reserving the newly developed heat-treated version for more profitable Western markets (Bogdanich and Koli 2003). Producers may be accountable for providing tools of repression; Amnesty International issued a report on American companies that export torture machinery (Amnesty International 1997).

As a source of capital, business may be complicit in human rights abuses. Banks, private and public investors, and international lending institutions have the power to finance or sanction repressive governments. Withdrawal of international capital, as in South African divestment, can prove a powerful lever for improving human rights (Klotz 1995). Private actors may also be liable if they finance unsafe, unfair, or violent activities. The campaign against "conflict diamonds" asked private companies to refrain from providing local diamond exporters in conflict-ridden African countries with the funding for weapons purchases (Tamm 2002). Finally, financial actors may launder or shelter the ill-gotten gains of dictators, murderers, and torturers. This is discussed in detail in Chapter 3.

The subsequent chapter's discussion of human rights and global health is situated in a larger, emerging field of the social responsibility of the professions as they cross borders. Should journalists be required to testify before international human rights tribunals or will it impede their professional function, with its implied higher purpose in promoting human rights monitoring? How do jurists from diverse legal backgrounds shape standards and procedures for accountability as they design those tribunals as well as national exercises in post-transition justice? Can aid workers remain neutral in conflict situations—and what should they do when their neutral role is breached or exploited?

Medicine and scientific research face specific obligations and challenges. The globalization of medical research has contributed to discrimination in health care and even denial of health rights. Risky drugs that would not be certified for use at home are tested in the developing world, and known treatments are denied to maintain the double-blind placebo structure (several African AIDS studies are reviewed in Farmer 2003: 197–199). At the same time, there is a dearth of research on the tropical diseases and malnutrition that cause most of the world's suffering, in favor of diseases of development such as obesity and cosmetic conditions. The commercialization of medicine leaves health resources increasingly at the mercy of market forces. ". . . [I]nequalities of access and outcome constitute the chief drama of modern medicine. In an increasingly interconnected world, inequalities are both local and global. . . ." (Farmer 2003: 164). The export of Western medicine and health technology can also create dependencies and foster discrimination (Mann et al. 1999). Indiscriminate promotion of antibiotics in the developing world has contributed to the evolution of resistant strains and diminished natural resistance. The diffusion of ultrasound technology for detection of fetal abnormalities and growth patterns has facilitated the practice of sex-selective abortion, especially in India. The struggle for AIDS pharmaceuticals, dilemmas of organ trafficking, and resistance to genetic mapping are markers in this wider field of medical modernization and its discontents.

Struggle at the Human Rights Horizon

This book documents and analyzes a set of human rights campaigns against global private wrongs. As an analysis of public claims and constructions, this study takes the form of a report synthesizing secondary material. Its goals are to document problematic practices, public challenges to those practices, and policy responses—without attempting a primary investigation of the motives or consciousness of claimants, decision makers, or global publics. Similarly, the mode of analysis is a middle-range attempt to aid in the diagnosis of the global condition and assess strategies for its amelioration. Such analysis can contribute to our understanding of the nature and dynamics of civil society, social norms, and human rights—but it cannot provide a grand theory of globalization or constructivism or definitive proof of any universal principle.

The next chapter provides a theoretical framework for norm change, through an extension of constructivist analysis of principled politics to the public-private divide. It also defines key terms of inquiry, such as civil society and human rights.

The following three chapters each consider a site of struggle over issues emerging as a human rights concern.

Chapter	Form of Globalization	Source of Authority	Type of Rights	Norm Change
2	migration	family state	children	new claimants
3	finance	business	accountability	new strategies
4	medicine	professions	health-access, privacy, self-determination	new boundaries

The chapter on children's migration shows how families and businesses push and pull children across borders; their presence is then adjudicated by states. In this process, children are increasingly constructed as new claimants: subjects of law and human rights standards.

"Follow the Money" explains how finance joins production as a field for claims of business responsibility for human rights conditions. Transnational litigation seeks retrospective accountability for both financial complicity and victims' property rights, and socially responsible investment constrains funding of both state and corporate abuse. Campaigns for financial accountability also contribute to a broader spectrum of human rights strategies—including litigation, investment, and state sanctions—to influence the full range of public and private abuses.

A set of global medical issues considered in Chapter 5 remaps the boundaries of rights. In some cases, health issues draw on new meanings for existing rights such as access to health care, whereas in others, health struggles actually introduce new claims in response to changing conditions. The collision of an unprecedented epidemic, rapid development of new tools to combat it, and the global corporate power of pharmaceutical manufacturers is seen in the struggle over AIDS treatment, which results in a new definition of the right to health access. Similarly, debates over organ trafficking develop new understandings of bodily integrity and economic coercion in medical decision making. The new research field of genetic mapping evokes old concerns about privacy—and new constructions of group rights.

Finally, the concluding chapter analyzes the cumulative change in global consciousness and global governance produced by these campaigns. The final chapter offers policy recommendations to enhance public control of private wrongs. And it briefly considers likely trends for the future.

2

Norm Change in Global Civil Society

The human rights horizon of private wrongs is at the edge of our vision. But principled politics operates across the spectrum, in ways that are both similar to and different from the twentieth-century model of the politics of human rights. The struggle against private wrongs draws on familiar elements of symbolic politics, transnational networks, and universal norms. Yet campaigns to limit private authority must also construct new rights and discover new wrongs, seeking state regulation and global civic control of areas previously labeled as apolitical. In this deepest form of political challenge, states—which may be thin, conflicted, or even repressive—ironically stand as the last best hope of civil society.

The Private Is Political: Civil Society and Nonstate Authority

Politics is the exercise of power—coercion, authority, allocation, and persuasion—among groups and individuals. The notion of civil society captures the idea that some set of institutions or relations outside the government structure also engage in politics. Civil society may consist of tribes or political parties, bird-watching societies or family businesses, universities or mosques, when and if they attempt to exercise power and political influence (Cohen and Arato 1992, Diamond 1999). Civil society is political but not authoritatively violent, in the sense of exercising a legitimate monopoly of force. It is civil in that it serves some social purpose, and the use of violence is not the primary purpose of association. Although many sectors and projects of civil society eschew or contest profit, market actors are not excluded from civil society when they pursue some purpose or program with political implications. The politics of civil society are deeply shaped by profit-making enterprises ranging from peasant craft cooperatives to pharmaceutical companies.

The term "global civil society" denotes patterns of political behavior by private actors across borders. One theorist defines global civil society broadly as "a dynamic nongovernmental system of interconnected socioeconomic institutions that straddle the whole earth" and demarcates this dynamic ensemble of activities as nongovernmental patterns of social interaction, nonviolent yet pluralistically conflictual, and stretched unevenly yet extensively across geographic boundaries. Keane also distinguishes between global civil society as an empirical description and global civil society as a normative project (Keane 2003: 8–17). Drawing on this conceptualization (without necessarily following all of its author's conclusions), my analysis does not assume that global civil society consists of transnational social movements, networks, or NGOs or that they pursue progressive or democratizing goals. Global civil society is simply an increasingly active and salient sector of global politics, whose effects in particular times, places, and issues are revealed by research (Tarrow 2001).

The political functions of civil society at both local and global levels may include authoritative *control* of the assets, behavior, and identity of individuals; education and *mobilization* for collective action; and direct attempts to *influence* the policies of states and international organizations. Thus, civil society can be both a source and a target of political action, as well as an interlocutor between state and citizen (Brysk 2000b). "Struggles over the public interest are not between civil society on the one hand and bad guys on the other but within civil society itself"(Carothers 1999–2000: 21).

When civil society crosses borders, its reach is extended and its potential is magnified. Citizen groups and international campaigns may mobilize quite effectively to influence global and national policies, as *agents* of global civil society—and often bearers of the normative political project of transnationalism. Meanwhile, global civil society is also an increasingly important *arena* of global politics, as transnational corporations, religious groups, and knowledge processors exercise growing authority and become the targets of local and global political action (Lipschutz 1992; Smith, Chatfield, and Pagnucco 1997; Florini 2000). The neoliberal privatization associated with globalization intensifies the latter dynamic of global civil society as arena, as international authority is delegated by states and international organizations to private actors (Sassen 1998). The main forms of transnational private authority are market authority (both institutional and normative) and moral authority based in expertise, neutrality, or normative claims (Biersteker and Hall 2002). In an era of globalization, private wrongs continue—with, below, and despite the state. Some private abuses have transnational sources, some are contested by transnational collective action, and some have transnational outcomes (Tarrow 2002).

When civil society itself is the problem, it may seek to undermine human rights and even to subvert democratic regimes (Armony 2001,

Berman 1997, Foley and Edwards 1996). We may further distinguish the range of roles civil society may play as a source of human rights abuse through analyzing the relationship between private authority and the state (Brysk 2000a). First, civil society may serve as a *handmaiden of state repression*: from Nazi doctors conducting medical experiments to Chinese physicians removing organs from political prisoners. Next, seemingly neutral private parties may *facilitate state abuse*. Swiss banks have sheltered the ill-gotten gains of concentration camps and African dictators, enabling the plunder of prisoners and national patrimony. When abuse emanates directly from the private actor, it may be through the exercise of *delegated authority*. Governments empower multinationals to administer extraction projects or export zones abusively or allow churches to run education and social service systems unaccountably. Finally, inadequately governed private parties may engage in truly *autonomous abuse*—political in its consequences and remedies but not its origins. Here we see child traffickers or pharmaceutical companies, acting for private profit to deny vulnerable citizens their liberty, dignity, or survival, without recourse to state protection. Overall, globalization has probably increased the potential and impact of private wrongs via delegated authority and autonomous abuse.

International law and standards for private accountability have tended to mirror the liberal NGO model, which assumes neutrality and voluntarism and seeks to shelter rather than regulate civic actors (Kingsbury 2002). But international human rights treaties and jurisprudence increasingly recognize private power and corresponding accountability for fundamental rights (Weissbrodt 2002). Furthermore, even the least recognized authorities—NGOs—face increasing scrutiny and assessment from a variety of sources and motives: from pressures for greater transparency, to projects monitoring impact, to direct partisan contests for political influence. A self-reflective project for greater accountability is the British government–backed www.oneworldtrust.org, and a political critique of the perceived growing power of NGOs is the American Enterprise Institute's www.ngowatch.org.

Potential governance of global civil society comes from two sources: the state and global civil society itself. In scenarios of abuse by global civil society, the role of the state ranges from repressor to referee. In the latter role, the state may become the most important source of protection for civil society against abusive private authority, just as it was domestically for advanced liberal societies during the phase of industrialization. Although globalization has created new international institutions and avenues of appeal for human rights violations, the globalized state has assumed a contradictory role in protecting citizens from abuse. States have taken on new issue-areas and adopted new human rights standards, but at the same time globalized states have sometimes delegated authority without accountability to both domestic and transnational private parties (Sassen 1996, Brysk 2002).

Another source of remedy lies within global civil society, which may be uniquely equipped to challenge private wrongs as a growing transnational *agent* of human rights claims. As one of its analysts defines the democratizing potential of global civil society, "For among the most promising features of global civil society is its self-spun traditions of civilizing politics—its actors' capacity to nurture networks of publicly organized campaigns against the archipelagos of incivility existing within and beyond its frontiers. . . . The vision of a global civil society is presented as a challenge to the normative silence or confusion within much of the contemporary literature on globalization and global governance. . . . Can this society perhaps help to redefine the *universal* entitlements and duties of the peoples of the world, across borders?" (Keane 2003: 153, xi–xiii).

To advance our understanding of how global civil society is constructed as both agent and arena, we must examine theoretical perspectives on power beyond the state. Several traditions of political theory elucidate the political roles of civil society and suggest responses to its abuse, although each approach focuses predominantly on one type of civic agent and its associated dynamics.

Feminist theory is grounded in the insight that a range of social relations previously viewed as private cultural practices constitute a political struggle for the control of women's production and reproduction. Although state and legal barriers to public equality are an important and obvious aspect of this struggle, feminist scholarship and political action have also targeted numerous forms of private authority: from domestic violence to religious control of reproductive rights. As Ann Tickner points out, "Importantly for feminists, gender is an analytical tool rather than merely a descriptive category . . . gendering is a mechanism for distributing social benefits and costs" (Tickner 2001: 134).

The feminist insight that gender is used as a strategy of authority encourages attention to the political construction of all forms of biological difference and the broader delegation of private authority to the family. This insight is critical under conditions of globalization, when the "natural" family unit of authority is displaced, stretched, splintered, and contested across state boundaries and jurisdictions (Enloe 1989, Pettman 1996).

But even beyond analyses of the condition of women, struggles over reproduction, and the shifting nature of the family, feminism offers a broader critique: "the personal is political." In this sense, feminist analysis initiates an unparalleled comprehensive examination of private authority and the politics of civil society across all issue-areas. Part of political power is the ability to define the public and private, and part of resistance is thus the questioning or reconstruction of that boundary (Elshtain 1981, Hartsock 1983).

A second approach, which has analyzed the private power of business and markets, is international political economy. In this approach, private profit-making actors control citizens' lives and distort public decision making in a variety of ways. Most directly, private firms may unaccountably control the resources and behavior of workers, host communities, and perhaps consumers. In a more structural way, private economic interests may shape the broader rules and roles of governance—regardless of whether they influence a particular decision. Finally, market actors may dominate political life through shaping knowledge and consciousness of what is possible and desirable (a somewhat Gramscian approach). Market logic may penetrate distinct domains of social relations, particularly the commodification of persons, activities, and products associated with identity (Cox 1996; Cutler, Haufler, and Porter 1999; Murphy 1994; Radin 1996). Each of these modes of private power is extended by globalization; the diffusion of multinational production and investment, the growing influence of multilateral economic institutions, and the increasing convergence of economic norms and practices such as privatization of state services. Rather than the conventional view of globalization as *deregulation* of the global economy, it may be more accurate to analyze the *shift* in the domain of regulation from the public and national to the private and transnational: including interstate organizations, transnational treaties, activist campaigns, and market-based codes (Lipschutz and Fogel 2002).

One branch of international political economy goes so far as to criticize the existence and usefulness of global civil society as a descriptor and source of resistance to economic globalization. According to this view, globalization is fundamentally an unregulated growth of the power of capital, best contested through national movements supplemented by traditional labor internationalism. "Global social movements cannot be the main vehicles for the achievement of human rights, the rule of law, peace, reclaiming the commons, and social justice" (Laxer and Halperin 2003: 15). This critical perspective tends to collapse transnational networks into local nodes, disembed markets from their social context, and reify labor (for related criticism, see Keane 2003).

Finally, several theoretical perspectives highlight the hidden power of expertise in shaping daily life and governing the allocation of resources. Sociological institutionalism documents the global diffusion of norms and institutions of scientific production (Finnemore 1996, Meyer et al. 1997, Boli and Thomas 1999). Thus, Western medicine exercises power through transnational professional networks that establish international organizations, homologous state institutions and policies, and norms of modernity. A more limited focus on the transnational networks of "epistemic communities" analyzes their ability to shape ongoing patterns of policy interaction via "international regimes"—loose patterns of regulation and expectation specific to an issue, combining state, international, and private authority (Haas 1992). In this sense, health professional organizations and designated experts would influence the pattern of policy and implementation toward a particular issue such as AIDS.

Postmodern perspectives offer a more pessimistic view of the private politics of expertise, particularly medical authority. In this reading, micropower penetrates daily life through the construction of conscious-ness and practices that redefine identities—all the stronger for their covert nature. Private authority forms an integral part of a complex of "govern-mentality" through professions, technologies, and languages of the mod-ern liberal subject (Foucault 1970). Nikolas Rose's extension of Foucault's approach shows how genealogies can diagnose the modern telos as a prob-lematic notion of freedom, enacting multiple forms of domination and discipline in the name of freedom—many via a constructed private realm. Yet Rose also points out that the norms and subjectivities of expertise can become a liberating norm from below (Rose 1999).

These perspectives offer varying levels of purchase on the genres of pri-vate authority investigated in this study. The struggle for children's rights would appear as a mere extension of liberal subjectivity to privatized objects—a petty boundary adjustment with no implications for sover-eignty. Similarly, financial accountability would register as an expansion of technologies of surveillance and norms of management for "good gover-nance" to financial flows. However, some of the contestations of health practices depicted here that are not yet social movements with policy pro-posals may be usefully understood as subversive remappings of "regimes of truth" and body politics, setting aside the "freedom" to sell one's genes and organs to assert deeper questions about knowledge, power, and boundaries.

Both critical theory and postmodern perspectives also caution us that agents of global civil society may participate unwittingly in the construc-tion of hegemony through their production of information and delegated authority as analysts. For example, grassroots women's movement activists may exhaust their representative function in producing information for the global arena (Riles 2000). Civil society may serve as a politically ambiguous gatekeeper; the Bush administration's Millennium Challenge Account foreign aid competition has designated NGOs such as Transpar-ency International the delegated analysts of states' qualifications for sup-port (Marquis 2004). Even projects such as this book help to shape global understandings of the nature and legitimacy of global civil society. Global civil society may still be a useful ground from which to contest globaliza-tion, and rights may be the best tools currently available to defend human worth, but critical perspectives can remind us that both concepts derive from the same governmentality—and are thus subject to the unintended consequences of participation in power.[1]

How can we synthesize these approaches to the politics of private authority? All agree that civil society exercises significant power, that part of its power derives from the concealment of its political role, and that pri-vate power depends on delegation and regulation by public authority. Whereas feminism and postmodern perspectives focus most on the consti-tutive and consciousness effects of private actors, political economy and sociological institutionalism look to private struggles for influence within states and international organizations. Each of these approaches does envisage change in private authority through the construction of new norms and institutions. The constructivist approach to globalization can be fruitfully combined with a critical theory perspective on civil society, to suggest that global civil society simultaneously constitutes and contests the hegemony of globalization. This means that global civil society can serve as a source of counterhegemony to both sovereignty and globalized private authority (Wapner 2000), but we must understand the source and limits of its legitimacy and leverage.

Constructing Norms, Expanding Rights

To reshape the exercise of private authority, activists must construct new norms that expand our understanding of rights and responsibilities. They must build new networks and coalitions across state and issue boundaries. Then, campaigns against private wrongs enter the familiar mechanisms of principled politics: agenda transformation, mobilization, influence, and institutionalization (also see Keck and Sikkink 1998).

In 2002, when a Pakistani woman was gang-raped by order of a tribal council—as punishment for a relative's alleged transgression—it was widely condemned as a human rights violation ("A Rape Victim in Pakistan," *New York Times*, September 2, 2002). Yet a decade before, multiple elements of private authority would not have been recognized. The classification of rape as a war crime in the International Criminal Court marks the culmination of a multifaceted international campaign identifying sexual violence as a political problem (Bedont and Martinez 1999, Keck and Sikkink 1998, McHenry 2002). The formal and informal judicial role of tribal, ethnic, and religious bodies has been increasingly subjected to universal standards, despite ongoing debates regarding self-determination of local groups (Stavenhagen 1996). The ancient principle of collective responsibility for crime by family members is largely considered illegitimate by national and international law, now imbued with modernist individualism. Although such heinous violations still occur, global consciousness of new human rights norms, international media coverage, and resulting pressure on the Pakistani state were strong enough to garner an investigation of both this case and this larger pattern of practice, as well as assistance to the victim.

How do the norms that both construct and castigate private violations emerge and change? Norms are widespread social values that define identities, roles, and forms of social interaction—norms create "social facts." Who counts as human? What is the function of government? These constitutive values and principles, in turn, instruct individuals and institutions on the appropriate behavior for an X in situation Y. For example, widely accepted international norms of sovereignty specify that governments must respect the authority of other legitimate state authorities within their territories. Norms of the medical profession stipulate that doctors should seek to preserve the life of the patient above all other goals, claims, and identities. As in the preceding example, norms also guide action in inevitable situations of ambiguity or conflict by providing road maps or focal points for decision making. Norms do not cause or guarantee any specific course of action; they simply provide legitimate rationales, rights, and responsibilities. These deep values about identities and rules will be referenced by most social actors, usually respected by many members of a society, and honored by some even when norms conflict with material interests (Ruggie 1998, Katzenstein 1996, Finnemore 1996, Goldstein and Keohane 1993, Hechter and Opp 2001).

The process of introducing or transforming a norm is a politics of persuasion, rooted in a dynamic of communicative action (Risse 2000, Price 1998, Nadelmann 1990, Klotz 1995). New norms must identify a problem, attribute causality for the problem, and politicize the problem by showing that it is public and amenable to governance (Brysk 1994). Finnemore and Sikkink argue that this process unfolds in stages of norm emergence, a "tipping point" of acceptance by a critical mass of relevant actors, a subsequent "norm cascade," and eventual institutionalization and internalization. Because private human rights are just emerging as an international norm, this general stage model predicts that the most important factors in introducing new norms will be domestic politics, norm entrepreneurs, and transnational networks. The few issues that may have reached a norms cascade—children's rights and financial reparations—should be analyzed in terms of international and state concerns with legitimacy and imitation, according to this account (Finnemore and Sikkink 1998).

A final aspect of norm change is understanding what types of emerging norms have a better chance of persuading and being accepted. A wave of studies of international norm transformation has identified diverse elements that seem to lead to success. New norms are more quickly and widely accepted when they: resonate with core principles of modernity such as equality and progress (Boli and Thomas 1999), appeal for physical protection of vulnerable groups (Keck and Sikkink 1998), develop naturally from preexisting principles (Snow and Benford 1988), follow a catalyzing historical event (Finnemore and Sikkink 1998), and are articulated by transformational leaders—individuals or groups possessing "moral capital" (Kane 2001). A number of these elements are clearly visible in the areas of struggle for private rights discussed subsequently, such as the appeal of vulnerable children and patients, and financial accountability focused on the catalyzing event of the Holocaust.

The primary preexisting norm in this area is human rights. What do we mean by the specific norm of human rights, and how can this definition expand to cover abuses by private authority? Human rights is a universal principle affirming the inalienable dignity and equality of persons, which limits legitimate forms of coercion and deprivation that may be used in the exercise of authority. Human rights may be conceived as a set of entitlements to the social prerequisites to human development: protection, security, freedom, and community. The norms of human rights are now considered a fundamental characteristic of the modern world order, a theoretical standard of legitimacy for governments, and a universal attribute of the individual (Schmitz and Sikkink 2002, Falk 2001).

Although the core values of human rights are inalienable and indivisible, specific forms of entitlement are evolving social constructions that originate in response to specific historical forms of oppression (Winston 2000: 15). New or newly visible rights are added to the validated canon through a process of "moral induction"—observation of a wrong, construction of a norm, mobilization of consensus, legalization, and subsequent application of the new principle to new cases (Winston 2000: 20). Although the historical focus of human rights has been to limit state power, the fundamental principles apply equally to any form of authority. Human rights theorists affirm that the duties implied by human rights "may be ascribed to various different agents, e.g., governments, individuals, or in some cases, non-governmental organizations such as private agencies or corporations, and may include duties to prevent deprivations of G as well as duties to provide access to G to the right holders" (Winston 2000: 5).

Human rights is a frame for collective action; a rationale that inspires mobilization. In general, it is easier to encompass new issues by amplifying an existing frame or bridging among several existing rubrics (Snow and Benford 1988). Private wrongs fit some aspects of the human rights frame easily but conflict with others. The human rights advocacy tradition draws on three historic modes of thought that justify rights, identify wrongs, and mobilize networks: Christian universalist altruism, Enlightenment humanist principles of freedom, and socialist struggles for justice (Passy 2001: 8). Private abuses readily evoke humanitarianism and justice norms, but only some private wrongs represent a denial of freedom—which is the heart and strength of the wider international human rights regime. For children's rights, the protection and security rationale is strong and can often be linked to illegitimate coercion; even deprivation is more widely recognized for children. Conflicts of human rights concepts occur to different degrees with individualism, equality, and freedom of children. The norms underlying business relations are almost exactly the opposite. Individualism and freedom are core values of the domain, but it is difficult to establish a case for protection and to classify economic activity as coercion. In addition, deprivation and equality are the most contested and relative of human rights values. Medicine presents a murky blend of principles; protection of individuals from coercion is fairly widely accepted, but situations of deprivation, equality, and diffuse accountability mirror the normative struggles over the social responsibility of business.

Emerging claims of new rights in the private sphere must also grapple with internal contradictions within the human rights frame. Equality and universality of private rights may conflict with collective rights of self-determination—such as cultural practices of ascriptive groups. Definitions of deprivation are highly relative, with unclear accountability from private actors and potential contradictions with private actors' freedom and property rights. Similarly, in the private realm, the inviolable boundaries of the individual may be breached by countervailing legitimate principles: such as the right to form and act in families, religious freedom, or delegated authority and care for individuals who lack full decision-making capacity.

The key *external* normative barrier to recognizing and debating human rights principles in the private sphere is the acknowledgment of a private authority relationship that should be subjected to scrutiny and accountability. Because each form of private authority depicts itself as natural, challengers bear the extra burden of politicizing long-standing social relations and questioning the consequences of socially approved delegation of power to legitimate private parties. In a more general discussion of authority, Kane reminds us that hegemonic ideologies displace moral choice by a logic of necessity. "The contrasting objective 'necessity' of one's own position may be founded on any of several bases—'scientific' rationality, an inexorable historical progress, the irresistible force of nature, inevitable economic development, or plain 'common sense'" (Kane 2001: 18). Even the principles of human rights initially shared the naturalized silences of liberalism. "With certain exceptions, rights-based discourse has generally ignored oppression in the private sphere, thus tending to reinforce the public/private distinction. . . ." (Tickner 2001: 115). However, feminism has provided a key normative innovation in politicizing the private sphere, especially in the campaign for "women's rights as human rights" (Charlesworth 1994). In the signal areas examined here, campaigns must introduce radical notions of private rights: the independent identity of children as persons, the social responsibility of business, and a universal right to health care and medical decision making.

Despite these challenges, global mobilization and dialogue can extend the vocabulary of human rights and expand the realm of global governance.

Contesting Private Authority

The struggle against private sector human rights abuse is a form of transgressive contentious politics: episodic public political claims by emerging political actors employing innovative forms of collective action (McAdam, Tarrow, and Tilly 2001). Challengers of both public and private abuse tend to mobilize through social movements and issue-networks. When the issue domain crosses borders, corresponding movements and networks are often transnational. But the additional agenda barrier of recognizing private authority and framing social practices as human rights violations tends to push campaigns against private wrongs into broader coalitions and looser campaigns (Khagram, Riker, and Sikkink 2001, for a discussion). Treatment of children's migration is not automatically accorded in migration organizations but crosses refugee, social service, and child labor networks. Socially responsible investment draws on environmental, religious, labor, and anti-globalization campaigns (although Holocaust reparations and asset seizures from dictators are based in traditional victim and human rights organizations). The AIDS drugs issue brought together physicians, development, and gay groups—even the narrow issue of organ trafficking links advocates of medical ethics with critics of human rights practices in China. These findings seem consistent with broader scholarship on global civil society movements: "our studies suggest that . . . forging non-traditional alliances and broad-based coalitions is just as important as working internationally" (Clark 2003: 166).

The mechanisms and strategies for contesting private authority are parallel to those used to challenge state actions but with some differences. Recent synthetic models of contention identify a range of critical elements (McAdam et al. 2001). The struggles for private rights chronicled subsequently show the importance of identities, brokerage, and diffusion. Construction of collective identities as child laborers, adoptees, Holocaust survivors, or AIDS patients was both a foundation and a result of collective action. Brokerage was provided largely by human rights activists in some cases and professionals such as doctors and lawyers in others. Diffusion of norms and tactics was important to mobilize transnationally.

Once contention is launched, broader analyses of principled politics suggest that norm transformation requires steps of: symbolic politics, monitoring and publicizing the problem, establishing channels of leverage, and institutionalizing new rules and procedures (Keck and Sikkink 1998). *Entering the political agenda* depends on the framing potential of the issue, strategic alignment of political communication, and effective use of symbolic politics (Ingram and Schneider 1993, Brysk 1995, Bob 2002). This has been especially important for children's rights: the emergence of a new category of rights-bearing individual. A critical component of most principled campaigns against public targets is legitimacy challenge—the claim that power holders have violated some aspect of the social contract or institutional mandate (Brysk 1994). "Political agents and institutions must be seen to serve and to stand for something apart from themselves, to achieve something beyond merely private ends. They must, in other words, establish a moral grounding. This they do by avowing their service to some set of fundamental values, principles and goals that find a resonant response in significant numbers of people" (Kane 2001: 10). States are challenged to honor treaties, businesses to respect political and economic freedom, doctors to provide care in exchange for special status.

But for private violations, often the institutional mandate and the attribution of abuse are unclear. Thus, in many cases the frame for private abuse will concentrate on the consequences rather than causes of violations. For child migrants, for example, causal pathways are complex, and family and state sovereignty cannot be directly challenged—so advocates emphasize children's abuse rather than structural reform. The default mode of human rights campaigns is a humanitarian mode of protection of vulnerable victims.

Information politics are especially important for exposing private wrongs. Activists must not only monitor instances of abuse but also document the wider pattern of violations. For children's undocumented migration, it is difficult to gather basic information on the scope of the problem. Business issues may be legally shrouded in secrecy. But even where economic reports provide ample data, establishing causality requires financial literacy and grassroots knowledge. Medical information gathering is also impeded by specialized vocabulary, patient confidentiality, and widely scattered practice. Disseminating information can be a challenge for all transnational movements, but publicity in some of these areas has been facilitated by the high symbolic valence of children, health, and the Holocaust. However, similarly situated issues, such as the asset seizures of assorted African dictators, have been much more difficult to publicize.

After issues are recognized and exposed, the next step is to establish channels of *leverage* over power holders—either the private authority itself or states with the power to regulate. Children's migration issues follow the general pattern of migration policy, with little or no leverage over sending countries or networks, but substantial potential for lobbying receiving states, especially via the U.S. Congress. Conversely, reform of medical issues founders precisely on the lack of leverage mechanisms over independent professionals and a quasi-commercial, quasi-principled domain. The AIDS drug issue was somewhat ameliorated because centralized pharmaceutical companies followed a business logic that was responsive to the "mobilization of shame." Campaigns against financial actors have been notable for pioneering or expanding diffuse transnational mechanisms of accountability: selective investment, shareholder resolutions, consumer boycotts, and transnational litigation. Many of these newer forms of leverage are based in civil society as well as targeting private actors.

Leverage over key states will be critical to regulate private authority. But different types of states have distinct relationships to globalization, which affect their incentive and ability to regulate private authority (Brysk 2002). State responsiveness to citizen campaigns also varies partly by issue-area. States have greater control over migration than medicine, but they may also respond more readily when their own policies are not the direct target. Overall, campaigns against private violations stake a broader claim to greater state accountability to civil society. At the same time, invoking the state as referee pushes human rights reformers to work with institutions rather than against them.

Finally, successful campaigns must *institutionalize* the influence of principled politics by changing rules, establishing institutions, or shifting the mandate or resources of existing rules and institutions. Although reforms in children's migration address only limited aspects of the issues, they have been institutionalized at a variety of levels: international treaties, U.S. law, changes in the Immigration and Naturalization Service (INS), and European policies. Similarly, the Holocaust reparations established a number of new funds and settlements—but other financial areas have been less institutionalized. The shift in U.S. asset control programs under the Office of Foreign Assets Control (OFAC) and the British pension fund social disclosure requirement are scattered reforms that illustrate the type of changes that would be necessary. Medical issues are the least institutionalized of the areas treated here. Nevertheless, intellectual property resolutions for health emergencies at the World Trade Organization (WTO) and new laws for organ donation show some initial evolution of institutions.

An important corollary of these strategies of leverage and institutionalization is the globalization of change. Many of the campaigns originate or have preferential leverage in the United States, yet they address global problems. In some cases such as transnational adoption, the United States exercises such control over a problem that any reform in the United States has a global impact. In other situations such as Holocaust reparations, U.S. hegemony permits the imposition of reform on the relevant private actor or foreign government. Sometimes practices such as socially responsible investment or transnational litigation spread to relevant jurisdictions through a process of diffusion or modeling. And some change is realized through the construction of multilateral regimes, with or without U.S. influence.

Principled campaigns against private authority thus contribute new subjects, new strategies, and new rights to global governance. Although all of the topics discussed subsequently embody all three elements, each case highlights one of these aspects. The emergence of children's rights illustrates how *new subjects*—a new category of persons—are recognized by the human rights regime, facilitated by the physical and social displacement of migration that makes children visible as individuals. Campaigns against financial actors show how activists construct *new forms of leverage* to limit private authority across borders. Struggles over medical care display the creation of *new rights*, through framing of new practices as rights relevant, new claims of accountability and access, and challenges to global cultural norms and boundaries.

Conclusion

Private wrongs *in* global civil society can be contested by constructing new norms, sectors, and strategies *of* global civil society. In order to mobilize support, private sector human rights campaigns must politicize unnoticed or naturalized abuses. Appeals must fit or build upon a human rights frame. Networks must be bridged or created. These networks will succeed to the extent that they persistently and creatively use symbolic politics, information, and leverage over multiple levels of global governance.

The study of human rights at the frontier can teach us about the nature of power and the process of social change. Because power is a relationship, we must search more broadly for the source, recipient, and modality of influence across boundaries and levels of analysis. Understanding the multiple forms and pathways of power can alert us to new threats to human dignity and suggest new strategies to address them. We will see that change comes when we expand membership in the human community, demand universal responsibility for the human condition, and defend the uniqueness of human identity. Thus, the ultimate lesson of these struggles is also a profound moral agenda.

3

Children Across Borders: New Subjects

... A person's a person no matter how small.

Dr. Seuss

The movement of children across borders—and state responses to this movement—challenges established systems of personhood and citizenship. But children's displacement has also drawn on and inspired the construction of new human rights norms. Children are a rapidly growing population with a history of special status as dependents, burgeoning universal rights claims, and vastly increased mobility. Millions of these children are at risk for human rights violations: doubly displaced from family and state in sweatshops, refugee camps, bordellos, and orphanages.

Ironically, children's displacement also makes them visible as individual subjects of private authority and increases the role of state regulation. This permits a struggle for children's rights as legal persons under international law. Children's rights combine the old and the new: a traditional extension of humanitarian norms to symbolically appealing victims but also the empowerment of new agents—problematic persons who possess full human identity without full human capacity. As one analyst explains, children's rights have moved "from protection to autonomy, from nurturance to self-determination, from welfare to justice" (Freeman and Veerman 1992: 3). An important part of expanding the human rights frontier has been the inclusion of such new groups, categories, and conditions as bearers of established rights, reshaping the human rights agenda. Another scholar concludes that, "The children's rights movement has moved forward one of the central challenges to the human rights movement; it has expanded the traditional human rights framework and now holds states accountable for violations carried out in the private realm" (Levesque 1999: 27).

The inclusion of children as a new subject of human rights has required the articulation of new claims on the *agenda*, the formation of new *coalitions*, and the use of *information politics*. New claims for children's autonomy collide with cultural norms of private authority and children's assigned social role as bearers of identity. Struggles over the rights claims of new groups often revolve around countervailing principles of cultural identity. New coalitions form, and traditional human rights movements shift, to craft a children's rights regime and lobby receiving states. These repertoires of identity claims and mobilization are established rather than innovative; the message is new but the media are well established. Such mechanisms are supplemented by the use of information politics: reports on child trafficking, juvenile detention conditions, and refugee testimony. Information politics, in turn, helps to legitimate new sectors of civil society and repertoires of governance—from the monitoring groups that produce the reports to transnational cooperation programs to stem trafficking.

Civil society is both a source of abuse and an agent of rights claims for children. The sources of violations related to children's migration include families as private authority, illegitimate criminal networks, and sending and receiving states. But *leverage* is mostly limited to migrant host states—with a few recent attempts to pressure sending states for greater regulation of domestic push factors. However, one of the first achievements of children's rights has been to broaden understanding of the sources of accountability for children's condition and the interdependence of various local and global causes. Thus, the United Nations Children's Fund (UNICEF 2001c) concludes that we must move beyond a view of violations of children's rights arising from family failure to a broader global responsibility because threats to children's survival and conditions are "sufficiently alarming to merit a reassessment of the traditional relationship between the family, the state and the civil society in matters relating to children's health, nutrition, education, and general well-being" (Himes 1994).

The global condition of children often threatens the fundamental rights clusters identified by the UN Convention on the Rights of the Child: survival, development, protection, provision, and participation (Wintersberger 2000). Half of the world's poor are children (UNICEF 1999). The ILO estimates that about 250 million children work—73 million under the age of 10—and that 111 million aged 5 to 14 participate in hazardous work. Among these, 8.4 million are in the United Nations' designated "worst forms" of child labor: trafficking, forced labor, armed conflict, prostitution, and crime. Child prostitution—within and across borders—is believed to affect approximately 1.8 million children (ILO 2002). More than 300,000 are child soldiers, some as young as seven years old (Coalition to Stop the Use of Child Soldiers 2001). All of these abuses involve a relationship between children's social and civil rights protections as well as a blend of global, national, and local causes. For example, AIDS orphans and child victims of armed conflict are at much greater risk for child prostitution and trafficking (UNICEF 2001c); there are over 11 million African children orphaned by AIDS, estimated to reach 20 million by the end of the decade (Wines 2003).

This chapter examines the special characteristics of children's migration, with an emphasis on transnational adoption—as a form of migration unique to children and a site where globalization, rights, and identities collide. After a discussion of the family as a form of private authority, the next section provides an overview of migration as a globalizing challenge to rights. The following portion describes the emerging international regime of children's rights. The chapter then considers the major modes of children's migration, resulting rights claims, and responses by states and international society.

Families as Private Authority

The private status of children shows that despite liberalism's claims to constitute a political community composed of public individual subjects, political membership in modern states has long been defined via a public-private distinction and collective subject: the family (Elshtain 1981, Sullivan 1995). The modern condition of childhood is part of the structuring of gender, privacy, regulation, and progress (Stephens 1995). Historically, political theory and corresponding legal doctrine offer three models of children's political status: property, progressive paternalism, and an ethic of care (Archard and MacLeod 2002). Children may be seen as the property of parents, the basis for the Roman law doctrine of *patria potestas* still influential in many continental legal systems—including features such as patriarchal permission for migration. The dominant liberal view treats children as incomplete adults, meriting a progressive paternalism constrained by children's potential future personhood, although with no claim to voice or justice. For example, by the 1830s, the United States had adopted the standard of "best interests of the child" in family law (Grossberg 1985). A more Kantian perspective on children, initially influential in international and nongovernmental groups, shifts debates on children's status to the grounds of a universal duty to care for all members of the human community but does not recognize rights for children.

In political practice, states construct children's status in tandem with private authority: through tutelary control of minors by delegated authority, private family legal codes, family- and gender-based assignment of membership/nationality, and differential rights by family status. Children's rights, behavior, and guardianship are generally governed by separate legal codes and juvenile systems—originally adopted for humanitarian protection—which often ironically offer *fewer* rights and guarantees than those available to adults, even adults accused of crimes. Children's status is peculiarly patrimonial; for all of the worldwide debate on the legal rights of fetuses, eggs, and even cell lines, once a child is born, she becomes the unquestioned property of her parents (and secondarily her state). States control children as both default parents and managers of social reproduction, with some recognized rights to control the number and functionality of future citizens (Archard 2003). The limiting features of children's lack of rights are usually invisible under the assumed norm of stable nuclear families, peaceful functional welfare states, and limited or temporary migration—but contemporary conditions often violate these assumptions. Because children lack full membership and participation rights, they have diminished access to resources—across generations, among nations, and even within families (Wintersberger 2000). At the same time, their lack of political voice and leverage impedes recognition of this gap.

Subjection to private authority is a significant determinant of children's exploitation and abuse. Children's freedom of movement, physical condition, access to education and health care, labor, migration, and marriage are universally controlled by families or some surrogate private authority (such as religious institutions). Until the passage in 1997 of legislation in the Dominican Republic, parents could legally sell their children's sexual services (UNICEF, "Profiting," 2001: 35). Similarly, in countries as diverse as Afghanistan, Bangladesh, Nepal, and Niger more than half of girls are married as minors by their parents—a violation of self-determination that is also strongly linked to lack of access to education, vulnerability to domestic violence, unhealthy early pregnancy, and infection with HIV (UNICEF, "Profiting," 2001: 15). State regulation of children's condition is often inferior to that of other dependents—including animals. The rights gap in tutelary delegation is not limited to resource-poor or traditional societies. For example, thousands of American parents have sent their troubled children against their will to unregulated overseas correctional schools, some of which provide inadequate living conditions and employ inhumane punishments (Weiner 2003).

Citizenship is the primary vehicle for individuals' realization of their rights in the contemporary world, and the state is the default addressee for rights claims. Yet children are systematically disadvantaged in access to citizenship—and children across borders are especially at risk. First, some states derive a child's nationality from its mother, others from its father, and some from both. Numerous international custody cases have arisen from the dissolution of marriages between U.S. mothers, generally presumed to pass citizenship to their children, and fathers from Arab countries, whose laws generally grant citizenship and control through the father. The foreign offices of Western governments deal with dozens of mothers each year whose children have been forcibly removed by their fathers to Islamic countries that are not signatories to the 1980 Hague Convention on the Civil Aspects of International Child Abduction, which has also inspired private recovery campaigns and the establishment of

NGOs such as Britain's Reunite (Alvarez 2003). Conversely, "In Egypt, as in most of the Arab world, children born to women who marry foreigners . . . are not considered citizens at all" (MacFarquhar 2001). The United Nations Development Programme (UNDP) estimates that millions of children in the Arab states are denied nationality in this way and consequently denied access to education, health care, and civil and political rights ("Experts Examine Nationality Laws," *Africa News Service*, September 30, 2003). Furthermore, in the states utilizing a blood criterion for citizenship such as Germany and Japan, children born to foreign parents within that state may not have the right to citizenship despite birth and residence.

Children may suffer special risks of lack of rights and citizenship if their birth is unregistered, either within a state, in a refugee camp, or in a state that is collapsing or at war. A recent study by UNICEF shows that as many as 50 million babies born in the year 2000 were never registered and explains the risks to these children of loss of nationality, vulnerability to exploitation and trafficking, and lack of access to citizenship functions such as formal employment, voting, legal migration, and marriage (Olson 2002a; also UNICEF 1998, UNICEF 2001—"Progress"). Beyond physical and social impediments to the registration of children's identities, some states discourage registration by refugees and ethnic minorities—precisely to avoid granting citizenship. Russia and Bhutan have been cited by refugee organizations for laws that deny nationality to children of nonethnic nationals, excluding sizable migrant populations, and Myanmar has been criticized for its failure to register minority groups. Similarly, during the Central American wars of the 1980s, Honduras and Mexico refused to register births of Salvadoran and Guatemalan refugees in border camps, consigning tens of thousands of children to a complete citizenship vacuum (United Nations High Commission on Refugees 2000).

Even registered children of secure nationality may be second-class citizens, insofar as their rights are dependent on their parents' marital status. "Illegitimate" children may be wards of the state, impeded in access to property rights or social services, or otherwise disadvantaged in legal standing. For example, in Ireland until the 1970s, children of unwed mothers were routinely removed by state and delegated Church authorities and placed for adoption without consent—including thousands of international adoptions (Milotte 1997). Several Latin American countries began to debate the rights of "natural" children during the 1990s, with reforms thus far in a few regional leaders such as Costa Rica. In the Philippines, children born out of wedlock still face barriers in law and social practices—often including denial of access to delegated Church-run schools. Even in Britain, fathers cannot transfer citizenship status to illegitimate children, affecting the immigration rights of such children.

Although childhood has traditionally been viewed by Western culture as a transient phase of incomplete adulthood for individuals, rights become possible as social science and international law increasingly treat childhood as a permanent marginalized social category with both universal and special standing—analogous to the disabled or the elderly. Although children are intrinsically dependent on some form of tutelage and lack full decision-making capacity, the "best interests of the child" standard initiated in liberal legal safeguards and enshrined in international law ultimately requires that the legitimizing purpose and legal limit of private authority over children is the protection and development of their identity as human persons (Freeman and Veerman 1992). Contemporary children's rights standards (detailed subsequently) go further, incorporating a norm of children's age-increasing right to voice and participation—"dynamic self-determination."

> . . . [T]he focus on dynamic self-determination, buttressed by other principles, essentially challenges the private, patriarchal nature of families. . . . [It] essentially seeks to re-image children's personhood . . . children belong to themselves. . . . Simply stated, children are no longer mere objects of rights; they are subjects of rights. (Levesque 1999: 26–27)

This norm of inherent, universal, and inalienable human dignity contrasts with social logics of children as projections or property of their parents and societies. Rather than a smooth evolution of universal individual rights to substitute for second-class citizenship, children have experienced a series of contradictory, ongoing struggles between identity, commodification, and rights. Like domestic public policy on children and families, international treatment of children reflects a fundamental ambivalence between logics of patrimony, property, and personhood.

The logic of patrimony views children as the bearers of a group identity for the family, ethnic, or nation, which trumps their rights or needs as individuals. Patrimonial identities and practices serve as a general source of resistance to both commodification and rights, with a rationale of protection and naturalized private life. In addition, patrimony has predominant policy influence over intercountry adoption—the only form of migration that automatically transfers citizenship.

Meanwhile, commodification displaces children into labor migration and trafficking, but there are unresolved tensions between children's economic value and their emerging liberal rights. In this sense, children as dependent humanitarian subjects are theoretically entitled to more rights than adult migrant workers, but their patrimonial invisibility within assumed family units reinforces the powerlessness of displaced second-class citizens. Working children may be protected property of their parents, states, or employers—but even protected property is not the same as personhood.

An inherent right to human dignity and protection for self-determination is emerging as a boundary condition for the abuses of patrimony and property. And although children displaced as refugees have gained rights more slowly than their adult counterparts, these newly recognized displaced persons have become the subject of new international norms and national practices. Even here, lingering patrimonial nationalist claims impede the expansion of rights for refugee children—but the humanitarian dependence of refugees is multiplied for children.

Private authority over children has been simultaneously stretched across borders and challenged by emerging rights norms in an age of globalization. Children are pushed and pulled across borders by families and fortune, made available for both protection and persecution.

Migration, Globalization, and Rights

Migration is much more than an individual response to domestic constraints—migration has become a major constitutive element of globalization. An invisible transnational estate the size of Brazil—175 million people—live permanently outside their own country. This constitutes 3 percent of the world's population, and it has doubled in the past 35 years. The largest receiving region is Europe (56 million), followed by Asia and North America. The largest single receiving state is the United States, hosting 35 million migrants. Sending states derive increasing proportions of their livelihood from the wages of migration. For example, Bangladesh—one of the poorest countries in the world—gets about half of its income from remittances (International Organization for Migration 2003).

Migration poses many challenges for rights. Most migrants lose the protections of citizenship when they leave home. Many are subject to private exploitation and law enforcement abuse in the receiving country. And a number of migrants are involuntary victims of human trafficking; an estimated 800,000 to 900,000 each year lose their freedom, suffer frequent violations of physical integrity, and may even be killed in the process (U.S. Department of State, "Trafficking in Persons Report," 2003). Even the international organizations mandated to assist them may abuse their vulnerability, as apparently occurred in African refugee camps where aid officials sexually exploited desperate girls and women (Crossette 2002)—similarly, UN peacekeepers in Cambodia (Levesque 1999: 79) and Mozambique (Kane 1998: 48) participated in and even sponsored child prostitution.

Within these overall patterns of migration, rights are based on an embedded domestic division of labor and woven through private authority. For example, the United States has created special visas for foreign domestic workers to accompany diplomatic families to the United States. In the past ten years, more than 35 thousand such visas have been issued

(Greenhouse 2001). Human rights organizations link this second-class "private" citizenship with widespread exploitation and abuse (Human Rights Watch 2001, "Hidden in the Home: Abuse of Domestic Workers with Special Visas in the United States"). Similarly, international matchmaking services in the United States arrange 4,000 to 6,000 marriages each year for foreign women who migrate to marry Americans. Domestic abuse of these vulnerable migrants, culminating in the murder in 2000 of a 20-year-old woman from Kyrgyzstan, has inspired legislation to mandate domestic violence background checks for U.S. men applying for visas to import brides (Crary 2003). Across the industrialized world, both domestic worker and foreign bride visa programs have been linked to trafficking for prostitution of both adults and minors.

For children, globalization disrupts private and state modes of incorporation—family and citizenship. Children are pushed and pulled across borders as dependents, laborers, refugees, and adoptees. As a negative consequence of globalization, children's migration is generated by underdevelopment, political conflict, and a new division of reproductive labor in which shifting patterns of private life in the North are enabled by the South's "people out of place": from maids to prostitutes to orphans (Maher 2004).

On the other hand, migration and new human rights norms make children more visible. In response to children's newly visible common identity and common plight, international organizations and transnational civil society monitor and advocate their rights across states. Globalization also makes some states more receptive to international norms, especially concerning noncitizens. Extending the general analysis of globalization and human rights (Brysk 2002) to children's migration, globalization is simultaneously the greatest threat and the greatest opportunity for children's rights, and different forms of migration have systematically different sources and consequences for children. A comprehensive international regime of treaties, transnational networks, and archipelagos of policy has developed to foster the rights of children, migrants, and child migrants.

The Children's Rights Regime: The Globalization of Personhood

What does it mean to say that children have rights? Children's positive (legal) rights have arguably outrun their unresolved moral and political status (Archard 2003), in a case of "moral induction" expanding the human rights agenda. The definition of rights for a class of individuals who are intrinsically dependent is problematic for the concept of rights, which is intimately tied to autonomy. Children's primary social role as bearers of identity also tests our notions of legal personhood, which is entwined with agency (Griffin 2002). As feminist theory suggests, cosmopolitan rights are based in a liberal order that cannot fully comprehend private identities. Subjects that are not capable of choice are consigned to

"1) nonpersonhood, 2) nonautonomy, and 3) illegitimacy" (Bibler, Maurer, and Yngvesson 2002). However, rights may also serve to protect interests—welfare and social rights are often justified on this basis, in contrast to liberty and participation rights (Brighouse 2002). Children may have age- and role-dependent "rights in trust" to self-determination, in which parent and state proxies seek children's "best interests"—defined to include maximizing children's future capacity for choice and participation—while also maximizing current feasible participation (Archard 2003). It is something like this package of protective rights and evolving, sometimes indirect self-determination that characterizes the contemporary children's rights regime.

The shifting status and increasing rights of children have developed along with liberalism, and the consolidation of an international children's rights regime is both a component of and a response to globalization. Protective rights for children were introduced as early as the 1920s, with the establishment of the Save the Children movement and the treatment of children's issues in the League of Nations (Kaufman and Rizzini 2002). Contemporary children's rights position children as universal and equal subjects of consistent international standards of freedom and entitlement. The landmark 1990 UN Convention on the Rights of the Child has been matched by the proliferation of comprehensive norms (Table 3.1), global agencies and advocacy groups (Table 3.2), new networks and coalitions (Table 3.3), conferences, and campaigns. As a legal analyst comparing international systems affirmed, "The case that children have rights has to a large extent been won: the burden now shifts to monitoring how well governments honour the pledges in their national laws and carry out their international obligations" (Freeman and Veerman 1992: 39). This international regime of norms and institutions has shifted the agenda on the treatment of children to a rights framework and established international benchmark standards that most liberal states strive to achieve.

This institutional and normative framework has been matched by a growth in monitoring and advocacy groups for children's rights. Children's rights have been constructed by and helped to construct global civil society. The Convention on the Rights of the Child was originated by the NGO Save the Children International, and NGOs played an important role in drafting articles as well as lobbying for its passage (Price Cohen 1990). Broader human rights organizations have founded special divisions and campaigns for children, and traditional humanitarian groups have adopted a rights orientation. Organizations have been established devoted wholly to children's rights, and children have even established peer advocacy campaigns across borders. Specific forms of abuse, notably trafficking, child labor, and prostitution, have generated specialized organizations and campaigns.

These groups and others have then combined with international organizations and sympathetic national officials to form transnational

TABLE 3.1 International Norms for Children's Rights (Selected)

Source	Norm	Features
UN Convention on the Rights of the Child	Name, nationality, family, sustenance, voice, protection, refuge, freedom of thought	190 signatories; optional protocols-trafficking, soldiers*
International Covenant on Civil and Political Rights	Protection, registration, nationality	Mainstreams children's rights as human rights
European Human Rights Convention (also American Convention, African Charter)	"best interests of the child"	Regional standards and jurisprudence
ILO 182—Child Labor	Bans prostitution, armed conflict	Ratified by over 100 countries
UN Convention on Migrant Workers and Their Families	Juvenile custody, family unity	Children's rights as migrants
UN High Commission on Refugees Guidelines on Refugee Children	No detention of asylum-seekers	Applies to international organizations as well as states

*Optional Protocols to the Convention on the Rights of the Child address Child Prostitution and Child Soldiers, and a separate 2000 Protocol to Prevent, Suppress, and Punish Trafficking in Persons, Especially Women and Children has been signed by over 88 countries (54/263—Optional Protocols to the Convention on the Rights of the Child on the Involvement of Children in Armed Conflict and on the Sale of Children, Child Prostitution and Child Pornography, esp. Annex II).

issue-networks. For example, the United Nations has become particularly active on the issue of transnational sexual exploitation of children, hosting annual conferences since a landmark 1996 Stockholm World Congress Against Commercial and Sexual Exploitation of Children and sponsoring multiple programs under the ILO, UNDP, UNICEF, and other agencies. The Stockholm conference involved 122 countries, but also 105 representatives of international organizations and 471 NGOs (Kane 1998). Global standards and networks have a cumulative and reinforcing relationship with international organizations—which eventually leads to the diffusion of local initiatives, such as the changes in U.S. policy toward trafficking described later.

Although host states differ in their classification of children's migration flows and level of adherence to international standards, international law and norms of children's rights do seem to be increasingly influential, even as developed states are overall less receptive to migration. ILO member states have readily incorporated conventions on child labor abuse, child trafficking, and child prostitution, and European Union (EU) institutions have initiated special programs in these areas. The U.S. Immigration and

TABLE 3.2 Global Advocacy Groups for Children's Rights (Sample)

Organization	Type
UNICEF	Intergovernmental, sponsors children's peer organizations*
Human Rights Watch (also Amnesty International)	Established Children's Rights Division 1994
Anti-Slavery International	Historic, violation vs. victim type focus
Save the Children	Humanitarian organization shifts to rights agenda
Defence For Children International	Founded to foster children's rights
Free the Children	Children's campaign for bonded laborers
ECPAT, Polaris, Captive Daughters	Vs. trafficking and prostitution
International Society for the Prevention of Child Abuse and Neglect (also International Union of Child Welfare)	Child welfare professionals, networks of national associations plus independent experts
Global Movement for Children	Coalition (see later)

*UNICEF has partnered with national children's empowerment organizations; in May 2002, the UN hosted a Special Session on Children to foster children's self-sponsored organizations, conducted by over 400 children from over 100 countries (UNICEF, "State of the World's Children," 2003).

TABLE 3.3 Children's Rights Issue Networks

Issue	Members
Coalition to Stop the Use of Child Soldiers	Amnesty International, Defence For Children International, Human Rights Watch, the International Federation of Terre des Hommes, the International Save the Children Alliance, Jesuit Refugee Service, the Quaker United Nations Office, World Vision International
Global Movement for Children	UNICEF, Plan International, Save the Children, World Vision, Bangladesh Rural Advancement Committee, Netaid (Cisco/UNDP)
Refugee children separated from families	UN High Commission on Refugees, UNICEF, the Red Cross, the International Rescue Committee, Save the Children, World Vision
U.S. immigration policy for juveniles	Amnesty International, American Civil Liberties Union (ACLU), American Bar Association, Human Rights Watch, Lawyers' Committee for Human Rights, Lutheran Immigration and Refugee Services, Women's Commission for Refugee Women and Children

Naturalization Service has referred to the United Nations' High Commission on Refugees' guidelines in reforming its procedures for the detention of unaccompanied minors. A U.S. immigration judge has ruled that deportation of a single immigrant parent must consider the "best interests of the child" (an American citizen who would be left behind)—explicitly citing the UN Convention on the Rights of the Child (Glaberson 2002).

In the identity-based area of intercountry adoption, international norms are stronger and more consistently incorporated by receiving states. The United States along with 65 other countries has signed the Hague Convention on Inter-country Adoption. Germany, Switzerland, Denmark, and the Netherlands have explicitly incorporated UN standards in their domestic legislation on intercountry adoption (Bagley 1993: 169). Sweden was forced to modify its adoption procedures by the European Court in two cases brought in 1987 and 1989 under the European Human Rights Convention (Smith 1993). When Australia sought to draft international adoption legislation in 1978, it sent delegations to the major Asian source countries to discuss the provisions (Picton 1986)—a subsequent set of standards incorporated the UN Convention on the Rights of the Child (Charlesworth 1993). The Hague Convention Conference has drafted model forms for adoption consent and recommendations for accreditation of adoption services that diffuse global standards across jurisdictions.

Given this panorama of evolving standards and emerging threats, how do states respond to the movements of children across national and social borders?

Movement #1: Displaced Workers, Misplaced Rights

As labor migration and refugee flows have increased worldwide, the participation of children within those flows has also intensified. Children are also a large proportion of "secondary migrants," who cross borders to join a parent or guardian who has previously migrated for labor or refuge. Although secondary migrant children are not displaced from family, they may be displaced from home-state protection from family abuse or exploitation. Furthermore, children do not always migrate in family units as the law assumes. Older children may be unaccompanied migrant laborers, and children of all ages may be trafficked by strangers.

Displaced Workers

There are no comprehensive data on the economic migration of children, but some indicators suggest that millions of children cross borders each year as workers. Immigration raids on U.S. sweatshops and fields regularly detain hundreds of children alongside adult workers. In 2002, Spain registered over 3,500 Moroccan child migrants, most separated from families (Miller 2003). Children's transborder labor migration within developing regions is generally more massive, undocumented, and often exploitative. In 1996, the ILO recorded 194,180 foreign child laborers in Thailand alone, most from Myanmar, Laos, and Cambodia—and many unaccompanied. In that country, there are estimated to be at least 5,000 foreign child prostitutes. An additional 49,000 child laborers have migrated from Nepal to India (www.ilo.org). International programs periodically attempt to improve these children's conditions, but they have few rights or advocates. The Geneva-based International Organization for Migration recently orchestrated the return of nearly 200 boys from Ghana—some as young as four—who had been sold to Lake Volta fishermen as nimble laborers, along with compensatory development aid to the families ("Ghana: Slave Boys Go Home," New York Times, September 12, 2003).

States' policies on "family reunification" generally determine children's rights and membership possibilities in economic or secondary migration. The United States has fairly broad provisions for secondary migration in which children join legally resettled parents, but the INS has deported as many as 10,000 undocumented children of legal residents (Johansen 1993). And children of illegal immigrants have no such rights to family. In recent years under public pressure, the INS has limited the conditions for "expedited removal" of juveniles and increased attempts to contact families. In Britain, the Immigration Act of 1988 removed the unqualified right to family unity, resulting in greater limits on secondary migration. Even in the Netherlands, a controversial ruling upheld by the European Court refused entry to the nine-year-old Moroccan son of a (widowed) permanent resident father with joint Dutch and Moroccan nationality (Bhabha 1998: 718).

Illegal, desperate parents have thus turned to illicit schemes of family reunification through smuggling, paying criminal networks to traffic children under difficult and dangerous conditions. Children travel with strangers, who may physically or sexually abuse them, often walking for days across deserts that kill hundreds of migrants each year, with inadequate food and medical care, and are passed along unaccountably to a series of secret locations over a period of weeks—often with little understanding of their situation and always with no recourse to protection. Hundreds of these children were located in one U.S. case alone (Schmitt 2002). U.S. authorities acknowledge the structural roots of this phenomenon, as increased border enforcement and security blocks resettled parents from returning to retrieve their children. Meanwhile, a U.S. immigration official explains that state policy has created an opportunity for a transnational network of ". . . cold-blooded capitalists. The smugglers have seen children as the next important exploitable population." In 2002, Mexico repatriated almost 10,000 unaccompanied minors, with a similar number apprehended just in the first nine months of 2003. An additional 2,900 Central American minors traveling with smugglers were caught in Mexico.

In response, the United States has increased enforcement against child smugglers, and UNICEF has worked with sending governments such as El Salvador to educate parents about the dangers. But these efforts seem wholly inadequate to counter structural pressures and parents' valuation of family reunification over children's safety—traffickers are jailed for mere months, and border children's shelters report the frequent return of deported children on subsequent smuggling attempts (Thompson 2003). The only mitigating feature of this trafficking for family reunification is that it is generally temporary.

Trafficking

More long-term involuntary trafficking of children for labor and sexual exploitation is estimated to affect 1.2 million worldwide, with most girls forced into prostitution and boys exploited in commercial agriculture and crime (ILO 2002). Recent estimates indicate that at least 11,500 and possibly as many as 20,000 foreign-born children are sexually exploited each year in the United States, generally unaccompanied or subsequently separated from their families (Hernandez 2001); an estimated 45,000 to 50,000 women and children are trafficked to the United States annually (UNICEF 2001, "Profiting": 13). Organized, lucrative, and brutal transnational criminal networks have developed subjecting Mexican girls to sexual slavery and physical abuse across the U.S. border, as well as selling children from Eastern Europe via Mexico (Landesman 2004). In terms of source country concentrations, various forms of international child trafficking are common in poverty-stricken Bangladesh: boys as young as four are shipped to the Persian Gulf for hazardous work as camel jockeys, while girls are sold to India and Pakistan to work as prostitutes and maids (Sengupta 2002). Although coercion and family failure may sometimes be factors, it is important to recognize that in most cases trafficking is deliberately promoted by children's families, from some combination of ignorance, desperation, exploitation, or even custom (Kane 1998, Levesque 1999).

Although commodification and border enforcement usually triumph over rights for economic migrant children, the particularly heinous abuse of child sex trafficking has generated significant international efforts at protection. Sex trafficking is uncontroversially recognized as a violation of rights of physical integrity; in 1990, the UN Human Rights Commission appointed a Special Rapporteur on Traffic in Children and Child Prostitution. In practice, trafficking is intertwined with sex tourism for child prostitution—they often overlap in victims, abusers, country patterns, and exploitation networks—so many measures address both forms of border-crossing violations of children.

Although the threat to rights continues, transnational action has clearly changed consciousness and the political agenda, generated information, and begun to increase options for some victims. In Cambodia, 31 percent of sex workers in one survey were aged 12 to 17, and significant numbers are trafficked to Thailand—where about a third of prostitutes are minors. As one response, UNICEF has established 52 village-based Child Protection Networks with local social workers and authorities who identify children at risk and intervene with educational, economic, and domestic abuse resources. One of the local Cambodian coordinators for the international program reflected on the impact of his experience and norm change,

> Formerly, people here didn't pay much attention to children. They considered that a child's problems were the result of his past life or because of private issues. . . . They now understand that children have rights. . . . (UNICEF 2001, "Profiting")

A similar local development initiative in northern Thailand, the Daughters Education Programme, is sponsored by UNICEF, the ILO, and ECPAT (End Child Prostitution, Child Pornography and Trafficking of Children for Sexual Purposes) (Kane 1998). For victim support in host countries, a U.S. NGO founded in 2002 has established a National Trafficking Alert System hotline (in several languages) and worked to train U.S. law enforcement to work more effectively with victims (Polaris Project; also see HumanTrafficking.com). The official Web site of the U.S. immigration agency now states that people who have been trafficked to the United States, even if they have entered illegally and participated in crimes such as prostitution, should be seen as victims and not criminals (www.hhs.gov).

On the demand side, campaigns target sex tourists, traffickers, and facilitating sectors of civil society. Industry associations such as the World Tourism Organization and the Universal Federation of Travel Agents' Association have initiated programs to raise awareness and set new standards and sanctions for their member organizations. Educational measures such as notices and warnings in air tickets to Asia have been introduced by Sweden, France, Australia, and Garuda Indonesia airlines (Kane 1998).

Beyond prevention and consciousness raising, selected international initiatives have ameliorated and remedied the plight of trafficked children. In October 2000, the United States passed the Trafficking Victims Protection Act, which increases penalties, protects witnesses, and provides immigration relief for victims. A 2003 reauthorization strengthened the U.S. measure by permitting prosecution of sex traffickers under racketeering legislation and allowing victims to bring civil suits. In addition, the United States has begun to issue an annual report on human trafficking, and countries deemed to make insufficient efforts to stop trafficking face the threat of a U.S. aid cut. Fifteen countries were designated as trafficking source countries eligible for sanctions in 2003 (Associated Press [AP], June

12, 2003)—economic sanctions were imposed on Cuba, North Korea, and Myanmar (AP, September 11, 2003). The United States now sponsors regular coordination programs with European governments, such as a recent visit to U.S. border areas with antitrafficking programs that included the Netherlands' chief police inspector and the chief of Latvia's Vice Squad. One San Diego program they were touring shut down 25 trafficking brothels in a two-year period and created a Bilateral Safety Corridor Coalition uniting more than 80 law enforcement and social service organizations for training to monitor and assist victims (Kabbany 2004).

Britain has legislation pending to close its legal lacuna and specifically penalize trafficking for the sexual exploitation of minors; Germany has also criminalized trafficking. Sweden has begun to prosecute customers of minor prostitutes, under its Violence Against Women Act. Interpol has a Standing Working Party on Offenses Against Minors, which has promoted police cooperation between Britain and the Philippines as well as Sweden and Thailand. In addition, by 1997 a dozen countries had passed legislation mandating extraterritorial accountability for sexual abuse of minors by their citizens, including France, Germany, the Nordic countries, Australia, and the United States (Kane 1998).

On the source country side, Albania, Bangladesh, Costa Rica, and the Dominican Republic have sharpened legal accountability, heightened penalties, and increased enforcement for trafficking and child prostitution. Thailand significantly tightened legislation and somewhat increased enforcement in 1996 (Kane 1998). Similarly, the Philippines reclassified child prostitutes as victims and increased prosecutions and penalties for foreign offenders (Levesque 1999).

Global consciousness has also translated into transnational action. Regional intergovernmental coordination initiatives have been launched with UN backing in southeastern Europe, West Africa, the Mekong Delta (UNICEF 2001, "Profiting"), and North America. In addition, the EU funds special programs, including victim reintegration by the 76-state International Organization for Migration (Kyle and Koslowski 2001). A recent regional crackdown in southeastern Europe identified 696 victims and prosecuted 499 suspects, reflecting an increase in monitoring and accountability by a dozen participating states (Binder 2003). The range of policies is profiled in Table 3.4.

Exploitative Enforcement

Despite some progress on trafficking, and in addition to the inherent abuses of smuggling, once child migrants arrive in developed countries such as the United States, they face further loss of rights. U.S. policy is generally emblematic of immigration enforcement abuses in the developed

TABLE 3.4 Global Governance Responds to New Norms and Information

Selected Policies on Child Sex Trafficking, 2000–2003	
Prevention	UNICEF village networks and education
Source country enforcement	Philippines legislation
Host country enforcement	U.S. Trafficking Victims Protection Act
Transnational coordination	Southeastern Europe regional initiatives
Direct assistance to victims	International Organization for Migration, ECPAT

host countries. In 2000, 4,136 unaccompanied minors were detained for more than 72 hours by the INS (Solomon 2002); by 2001, the INS reported 5,385 apprehensions of unaccompanied minors (www.immigration.gov, Office of Juvenile Affairs). INS detention of children under punitive conditions, in inappropriate facilities, and without access to legal counsel or interpreters evoked condemnation by Human Rights Watch, a 1985 class-action lawsuit (Flores v. Reno), and some reforms in 1998 (Human Rights Watch 1998, Amon 2001). Thus, the INS established several special Youth Shelters for detained unaccompanied minors. But thousands of children are still detained for months or years—over one third are held in prisons, up to 80 percent of unaccompanied juveniles still lack legal representation, and their medical, educational, psychological, and language needs are often ignored. A 2003 Amnesty International report shows that child migrants in INS contract facilities are still routinely denied attorneys, jailed with criminals, shackled, and strip-searched (Amnesty International 2003).

After exposure and advocacy by a coalition of legal, human rights, and refugee advocacy organizations, legislation was introduced to shift the U.S. system for processing unaccompanied minors (a proposed new office in the Department of Justice). In joint testimony before the Senate Subcommittee on Immigration, the U.S. Conference of Catholic Bishops and Lutheran Immigration and Refugee Service made an explicit appeal for universal rights transcending citizenship:

> The main theme of our testimony today is that unaccompanied alien children should be treated under the same standards and be afforded the same child welfare protections that are available to other children in the United States. Such standards were developed to protect children as vulnerable human beings; they should not discriminate based upon legal status or national origin, but they currently do. (Duncan 2002)

Meanwhile, the framework of U.S. immigration policy experienced a seismic shift with the combination of post-9/11 security concerns and long-deferred administrative reorganization of the much-criticized INS.

In 2002, the Homeland Security Bill moved responsibility for unaccompanied minor refugees from the INS to the Office of Refugee Resettlement in the Department of Health and Human Services ("Shift of Care For Immigrant Children Alone," New York Times, November 27, 2002). Although the program formally covers only refugee minors identified for resettlement overseas, illegal minor entrants and victims of trafficking may be reclassified as refugees for resettlement by this agency, which is currently serving around 700 children each year (www.hhs.gov). Britain has adopted a similar system, in which unaccompanied minors are referred to the health board as a guardian—administered by a social worker (Bushe 2003).

As for economic migrants or unaccompanied minors with undetermined status, the INS has been broken up into a Bureau of Border Security and a Bureau of Citizenship and Immigration Services, both under the Department of Homeland Security. Under the new structure, unaccompanied minors are assigned case management officers, who make decisions regarding their placement and removal. The Office of Juvenile Affairs now supervises contract facilities for the detention of minors, which are supposed to meet the same standards as juvenile facilities for citizens. However, recent reports record continuing confusion, mistreatment, prolonged detentions, frequent deportations, and bureaucratic lacunae between Homeland Security and the child welfare system (Bernstein 2004).

California Democratic Senator Dianne Feinstein has proposed an Unaccompanied Alien Child Protection Act that would also establish minimum standards for custody, establish a special immigrant juvenile visa, require family reunification or foster care where possible, and appoint child welfare professionals and legal representatives to represent unaccompanied minors (Unaccompanied Alien Child Protection Act, S.121—available at http://thomas.loc.gov). Senator Feinstein sponsored a news conference to promote the passage of this now-bipartisan bill the day after the release of the 2003 Amnesty International report criticizing both INS and new U.S. Citizenship and Immigration Services (USCIS) practices; she was accompanied by a representative of the United Nations' High Commission on Refugees. The bipartisan congressional proposal and the movement it draws on show a burgeoning recognition of children's universal rights and international refugee norms—despite declining general protection of migrants in the post-9/11 United States.

Movement #2: Refugee Minors—Dependent Rights

In terms of refugees, the United Nations High Commission on Refugees (UNHCR) estimates that 10 million of the world's 22.4 million refugees are minors, and 2 to 5 percent of typical refugee movements are unaccompanied children (Doek, van Loon, and Vlaardingerbroek 1996). Children form such an important component of the refugee population that the

UNHCR has a special set of guidelines for "Dealing with Unaccompanied Children Seeking Asylum" and recently established Regional Policy Officers for Children in half a dozen regions. In Europe, 13,600 unaccompanied minors applied for asylum in 1999 (UNHCR 2001). The United States in 1996 admitted 74,491 refugees, many children (there are no separate figures). In 1998, the INS also established special Guidelines for Asylum for Children (Human Rights Watch 1998). The largest single case of unaccompanied minor refugees in the United States, in 2000, involved 3,800 Sudanese war orphans who had walked to refugee camps in Kenya and were subsequently accepted for resettlement in the United States (*Economist*, November 18, 2000: 5). Unaccompanied child refugees bring two additional issues to the determination of refugee status: the determination of adoption or foster care in the absence of either parents or home state and the small but growing phenomenon of families that send an unaccompanied child to seek refugee status in the hope of subsequently securing migration for the parents (Doek et al. 1996).

In the United States, juvenile asylum seekers go through a process similar to that of adult refugees but often lack legal representation and sometimes translators. All refugee applicants must demonstrate a "well-founded fear of persecution" by their government. When asylum claims are accepted, the U.S. Office of Refugee Resettlement provides financial support to unaccompanied minor refugees and foster placement via the U.S. Catholic Conference and Lutheran Immigration and Refugee services (www.ins.usdoj.gov). But rejected petitioners can be deported, and conditions of detention and assessment of child refugees have been sharply criticized by human rights groups. In 2002, lawyers for a mentally retarded Guinean teenage orphan fleeing political persecution sued the INS for detaining him for nearly nine months in adult jails, where he had been beaten and placed in solitary confinement ("Illegal Guinea Immigrant," *New York Times*, November 2, 2002). More recently, the National Association for the Advancement of Colored People (NAACP) and the Congressional Black Caucus appealed directly to the Under-Secretary for Border Security, Asa Hutchinson, for asylum for this cause célèbre (Files 2004). Furthermore, since 2001 security reforms, all applicants including children seeking refuge from 25 specified countries are subject to detention and lengthy background checks, which have often resulted in prolonged detentions for both unaccompanied child refugees and entire families—in some cases separating detained children from their accompanying family members (Taylor 2002).

By contrast, in many Organization for Economic Cooperation and Development (OECD) countries, immigration policies for children persecuted by their states or families go further than the U.S. norm of screening and selective resettlement and offer the legal representation and deportation limits proposed by Feinstein's Unaccompanied Alien Child Protection Act. In Britain, Norway, Switzerland, Holland, and Canada, children cannot be returned to a home country without a suitability assessment of both country and caretaker conditions (Duncan 2002). Britain and Spain have experienced increasing numbers of unaccompanied children seeking refugee status and have instituted greater age screening, although both retain significant resettlement services for those accepted (Bushe 2003). In similar fashion, Sweden froze Iraqis' eligibility for asylum during the 2003 war but exempted unaccompanied minors (Agence France Presse, March 30, 2003). In the Nordic countries, children are appointed a court-ordered legal representative and placed with a foster family during the assessment of their status. And in most European countries, refugee status and family tracing must be determined within six months. The major negative feature of European policy is the refusal to grant asylum if the applicant has arrived from a "safe third country" (Doek et al. 1996).

Dependent Rights

The range and basis of U.S. migration policy for children are displayed by three recent cases that display "dependent rights": rights outcomes for similar persons depend on disparate legal classifications that reflect uneven global norms. Economic migration by unaccompanied minors is generally denied even when it challenges family ties and the rights of the minor. In June 2000, an eight-year-old girl from Nigeria arrived alone in the United States and was detained by immigration authorities. It is believed that the child planned to join her mother, who had previously migrated illegally to the United States for economic reasons, but that the mother was unwilling to pick up the girl because of the prospect of deportation (this type of situation is apparently not infrequent, and the INS has been criticized for detaining undocumented children as "bait" to lure undocumented parents already resident in the United States). Because the INS was unable to locate family in the sending country, the girl remained in an INS foster care facility for over a year. Subsequently, a Nigerian claiming to be her father came forward—but he is living illegally in London. She cannot be admitted to the United States or Britain or released for adoption or even private foster care. Although this case is unusually extended, INS children's shelters house hundreds of children for months at a time, indicating the scope of unaccompanied minors caught in similar immigration dilemmas (Schmitt 2001).

Meanwhile, in the infamous case of Elian Gonzalez, patrimony trumped rights and refugee status despite tremendous controversy and transnational lobbying. In 1999, this five-year-old Cuban boy was rescued from a raft approaching U.S. waters, where his mother had perished. While the boy's (noncustodial) father petitioned for his son's return to Cuba, Cuban-American exiled relatives of the mother demanded custody and pleaded for Elian to receive refugee status. After months of legal maneuvering, diplomatic tension, and exhaustive press coverage, a U.S. court finally ruled that the father's rights to his son and standard diplomatic practice determined the boy's return to Cuba. In a memo to Immigration Commissioner Doris Meissner, the Department of Justice noted that the key legal principle was who had standing to represent a minor's immigration claims. The finding concluded that Elian's father remained his legal representative under the Cuban Family Code, following U.S. practice of assigning jurisdiction to the legal system in which the family relationship arose (www.ins.usdoj.gov). An interesting feature for children's rights was the U.S. acceptance of the Cuban code's recognition of unwed paternity—and the United States did briefly consider and discard the child's potential individual fear of persecution (Abraham 2001, Rabkin 2000).

But occasionally, humanitarian and rights considerations do triumph over both patrimony and property. On July 23, 2001, the U.S. Attorney General granted "humanitarian parole" to a Thai boy who had been trafficked to the United States by smugglers and was later discovered to be HIV positive. The four-year-old had been rented by his Thai prostitute mother to a Thai trafficker, who was using the boy to pose as his son to facilitate the entry of another Thai prostitute into the United States. In the year following the boy's apprehension, he was cared for by a Los Angeles Thai community organization, which has acted as his medical and legal advocate. Even though HIV status has been used to exclude adult migrants from the United States, in this case it was viewed by the courts as a condition mandating a right to treatment available only in the United States. The legal claims of the biological family (although supported by the Thai government) have also been questioned by U.S. courts in terms of the "best interests of the child" because his mother rented the child, his father had previously committed suicide, and the paternal grandparents seeking custody include a convicted heroin trafficker who served 12 years in a Thai prison. The boy will also be eligible for a new visa mandated by the 2000 Victims of Trafficking and Violence Protection Act, which grants rights-based asylum to many who have been coercively commodified. Meanwhile, the transnational Thai community group has placed the boy with a Los Angeles couple who wish to adopt him (Whitaker 2001; "Ashcroft Wants Thai Boy Used By Smugglers to Stay in U.S.," *New York Times*, July 24, 2001)

Movement #3: Transnational Adoption—Identity Rights?

Transnational adoption, although numerically small, has increased dramatically and reveals critical aspects of children's ambiguous rights and status. Debates on intercountry adoption dramatically highlight the competing policies of patrimony, property, and personhood that govern regulation of the movement of children. Thus, the First Lady of Soviet Georgia announced her state's restriction of transnational adoption during the post–Cold War economic crisis in the following terms of state identity over children's individual rights: "I am categorically against foreign adoption. Our nation's gene pool is being depleted. All the Georgian people are suffering hardships. Let our children suffer, too" (Simon and Altstein 2000: 109). In a more privatized assignment of patrimony, many Islamic countries forbid all adoption because Islam states that children's identity and inheritance belong to their biological families and cannot be transferred to another family. Meanwhile, liberalism in receiving states shows a mix of property and personhood, balancing the "best interests of the child" with commodification. Within the United States—the same liberal state that admitted the Thai boy based on his universal right to medical care—one of the sponsors of U.S. legislation facilitating intercountry adoption referred to it as a "consumer protection" measure (for adoptive parents) (HR2909, Comments by Chairman Gilman, March 22, 2000, House Committee on International Relations).

Since World War II, there have been hundreds of thousands of intercountry adoptions—possibly as many as half a million (Altstein and Simon 2000: 8; Bagley et al. 1993: 135), and this migratory flow has increased with globalization. "The number of children adopted internationally has doubled since 1992" (Freundlich 1999). The United States currently admits 15,000 to 20,000 children per year via adoption, and the major European countries together take in a similar number. The United States 2000 census registered 200,000 foreign-born adopted children (Armas 2003). On the sending side, it is estimated that Korea exported almost 100,000 children from the 1950s through the 1980s (Altstein and Simon 1991). Since 1990, more than 25,000 children from Russia, Romania, Bulgaria, and former Soviet republics have been adopted by American families (Judge 1999).

Formal programs of intercountry adoption began after World War II, with the dual rationale of humanitarian rescue of war orphans and patrilineal resettlement in the father's state for children of returning soldiers. In the United States, the Displaced Persons Act of 1948 admitted 10,000 war orphans of specified nationalities (Bagley et al. 1993: 148).[1] Since that time, large-scale intercountry adoption has usually resulted from some combination of recent war, socioeconomic imbalance between sending and receiving countries, and organizational linkages to facilitate the process (Altstein and Simon 1991)—the same factors that produce labor migration and refugees. Thus, postwar European orphans were quickly replaced by Korean children, who have been a major source through the 1990s. The 1970s saw an increase in Latin American adoptions along with political conflict in that region, and the 1990s introduced large-scale post-Soviet and Chinese adoptions. Currently, more than half of U.S. "immigrant-orphans" come from Asia—almost one third from China alone. In 2002, more than 5,000 Chinese children were adopted by U.S. citizens (Elliott 2003).

Despite the term and image of "orphans," the majority of internationally adopted children have at least one living parent—usually the mother, who has generally abandoned or relinquished them under intense economic and social pressure. About two thirds of foreign adoptees are female, and gender preferences in the sending country contribute heavily to adoptions from many countries, especially China, Korea, and India. This reiterates the patrimonial logic whereby females' identity is mutable and their citizenship correspondingly disposable. On the demand side, most U.S. and European prospective parents exhibit a preference for female children, often expressing a belief that girls are more adaptable to resettlement (Pahz 1988: 64).

At the same time, liberal states' changes in family patterns, globalization of markets, and communication links have increased the general demand for and feasibility of intercountry adoptions. Developed societies' changes in markets and mores have combined to produce an increased number of childless couples seeking adoption and a reduced pool of children available within those countries. As citizens of developed countries increasingly delay childbearing to an age of decreasing fertility, more couples are unable to become biological parents, increasing the demand for adoption. Meanwhile, the domestic supply of unwanted children is reduced by the increased availability of abortion and alternatively increased support for unmarried mothers. Thus, the focus of intercountry adoption has somewhat shifted "from parentless children to childless couples" (Altstein and Simon 1991). International regimes and state policies are thus pressed also to incorporate the rights and needs of adoptive parents.

Today, international adoption constitutes about 15 percent of U.S. adoptions but one fourth to one third of adoptions in European countries such as Germany, Holland, and Sweden (Altstein and Simon 1991). Sweden, Denmark, and Norway have the highest proportions. Sweden alone currently adopts 1,500 to 2,000 children per year from abroad and had received 30,000 adoptees from 40 countries by 1990 (Jantera-Jareborg 1990, 1994). The Netherlands has also adopted over 32,000 foreign children, and more than half of Dutch adoptions are international (Hoksbergen and Bunjes 1986). "Foreign" adoptions in Germany include the German-born abandoned children of noncitizen guest workers (Baer 1986).

Objections to intercountry adoption range from the patrimonial to rights based and speak to the interests of each participant in the "adoption triangle": birth parents, adoptive parents, and children. First, some contend that displacement and adjustment ultimately harm the children. Because numerous studies seem to refute this charge at the individual level (Simon and Altstein 2000, Bagley 1993), this argument shifts to a collective identity claim—or at best a psychologically latent child's right to racial identity. A related concern is whether adopted children from a racial group stigmatized in the host society, no matter how well cared for and secure in the adoptive family, will become second-class citizens as adults. Arguing against this identity-based blocking of transracial adoption in the United States, two social welfare professionals who have documented positive placement outcomes for the children contend that it violates children's "rights as citizens as called for in the 14th Amendment to the U.S. Constitution" (to equal protection and equal opportunity for placement in a family) (Simon and Altstein 2000: 144–45, 150).

A second set of arguments focuses on the sending states. Image-conscious states see the export of dependents as a mark of failure, and countries decry the loss of future productive citizens. A Thai social service official explains that "Handing Thai children over for adoption by foreigners is seen by policy-makers as a loss of dignity and a waste of human resources" (Dharmaruksa 1986: 128). It was also on this basis that Nigerian officials following the Biafran war refused to release an estimated 10,000 war orphans, insisting on resettling them within the nation (Bagley 1993: 180).

At the same time, some children's rights advocates claim that intercountry adoption allows sending states to evade their social obligations to children by exporting the unwanted. Instead, they argue, the resources devoted to adoption should be invested in local development to serve the best interests of *all* the society's children. For example, in Belarus adoptions rose 160 percent over a decade of economic crisis—but the proportion of children younger than three living in orphanages rose 170 percent (UNICEF 2001). Critics reply that absent structural leverage and resources for improving children's welfare, in the short and medium term restricting adoptions simply condemns hundreds of thousands of children to abysmal conditions and even death in domestic institutions (Human Rights Watch/ Asia 1996).

Finally, critics from all camps condemn the numerous cases of trafficking of children and coercion of birth parents (Bagley 1993: 172–173). In its milder form, trafficking may refer simply to inadequately supervised and financially tainted adoptions—which are problematic and often exploitative of birth parents but do not necessarily harm the child. A less recognized problem is that the growth of transnational adoption has also fueled the growth of an unsavory element of global civil society: adoption profiteers, including unethical overseas attorneys who exploit their access to state policy to coerce birth parents, extort adoptive parents, and/or endanger children through hasty or inappropriate adoptions (Pahz 1988: Chapter 3).

One response to this phenomenon simply seeks greater regulation and control of international adoption along with other global flows. For example, some sending countries and several states within the United States now prohibit private transnational adoption, in order to ensure government supervision. And U.S.-based adoption agencies have formed councils for self-regulation, such as the International Concerns Committee for

Children (Pahz 1988: 17). But a stronger version asserts that the inter-country adoption process is inherently and irremediably exploitative as soon as children are assigned exchange value. In addition, in rare but horrifying cases, children released for adoption have been illicitly trafficked for commercial and/or sexual exploitation. For example, a 2002 raid in Pakistan uncovered 11 infants held by a long-standing kidnapping ring—including three Pakistani nurses, along with three Maltese traffickers carrying passports and adoption papers to facilitate the children's sale in Malta (Bonner 2002).[2]

In response to these issues, parallel to the children's rights regime an overlapping international regime for intercountry adoption has developed, with universal, regional, and bilateral components. At the global level, general human rights treaties, the UN Convention on the Rights of the Child, and the Hague Convention on Protection of Children and Co-Operation in Respect of Inter-country Adoption all address the rights and safeguards of children and parents (see Table 3.5). Earlier and less comprehensive inter-American, European, and Nordic conventions on adoption facilitate legal recognition of adoptions among countries with close historic ties. This is all supplemented with bilateral agreements between countries with high flow levels (such as Sweden and the Philippines, Sweden and Ecuador, the Netherlands and the Philippines, and Norway and the Philippines), which generally reduce waiting periods, clarify jurisdiction, and sometimes guarantee repatriation if the adoption is disqualified.

The UN Convention asserts the best interests of the child and respect for the child's opinion but also specifies that children have the right to "be cared for by his or her own parents . . . as far as possible" and the right to protection from unjustified separation from parents (Lucker-Babel 1991). The Rights of the Child Convention clearly specifies that intercountry adoption should be a subsidiary option only when the child cannot be

TABLE 3.5 International Adoption Regime

Source	Norms
UN Convention on the Rights of the Child	"Best interests of the child," voice for child, preference for family and state care
UN Declaration on Protection and Welfare of Children, with special reference to Foster Placement and Adoption (41/85, 1986)	Prevent profit and trafficking
Hague Convention on Inter-Country Adoption (66 states)	"Best interests of the child," state must est. central authority to process, parental consent cannot break all ties, parent must consent *after* birth
Regional and bilateral accords: European, Inter-American, African Charter	Legal reciprocity, guarantee repatriation

cared for in the country of origin (Article 21(b)). In such cases, the 1993 Hague Convention mandates that signatories establish a responsible central authority within each state to monitor, adjudicate, and administer intercountry adoption. It does not definitively establish jurisdiction ("choice of law") but in aspiration to universality admitted 30 nonmember states with full voting rights to the drafting convention—largely states of origin for adopted children. The key innovation of the Convention is to raise the standard for transnational translation of consent: more limited parental consent in the country of origin for a "simple adoption" cannot be translated in the receiving country into a "full adoption" breaking all legal ties with the biological parent(s).[3] The Hague Convention also specifies that the mother must consent to adoption *after* the birth and encourages adoptive parents to transfer the child personally from the country of origin (Jantera-Jareborg 1994, Doek et al. 1996).

Transnational adoption depends on and stimulates the formation of global civil society in several senses. Most directly, transnational adoption globalizes families—the most private and local social unit. Transnational adoption also often draws on previous patterns of travel, marriage, and migration across borders. One hotel in China hosted 1,500 American families waiting for adoptions in a single year (Barboza 2003). And some adoptive families develop new relationships to the child's country of origin, including the growing tourist flow of "heritage tours" retracing the child's roots (Zhao 2002). At the organizational level, there are several types of distinctive transnational adoption NGOs. Historical humanitarian organizations, often based in relief efforts, promote the private liberal interests of children and families: prominently Holt International in the United States and Terre des Hommes in Europe. On the other hand, transnational professional groups of social workers (International Social Services) explicitly seek to regulate states and are often delegated administrative responsibility and granted policy influence.

How do individual states deal with this anomalous form of migration of their most ambiguous citizens? Some sending states restrict while others facilitate the export of "surplus" children; standards reflect the state's strength, history, and relationship with globalization.[4] A few countries, which constitute the major sources of adopted children, actively promote international adoption as a solution to domestic crises and inadequate domestic institutions. Although sending states' regulation is largely patrimonial, there is some increasing recognition of the best interests of the child and the dangers of trafficking.

Korea passed an Extraordinary Adoption Law in 1961 that encourages international adoption, citing a low domestic social welfare budget because of the expenses of protracted military confrontation with North Korea. Despite some bilateral modifications during the 1970s and an attempt generally to decrease adoptions along with development, Korean policy and intermediary organizations remain committed to intercountry adoption. Almost 50,000 Korean children have been adopted in the United States alone, according to the 2000 census (Armas 2003). Korea's adoption program sends internationally placed children books and cultural materials on their country of origin and will subsequently help adopted adults to locate and visit their biological parents (Tahk 1986).

Similarly, China has generally welcomed international adoption as a source of relief for its overflowing orphanages. In that country, the economic pressures of poverty and globalization combine with a uniquely draconian population policy to produce a significant "surplus" of children without families. Accordingly, China set up a special intercountry adoption office in 1992 (Bagley 1993: 190). Although birth parents are not subject to direct coercion, their choice to relinquish a (usually female) child for adoption is severely circumscribed by globalizing economic pressures and their state's denial of reproductive rights, combined with patrimonial preferences for male lineage. Even in a nominally socialist state, children are commodified—China receives an average of $15,000 per adoption (Simon and Altstein 2000). Meanwhile, adoptive parents seek to secure their right to form a family. Thus, lesbian and gay couples effectively excluded from adoption in the United States have sought adoptions in China, which permits single parents to adopt.

For reasons similar to those of China, in the early 1990s Romania housed vast numbers of orphans who were initially released wholesale for adoption. But following adoption abuses, adjustment difficulties, and national embarrassment, Romania temporarily instituted a ban on international adoptions. Shortly thereafter, Romania created a state committee to redesign the adoption process—with a prominent U.S. consultant (Simon and Altstein 2000: 17). In Latin America, Colombia has sent large numbers abroad relative to its level of development—because of internal political conflict. Because of trafficking problems, during the mid-1980s Colombia banned private adoption and now requires that all adoptions be regulated through a government agency (Pahz 1988). Guatemala, one of the countries most negatively influenced by economic globalization, is currently the leading Latin American source for intercountry adoption.

It is also interesting to note that several countries that generate large numbers of abandoned children possess the requisite linkages but choose to limit international adoption drastically. Thailand sets a modest quota, permitting only a few hundred adoptions a year. After a series of scandals in the 1970s, Thailand reorganized its adoption process and transferred passport control to the Ministry of Foreign Affairs and Interior (Dharmaruksa 1986). It is suggested that one factor in this difference is the greater potential value of girls as continuing income earners in the Thai family, compared with its more Confucian neighbors. With similar patrimonial rationale, Indonesia requires foreigners to live and work in Indonesia for three years to qualify as prospective parents (Indonesian National Council on Social Welfare 1986).

On the other side of the equation, receiving states differ in whether they treat international adoption as primarily an immigration or a private family matter. Do they grant automatic citizenship or require separate screening? Is the state's policy influenced by international standards? What is the role of private adoption and intermediary organizations? Immigration-oriented receiving states (mainly the United States) have shown a marked increase in rights-based protection, although privatized adoption systems may initially offer greater humanitarian protection for children—but will not be adequate to the demands of globalization until they enter the institutionalized international adoption regime.

Because the United States is the destination for at least half of the world's international adoptions, U.S. policy is especially significant. U.S. policy is among the most restrictive and immigration oriented, but nevertheless this is the loosest area of U.S. immigration law. U.S. law requires that international adoptions meet three sets of standards: the sending country, the immigration agency (formerly the INS), and the U.S. state in which the adoptive parents reside. Usually the INS requirements exceed those of the other parties because the INS in these cases is mandated to investigate both the child's immigration eligibility and the adoptive parents' qualifications. As they remind prospective parents, "adoption of a foreign-born child does not guarantee the child's eligibility to immigrate to the U.S." (U.S. Department of Justice, "Immigration of Adopted Children," Pamphlet M-249 and M-249Y). Only U.S. citizens—not legal aliens—may file for a foreign adoption, which is technically known as a "petition to classify an orphan as an immediate relative." In addition to miscellaneous paperwork and fees, the parents must provide INS with a fingerprint background check, certification of marital status, proof that they have personally examined the child and satisfied the requirements of the sending country, and a "home study" documenting their domestic and psychological suitability for parenthood, conducted by a licensed agency.[5] Regarding the child, they must show that the child is younger than 16 years, free of specified communicable diseases, and meets the legal definition of an orphan: a child whose parents are dead, disappeared, or have relinquished the child in writing for emigration and adoption because "the sole parent cannot provide basic needs by local standards" (U.S. DOJ, M-249). In 2000, the United States issued nearly 18,000 immigrant visas for adoption of foreign-born children (Armas 2003).

However, popular pressure and sympathetic legislators (including several adoptive parents) have recently passed two key reforms that ease and coordinate the implementation of these requirements: the Inter-country Adoption Act of 2000 and the Child Citizenship Act of 2000. Under the Child Citizenship Act of 2000, adopted children now receive citizenship automatically rather than facing an additional set of applications and screening to naturalize the immigration visas formerly issued upon adoption. At the same time that U.S. policy has eased adoption flows and facilitated U.S.

parents' rights, it has also strengthened the children's rights side of the liberal agenda through increased vigilance of suspected trafficking. Eight American couples were denied visas to bring home babies from Vietnam when their partner agency was investigated by the INS, despite pleas by a U.S. senator on behalf of his constituents who were prospective parents (Gootman 2002). Similarly, the U.S. Embassy suspended all adoptions from Cambodia—which had been supplying almost 100 children each month to American families—when it uncovered evidence of trafficking. Local NGOs have tried to monitor trafficking and corruption in Cambodian adoptions (Mydans 2001).

In general, the other major destinations treat adoption as a more private issue, consult more with international counterparts, and incorporate the child's rights and interests more systematically. In 1973, Sweden established a National Board for Inter-country Adoption composed of political party representatives and experts, which certifies domestic and international counterpart adoption organizations (Andersson 1986). A 1979 adoption act restricted and regulated private international adoption in Sweden. Since 1988, the Swedish government has compensated adoptive parents for half the cost of international adoptions. However, Swedish courts have been presented with a series of cases in which adoption of adolescents and adults appeared to circumvent immigration regulations—these adoptions were generally rejected on that basis (Jantera-Jareborg 1990). Denmark requires dual adoption under Danish and sending country law but also permits the maintenance of dual nationality by the adopted child (Melchior 1986). In the Netherlands, a child-oriented foreign adoption policy privileges the child's interests over those of the (Dutch citizen) adoptive parents, encourages Dutch adoption agencies to work closely with sending country counterparts, and expects adoptive parents to engage in "project help" activities for their children's country of origin (Hoksbergen 1991). Intercountry adoption stimulated the formulation of a national adoption policy in Australia, which had formerly relegated family law to state governments on the U.S. model (Charlesworth 1993).

Finally, patrimony exerts a greater influence on both sending and receiving countries with conflicted religious identities. In many sending countries, biological parents' sole specification regarding an adoptive placement is the religion in which the child will be raised. On the host side, Israel's state monopoly on domestic adoption and lack of international regulation have shifted demand overseas, resulting in a high proportion of intercountry adoption without a clear institutional structure to process it. Thus, children brought privately on foreign passports readily receive Israeli identity cards—but those cards carry a special notation, and there is the additional element that the children must be converted to Judaism to receive the full spectrum of membership in Israeli society (Jaffe 1991).

India, a prominent source country, does not have any official adoption law because Indian Muslims have blocked such legislation. Instead, Indian institutions operate under a substitute regime of "guardianship," which is functionally equivalent but widely variable in its application by local administrative units (Pandit 1993). India's guardianship laws apply only to Hindus and Buddhists, rendering Muslim children ineligible for the option of international adoption, and members of smaller religious minorities in anomalous status. "Indian law requires that before a child can be adopted by foreigners she must first be offered to an Indian couple; then to an Indian couple living abroad; then to a couple with one Indian spouse." Despite these restrictions, in 2002, about 800 Indian children were adopted by U.S. and European families (Bonner 2003a).

But a 2001 baby-selling scandal has combined with a campaign by local activists to block international adoptions from India. The Solomonic case of an Indian girl named Haseena is a microcosm of the struggle between patrimony allied with structural critique versus liberal rights of the child combined with adoptive parents' "freedom of choice." A grassroots group led by a former union organizer argues that a corrupt local system, poverty, and sexism push and wealthy Westerners pull Indian mothers to sell their daughters—and advocates a moratorium on foreign adoptions. The American couple who had been approved to adopt the cause célèbre child has invoked letters from U.S. senators and inquiries from the American Embassy. An Indian family has come forward to adopt the girl, now a toddler, but the Indian family was evaluated by the Indian state's own child welfare agency to "not come out of love and affection for the child" and act from "certain external pressures." Meanwhile, the child herself has been removed from the export-oriented Catholic orphanage in which she was raised and placed in a state facility (Bonner 2003).

New Subjects: From Patriarchy to Personhood

Children are one of the largest and most vulnerable groups across many types of social and political systems. One of the most promising features of the emergence of international human rights is the potential to extend legal personhood to such privatized, powerless, and socially anomalous groups.

Children's status and membership are still largely subsumed under patrimony, which treats children as embodiments of the identity of their family, ethnicity, or state. Meanwhile, children's migration increasingly reflects commodification, which positions children as a uniquely vulnerable sector of the labor force. Even refugee children do not always receive the legal personhood to which they are entitled by international law, although the small subset of unaccompanied minors who are victims of trafficking or severe civil conflict are increasingly recognized by the liberal developed countries.

Transnational adoption, the smallest and most specialized flow of children across borders, is the area that most systematically transfers membership and considers rights. Rooted in the patrimonial assignment of identity through family, transnational adoption now reflects the competing logics of globalization. Surplus children are produced by developing nations, and developed countries increasingly import all forms of reproduction. But in response to this commodification and transnationalization of the private realm, a strong sector of transnational civil society has developed to assert the rights of women, children, and migrants. Thus, evolving state policies and international agreements seek to realize an uneasy blend of collective cultural rights, individual "best interests of the child," and rights of the (birth and adoptive) family vis-à-vis the state. Although states continue to exercise immigration vigilance over adoption flows, receiving states in this area are unusually responsive to private and transnational concerns and to children's rights.

Overall, the emergence of children's rights across borders is a process of "moral induction" (Winston 2000) that has bridged humanitarian protection and legal personhood. However, the children's rights regime is incompletely developed, is unevenly internalized within domestic state structures, and thus far proves inadequate to the demands of globalization. Children's rights has introduced new subjects to the human rights agenda, and new streams of information that reshape state policies in selected areas, but falters in the quest for leverage over private actors—the theme of the next chapter.

4

New Strategies: "Follow the Money"

A growing web of political accountability is emerging for the human rights impact of global financial flows. International finance now comprises an unprecedented exchange of trillions of dollars a day, generating a high proportion of value in the world economy. Contemporary financial flows are governed primarily by the norms of free-market capitalism. But in recent decades, principles of human rights and social equity have inspired attempts at increased governance of economic exchange. Human rights campaigns contend that private financial actors may facilitate state abuse and sometimes autonomously impinge on social and economic rights. Although finance is still less regulated than any other flow, a cluster of recent challenges pioneers new mechanisms of human rights conditionality in the core domain of global capital. Conversely, human rights campaigns that have focused previously on trade, aid, and investment may now be applied to the most dynamic sector of the world economy, which could provide increased leverage for the transnational human rights regime (Singh 2000).

The most visible and contested challenge occurs when financial flows result from or reward human rights violations.[1] The pursuit of reparations from financial intermediaries uses international law to stimulate increased accountability for prior abuses. Socially responsible investment is a direct attempt by civil society to withdraw or leverage the capital of repressive regimes and complicit corporations through existing market mechanisms. At another level, states have expanded the security basis of capital controls to incorporate pariah regimes, in part responding to human rights campaigns and principles. Governments have developed new norms of multilateral tracing and freezing of financial assets of individuals who violate international norms, sometimes including human rights, which go beyond earlier practices of sovereign expropriation.

Under the political economy of neoliberalism, financial markets aspire to be anonymous, autonomous, and apolitical. Contemporary conditions increasingly yield national control to transnational private flows of banking, exchange, and finance (Strange 1998, Cerny 1993). Yet states retain the power to regulate capital flows for fiduciary trust and to ensure social purposes such as national security. Now, challengers from civil society demand the transparency and redirection of international finance in pursuit of purposive ethical agendas. Their legitimacy challenge highlights the social responsibility of business and reminds us that profit is a social construction—not a law of physics.

In addition to reshaping the *agenda*, financial accountability struggles use *information politics*. Litigation requires or inspires the disclosure of historic economic relationships between firms and regimes. Social investment organizations research and publicize investment patterns and corporate ties to specific countries and production practices. As an international political economy perspective would suggest, such struggles are also a result and target of state regulation and delegated authority. And professionals are important brokers for seeking information and leverage: lawyers for litigation—who are sometimes critiqued for pursuing professional gain alongside the principled goal, and economists for researching and evaluating socially responsible investment.

Reparations, socially responsible investment, and economic sanctions provide new forms of *leverage* for this expanded human rights agenda. The potential impact for human rights conditionality of financial flows is substantial. "The growing intensity and extensity of global financial flows, combined with the trend towards the liberalization of national financial markets, the absence of national capital controls, and the move towards flexible exchange rates, suggest that a qualitative shift is underway involving deeper global financial integration" (Held et al. 1999: 216). Transnational banking is a key element of the contemporary global economy. In 1995, non-residents controlled $7.9 trillion of world bank deposits. Within the world financial centers such as London and New York, 40 percent of deposits were held by nonresidents. (Scholte 2000: 79). On another front, of the world's estimated $2.5 trillion per day in international equity flows, developing countries where human rights violations are concentrated now receive about $40 billion. These flows are particularly influential within the economies of the countries most at risk—bond finance now constitutes over 28 percent of less developed countries' (LDCs) financial flows (compared with 19 percent for foreign aid and 19.8 percent for foreign direct investment) (Held et al. 1999: 208, 211).

Global Finance Norms: Human Rights versus Business as Usual

The fundamental assumptions of international finance rest on the legitimacy and fungibility of money as well as the institutional coherence and isomorphism of its repositories. Money must be a morally neutral store of value that can be exchanged for resources. Assets must be transferable across borders via institutions that operate under predictable and coordinated rules. These private institutions must be insulated from the exercise of public authority and its shifting policy objectives (Helleiner 1994, 1999).

In the traditional liberal economic view, human rights are "social externalities" whose existence must be guaranteed by the state and are properly ignored by the market. It is the state's function to set boundaries to fair competition in a way that provides nonmarket goods deemed desirable by the society (Bluestone 1986). However, this division of labor provides no remedy for two kinds of human rights violations committed by actors above, below, or across states—the transnational and the private (Brysk 2002, Cook 1994). The private norms of global finance are a form of "private authority," which operates where public governance cannot but does result in an allocation of legitimate decision-making power based on state delegation, historical practice, and expertise.[2] By its nature, private authority is generally less accountable than its public counterpart (Cutler, Haufler, and Porter 1999).

According to the historically prevalent view, private banks and businesses should not be held responsible to political or ethical standards governing the source or use of their resources. A vivid illustration of the role played by German finance in supporting human rights violations is the case of Deutsche Bank, which financed the construction of Auschwitz—including providing credit lines explicitly dedicated to building SS barracks and installing the crematoria. The 1999 revelation of this role came while Deutsche Bank faced U.S. scrutiny for its proposed takeover of New York–based Bankers Trust. ("Holocaust Reparations: German CEOs Unlock Their Vaults," *Businessweek*, February 22, 1999) The case for business as usual is expressed succinctly by an international law expert (ironically, one of the American prosecutors of German industrialists at Nuremberg), rejecting 1990s international legal prosecution of Swiss banks for Holocaust abuses. He argues, "A substantial aspect of the business of banking for profit is acceptance of deposits without regard to the history of the money being deposited. Swiss bankers are not unusual in this practice. . . . [I]n the matter of the claims of survivors to deposits of the murdered persons in Swiss banks, the Swiss bankers seem to have behaved badly, but like bankers" (cited in Ramasastry 1998: 30).

However, the growing globalization of markets has been paralleled by other forms of globalization that provide a basis to challenge business as usual—such as global civic linkages, international law, and an "international human rights regime"(Matthews 1997, Donnelly 1986, Sikkink 1986). The international ideology of liberalism held by hegemonic powers and global institutions has come to incorporate a minimal package of democracy and basic security rights along with free-market economics (Fried 2000). And critical scholars of globalization increasingly tie the realization of human rights to reforms in the governance of finance. Held's "cosmopolitan democracy" model includes proposals for community representation in pension funds and financial institutions (Held 2000). Another scholar of globalization recommends capital controls and the abolition of offshore finance to promote social rights (Scholte 2000). Others advocate reform of the International Monetary Fund (IMF) and a "Tobin tax" on foreign exchange (Singh 2000, Muro 2003).

Campaigns for financial conditionality shift private incentives and state regulation and promote linkages between private authority and public accountability. Global governance is a process of generating transnational rules (Sandholtz 1999) as well as subsequent enforcement mechanisms. In the cases discussed here, we see a conflict between two facets of liberalism: formal general rules of property rights versus informal specific rules about the violation of individual freedom. As a result of this struggle over norms, investors' right to privacy is sometimes trumped by the claim to social regulation of illegitimate coercion. The domestic principle that property rights may be abrogated when property is acquired by force is extended to the anarchic international realm. Thus, former U.S. Treasury Secretary Paul O'Neill, explaining financial pursuit of terrorists, expressed a new understanding (employed more broadly by human rights activists)—"Those who underwrite violence bear equal culpability to those who perpetrate it. Feigned indifference, willful blindness and the appearance of normalcy and status in the world of business or commerce will no longer provide cover" (Hill 2001). This shift in norms has been constructed by and resulted in new forms of leverage in the global economy.

Reparations: Putting Past Profits on Trial

Financial sector reparations are a direct, punitive, and retroactive response to human rights violations perpetrated or perpetuated by the private sector. Although activists have also pursued significant civil actions against former dictators and torturers, financial intermediary reparations target private parties rather than public authority, linking financial malfeasance to direct violations of security rights. Although government reparations for human rights abuses of former regimes are increasingly common (Torpey 2003), they are primarily oriented toward compensating and healing of victims. Private sector reparations may have a compensatory element, but the underlying rationale is to remove the profit motive and establish accountability for complicity and/or delegated deprivation of economic and property rights. Furthermore, public reparations are usually possible only when regimes are overthrown dictatorships or historically chastened democracies—private sector reparations do not depend on government status in the repressive state. Financial sector reparations actions are brought by and for private victims, but they tend to involve interactions among four types of parties: national and transnational organizations of victims and their representatives, victims' governments, corporate bodies of financial intermediaries, and financiers' host states.[3]

Private sector Holocaust reparations represent the most developed case so far of transnational private accountability for human rights violations by financial actors and a possible precedent for future governance attempts. The state-sponsored murder of six million Jews and millions more Roma, disabled, and dissenters, along with the torture, forced labor, and displacement of ten of millions more, has generated a panoply of reparation policies and demands over the past half-century. Following the defeat of Germany, Allied forces drafted legislation mandating government reparations to (mostly Jewish) survivors of concentration camps, which was subsequently endorsed by the new German government. In the wake of these payments, the Conference on Jewish Material Claims Against Germany was established by twenty-three Jewish organizations and the state of Israel; the Conference has processed compensation to more than 500,000 Holocaust victims (www.claimscon.org). A generation later, victims of slave labor began to pursue German corporations for their role. In parallel actions, by the 1980s aging survivors and heirs sought to trace bank accounts, insurance policies, and other assets such as art that had been usurped from Holocaust victims and retained by private intermediaries in several European countries. Finally, as revelations of neutral Switzerland's financial collaboration with the Nazis surfaced, survivors of Jewish refugee families deported from Switzerland to concentration camps sued the Swiss government for its political complicity via discriminatory refugee policies.[4]

Although the German government had provided more than $60 billion in reparations to over four million direct victims of Nazi state policies of persecution since the 1950s, many German companies that employed slave labor had never been brought to account. An estimated one million of approximately 10 million slave laborers survive. The victims of Nazi industry were represented by 30 law firms, five governments from Central and Eastern Europe, the Conference on Material Claims Against Germany, and the state of Israel. On July 17, 2000, a $4.5 billion joint state-private fund was created to compensate slave laborers and their heirs, estimated to encompass one million people. The foundation was proposed by leading German firms such as Bayer, DaimlerChrysler, Deutsche Bank, Krupp, and Volkswagen—the establishing agreement explicitly cites "the moral responsibility of German business." Half of the fund will be provided by the German government and half by thousands of German corporations—including a number of transnational firms established *after* the period when the violations occurred, which were not legally at risk. The foundation's Web site states that participating firms include 70 percent of German manufacturing, over 90 percent of banking, and almost 100 percent of insurance companies (http://www.stiftungsinitiative.de/eindex.html). Further evidence of the expanding moral claims of the foundation is the extension of compensation to survivors with no direct claim on German business: victims of defunct German companies, state- or SS-owned companies, and agricultural workers (U.S. State Department, "Remarks of Stuart E. Eizenstat," July 17, 2000). Overall, this measure provides payments to persons who suffered any form of personal injury or property damage at the hands of German companies, including their foreign holding companies or subsidiaries. The foundation has also made progress toward its stated goal of achieving "all-embracing and enduring legal peace . . . for the companies"; 68 pending cases have been dismissed (http://www.stiftungsinitiative.de/eindex.html). The foundation's board of trustees includes representatives of the plaintiff countries, the United Nations High Commissioner for Refugees, the International Organization for Migration, the Conference on Jewish Material Claims Against Germany, and the Sinti and Roma (Gypsy) communities.

Holocaust survivors had also brought suits against German banks, which were dismissed in May 2001 following the establishment of the German compensation foundation. Besides forced labor and other physical injuries such as medical experimentation, the German foundation provides compensation for property loss or damage by German banks and insurance companies (U.S. Department of State, Office of Holocaust Assets Issues, Fact Sheet, August 18, 2000). In 2003, a survivor of Nazi medical experiments painfully injected with sterilizing chemicals at Birkenau rejected the $8,000 offered by the German fund and brought suit against Bayer and Schering—the pharmaceutical companies that provided experts and drugs to Nazi doctors (Greenhouse, S. 2003).

But Swiss banks offered the most accessible source of compensation for the broader set of victims and their heirs, via Swiss stewardship of contested assets. Switzerland holds two classes of assets linked to Holocaust victims: dormant accounts that may have belonged to victims and gold reserves allegedly looted from concentration camp prisoners. Swiss banks had also facilitated the financial plunder and security rights violations of the Nazi regime, such as opening an account for the SS and laundering Nazi gold via Canada and Portugal. The Nazi regime had stolen gold from the central banks of occupied countries and the assets of "Aryanized" Jewish businesses, as well as the gold dental fillings and wedding rings of millions murdered in the camps—all of these assets were believed to be held in Switzerland (Bower 1997). At the conclusion of the war, Switzerland made an agreement with the Allies concerning gold holdings, under which Switzerland agreed to pay $58 million toward European reconstruction and the Allies agreed to drop any further claims on gold holdings.[5] More recent reports suggest that Switzerland may have held up to $20 billion in gold looted by the Nazis (Ferguson 1998), that Switzerland "formed part of Germany's economic lifeline," and that Switzerland returned millions of dollars in assets to Germany in violation of the 1946 agreement with the Allies (Olson 2001b).

As for the dormant accounts, Switzerland claims that its banking secrecy laws were originally enacted to protect German Jews transferring their assets in response to Nazi persecution and that good-faith efforts were made in the postwar years to track account holders and heirs. After over a decade of fruitless negotiation with Jewish groups, Switzerland did pass a 1962 resolution that allowed the tracing and dispersal of a small portion of the dormant accounts—but which omitted major categories of claimants such as those who died from "natural" causes such as hunger and depositors living in Eastern Europe (Ramasastry 2001: 17). After a massive audit of four million Swiss accounts from the war years, the Volcker Committee (see later) concluded that,

> The auditors reported no evidence of systematic destruction of records of Nazi victims' accounts, organized discrimination against the victims of Nazi persecution, or concerted efforts to divert the funds of Nazi persecution victims to improper purposes. However, they did find confirmed evidence of questionable and deceitful actions by some individual banks in the handling of victims' accounts, including withholding of account information from Holocaust victims or their heirs, inappropriate account closures, failure to keep adequate records, many cases of insensitivity to the efforts of victims or their heirs to claim dormant or closed accounts, and a general lack of diligence—even active resistance—in response to earlier private and official inquiries about dormant accounts. (Geneva Financial Center—The Volcker Report, http://www.geneva-finance.ch/e/volcker.htm)

During the 1990s, Holocaust survivors and heirs brought a series of class action suits against Swiss banks in U.S. courts. Plaintiffs included U.S. and foreign citizens, and charges included complicity in violations of international law, breach of fiduciary duty, unjust enrichment, and fraud (Ramasastry 1998). By 1997, California, Maryland, Illinois, New Jersey, New York, and Rhode Island had passed laws requesting release of information, compensation, or even forbidding state use of Swiss banks with unresolved accounts ("States act on Jewish assets in Swiss banks," *State Legislatures*, v. 23, n. 7, July-August 1997). New York State's Banking Department established a Holocaust Claims Processing Office, pressed Swiss banks holding its pension funds to contribute to reparations, and barred Union Bank of Switzerland from participation in a billion-dollar bond offering in 1997. Later that year, the State of California froze all commercial relations with the three big Swiss banks. In addition, the World Jewish Congress and the Jewish Agency for Israel had threatened to coordinate a boycott of Swiss banks ("The search is on . . . ," *The Economist*, v. 342, n. 7999, January 11, 1997). Shortly afterward, two of the major Swiss banks merged, creating the world's second largest financial institution: United Bank of Switzerland. The merger was closely scrutinized by New York's Banking Commission because of the Holocaust claims.

Nevertheless, Swiss banks and government initially resisted all attempts at accountability. Swiss banking secrecy embodied twin principles of investor privacy and Swiss sovereignty; Swiss law provides civil, administrative, and criminal accountability for release of information. Switzerland's right to privacy encompasses businesses as well as individuals (Ferguson 1998). Swiss political figures labeled the reparations demands as "blackmail" and threatened a counterboycott of American goods to address their perceived loss of sovereignty. The Swiss government did establish an independent group of historians to clarify Switzerland's wartime role, headed by Prof. Jean-Francois Bergier and composed of five Swiss and four foreign experts (reports available at www.uek.ch). The Bergier Commission's 25-volume report, released in 2002, concludes that Switzerland knowingly turned away tens of thousands of Jewish refugees to near certain death, allowed economic transactions that distorted neutrality, and failed to cooperate constructively with the return of victims' assets—although rejecting charges of conspiracy and active collusion with the Nazi regime (Olson 2003).

One of the banks' responses to legal challenge was the appointment of an independent investigatory commission in 1996, headed by Paul Volcker, former president of the American Federal Reserve Bank (the Independent Commission of Eminent Persons, reports and publications available at www.icep-iaep.org). Later that year, the Swiss government authorized the lifting of banking secrecy for five years for research on unclaimed assets. In 1997, the New York State Banking Department was granted unprecedented access to wartime records, in response to the regulatory controversy. Following the recommendations of the Volcker Committee, the banks released several lists of dormant account holders in waves, suspending banking secrecy (in 1997, approximately 16,000 names; 2001, 20,000 names).

Meanwhile, in 1997 the three major Swiss banks set up a humanitarian fund for victims of the Holocaust (not linked to assets or compensation). This fund paid out $179 million to 309,000 needy survivors around the world by 2002. Small payments to elderly survivors were concentrated in Eastern Europe. This was a goodwill gesture separate from the legal cases (Olson 2002b). Independently, the Swiss government proposed a multibillion-dollar Solidarity Fund based on reevaluation of the Swiss National

Bank gold reserves, for current victims of poverty and human rights abuse worldwide. This measure required voters' approval of a new constitution to remove the gold backing of the Swiss franc. Later, the Swiss Department of Foreign Affairs opened a historical office to reexamine Switzerland's human rights policies and financial role in South Africa, Argentina, Chile, and Rwanda (www.giussani.com/holocaust-assets, 25.1.99).

Throughout 1998, negotiations ensued as pressure mounted on the still-recalcitrant Swiss firms: Florida canceled lines of credit with Swiss banks, the European Parliament and Cardinal John O'Connor called for restitution from the banks, and the U.S. Senate Banking Committee held hearings.

On August 12, 1998, Swiss banks reached a $1.25 billion agreement to settle the pending class action suits by victims (approved in July 2000). The 1998 Global Settlement explicitly extinguished pending legal action and specified that the U.S. government would protect Swiss banks from any future lawsuits by filing friend-of-the-court briefs asserting a U.S. foreign policy interest in "legal peace." By mid-2001, more than half a million claims had been received under this program. Meanwhile, U.S. courts have dismissed 55 cases (U.S. State Department Web site, Press Statement, March 15, 2001). U.S. states dropped their boycott measures. Thirty-six Swiss companies implicated in wartime forced labor through their German subsidiaries have announced their intention to participate in the settlement to avoid future litigation; they include Nestle, Novartis, Ciba, and Roche. The Swiss government repeatedly removed itself from the issue, and the Swiss National Bank is not included in the settlement. Two class action suits were brought against the central bank in 2000, in both the United States and Croatia. The Volcker Commission's Claims Resolution Tribunal for Dormant Accounts eventually recovered $10 million for victims' families from 207 dormant accounts as well as $40 million from dormant accounts unconnected to the Holocaust (Olson 2001a). (For further information and analysis, see Levin 1999.) Because a significant proportion of the $1.25 billion settlement has been unclaimed by specific depositors and more difficult to attribute than anticipated, a New York federal court judge is adjudicating competing proposals for dispersal to survivors' groups of various religions and ethnicities, human rights groups, and related educational and cultural projects—revealing both the range of Nazi victimization and the diversity of civil society claims (Glaberson 2004).

Meanwhile, survivors and heirs also sought compensation from European insurance companies, which had failed to publicize policies or locate designated beneficiaries and often refused to pay identified claims on grounds such as the lack of death certificates for those murdered in concentration camps. In early 1998, two U.S. congressional representatives introduced the "Holocaust Victims Insurance Act," which would fine

European insurance companies that failed to pay claims. Legally besieged insurance companies established the International Commission on Holocaust Insurance Claims in October 1998, with representatives from the companies, European regulators, Jewish and survivor organizations, and the state of Israel. Chaired by former U.S. official Lawrence Eagleburger, the Commission conducted an investigation of claims that major European insurance companies such as Allianz, Axa, Generali, Winterthur, and Zurich had failed to honor life and property policies purchased by Holocaust victims. The Eagleburger Commission also published lists, of approximately 19,000 policy owners in 2000. This commission has operated very slowly; from around 80,000 claims it has offered settlements to 2,420 people. A U.S. court recently accepted a pending class action suit that the companies had sought to divert to the Commission, citing doubts about its independence and reliability as a source of remedy (Treaster 2002, 2003a). By September 2003, even Chair Lawrence Eagleburger complained that the Commission on Holocaust-Era Insurance Claims had spent more for operations than it recovered and that insurance companies had paid only about 6 percent of the 54,000 claims the commission had identified as valid (Treaster 2003b).

Thus, some insurance companies have also settled one by one under national processes. Swiss and German insurance companies have generally sought to participate in their respective bank settlements. Italian insurer Assicurazioni Generali has agreed to pay out $100 million in claims through the Commission, but the French company Axa's settlement has foundered on French privacy laws that forbid the release of names of policyholders (Lipkin, "Tracking down all the Holocaust beneficiaries," *Insurance Day*, July 10, 2001). Although a U.S.-Austrian reparations agreement that included a limit on insurance companies' liability was reached in January 2001, attorneys for 230 survivors have brought suit against the Austrian government, 15 European insurers, and a Viennese auction house, claiming that the agreement is illegal ("Legal battle looms as Holocaust survivors ignore U.S.-Austria deal," *Insurance Day*, June 21, 2001). (Also see Braillard 2000.) About a dozen U.S. suits are still pending.

The U.S. government played a significant role at several critical junctures in this process. The Swiss bank controversy was catalyzed by several U.S. states' purchasing restrictions and boycott threats. In addition, U.S. insurance and bank regulators were considering revoking the licenses of companies with "unfulfilled obligations contracted during the Holocaust years." In 1998, the German government asked the U.S. government to use its "good offices" to mediate. (U.S. Department of State, Ambassador J.D. Bindenagel, "Remembrance, Responsibility and the Future: Fulfilling the Promise of Justice through Dignified Payments," September 22, 2000). Clinton's Treasury Secretary Stuart Eizenstat then assumed a key role as broker of the settlement, mediating numerous conferences among plaintiffs, banks, Jewish organizations, and governments over a period of several years (Eizenstat 2002). An unprecedented U.S. government commitment to extinguish legal action provided the leverage for the establishment of both the Swiss settlement and the German foundation; Madeleine Albright cited 600,000 U.S. jobs provided by German companies and 1,800 U.S. companies operating in Germany (U.S. Department of State, Statement on the Establishment of the German Foundation "Remembrance, Responsibility and the Future," October 20, 2000).

The international debate on financial reparations has also spilled over to previously uninvolved countries. France established a special fund to restore property alienated by the Vichy regime; nevertheless, in 1998 heirs filed suit in New York against nine international banks that operated in France under Vichy (Samber 2001). When the French government asked a U.S. federal court to dismiss the suits in 1999, the plaintiffs' attorneys argued that "we are not suing the government of France, but individual banks" (www.giussani.com/holocaust-assets, 30.3.99). The British Bankers' Association published a list of dormant Holocaust-era accounts to facilitate claims. Britain also cosponsored another special fund with the United States for aging Holocaust survivors. In addition, the Austrian Postal Bank issued a new report identifying 7,000 dormant accounts of deported Jews and extending an earlier partial repayment process. Bank Austria settled a class action suit for $40 million in 1999 (Holocaust Reparations: *Watman v. Deutschebank*).

The mechanism of transnational financial accountability for human rights violations, pursued through litigation, has diffused widely. Former prisoners of war and slave laborers in Japan have filed 28 suits against implicated Japanese firms, such as Mitsubishi (Chang 2001, Liptak 2003).[6] African Americans have sought reparations for both enslavement and financial complicity, in nine suits naming 19 corporations—including Aetna Insurance and R.J. Reynolds (U.S. Newswire, 6/24/03). This initiative has diffused through the United Nations' Global Conference on Racism to an October 2002 Pan African movement conference in Barbados at which 500 participants voted to launch lawsuits against the major slave-trading nations (Inter-Press Service, 1/21/03). In response, Los Angeles and several other cities have required firms seeking municipal contracts to disclose their historic connections with slavery.

In a more contemporary vein, three American law firms have joined with a South African firm to bring suit in U.S. courts against U.S. companies for facilitating forced labor and torture under the apartheid government. For example, IBM provided computers and systems to maintain the national identity system that classified people by race for the South African government. In addition, some of the same lawyers involved in the Holocaust reparations cases have pursued transnational corporations such as Anglo-American Mining for general complicity with apartheid, under the Alien Torts Act (*Financial Times*, 5/20/03). The Holocaust reparations lawsuits against Swiss banks were cited by a group of Philippine victims suing the same Swiss banks for release of frozen assets to satisfy a civil judgment for human rights violations against former dictator Ferdinand Marcos (Ramasastry 1998)—a complementary mechanism of accountability discussed later.

In addition, half a dozen human rights lawsuits have been filed against multinational corporations for contemporary complicity with repressive regimes in production and/or investment. The best-known case, citing oil giant UNOCAL's collaboration with the Burmese government, was initially rejected in June 2003 but continues under appeal in U.S. courts. Similar suits have been filed against ChevronTexaco for its behavior toward minority groups in Nigeria, and ExxonMobil for supporting government repression in Indonesia. Occidental Petroleum has been sued at its U.S. corporate headquarters for allegedly aiding a Colombian government bombing of a village that killed dozens of civilians. In a further extension of the call for corporate accountability, citizen campaigns have petitioned for the revocation of corporate charters on the basis of overseas violations of environmental, labor, and human rights laws (Avery 2000).

Although these cases will meet diverse legal fates, the publicity and any settlements generated already contribute to the growing web of awareness and accountability. They add another tool to the repertoire of human rights activists and help construct the principle that businesses are accountable for more than balance sheets.

Socially Responsible Investment: Global Governance from Below?

Human rights activists can also "follow the money" bankrolling current political systems and practices. Politically selective investment is an attempt by consumers to "vote with their dollars," to influence the current and future behavior of private financial actors. As the founders of a leading socially responsible investing fund explain, "The power in guideline investing comes from linking a private act with public acts" (Kinder, Lydenberg, and Domini 1993: 4). Socially responsible investment may involve some combination of three activities. First, consumers, investment advisors, or mutual funds may engage in passive screening of the social behavior of companies, sectors, or countries contemplated for investment. This is the most common and consequential form of investment conditionality, detailed later.

Second, any of these agents—especially institutional or social movement investors—may purchase small amounts of stock in socially undesirable corporations, in order to file shareholder resolutions challenging their conduct. Each year, investors file over 100 such resolutions, targeting dozens of corporations (Interfaith Center on Corporate Responsibility, www.iccr.org, also see http://shareholderaction.org). Such activist investors are estimated to control about 5 percent of managed funds (French 2000: 9).

Finally, investors, funds, or credit unions may preferentially offer socially desirable investment opportunities, commonly referred to as "community investment." Although community investment can be influential in the United States, international community investment is somewhat marginal in size, activity level, and profitability. For example, Calvert's New Africa Fund has lost money every year since its inception in a bull market. An emerging parallel mechanism is the establishment of socially screened mutual funds by advocacy groups to fund their campaigns, pioneered by the Humane Society and proposed by the Sierra Club (Cushman 2001).

The deep historic roots of socially responsible investment come from seventeenth century Quakers' refusal to profit from war or slavery. During the nineteenth century, Protestants who eschewed investments in alcohol and tobacco founded the Pioneer Fund. The practice was revived in the United States during the 1960s, through a 1965 civil rights proxy voting campaign against Kodak, Ralph Nader's 1966 resolutions against General Motors, and the establishment of the Pax World Fund in 1970 by Methodists opposed to the Vietnam War (Kinder et al. 1993). The 1970s boycott campaign against Nestle for unsafe marketing of infant formula also targeted investors (Sikkink 1986). In response to shareholder pressure and disinvestment throughout the 1980s, around 350 companies eventually withdrew from South Africa (Rodman 2001, Klotz 1995).

Social screening is the dominant form of socially responsible investment. By 2002, there were 230 socially screened mutual funds according to the Social Investment Forum. Including all forms of social screening, over $2 trillion—around 12 percent of managed funds—are invested in screened portfolios, with continued absolute and relative growth even in declining markets (www.socialinvest.org). Several large, billion-plus players dominate the market. Dreyfus Premier Third Century has been in existence since 1972 and now controls over $1 billion. An equally large index fund is the Domini Social Equity Fund—which also designed the Domini Social Index, a socially screened alternative to the Standard & Poor's 500. Domini has recently been added to the pension menu at major corporations such as Ford and Hewlett-Packard (Hakim 2001). Socially responsible investment options within major financial players include the $4 billion TIAA-CREF Social Choice Equity Mutual Fund (part of the largest pension fund in the United States), and the Vanguard Calvert Social Index Fund—a collaboration between the U.S. second largest mutual fund and the largest family of nine socially responsible funds. In addition, California's $165 billion public employees pension fund—the nation's largest investment fund—agreed in 2001 to divest tobacco companies and investments in countries that restrict press, political, and labor freedoms (Hakim 2001).

Several smaller funds deepen social responsibility beyond avoidance: Green Century donates its profits to NGOs, DEVCAP allows investors to allocate to microenterprise projects in the developing world, and Bridgeway shares 50 percent of its profits with charity. In addition, over $1 billion of private portfolios are socially screened (Social Investment Forum 1999). Amy Domini, the founder of the $1.89 billion Domini Social Equity Funds, also manages $1.17 billion in private portfolios (Roosevelt 2000: 79).

International funds especially relevant to countries at risk for human rights violations include Citizens Global Equity, which partners with local NGOs, and the Calvert World Values International Equity. The Calvert Group has prepared internal policy papers on Burma, Mexico, China, and Nigeria, including minimum standards for investment in China. Another leading socially responsible international investment fund, Walden Capital Management, has screened out companies with repressive regimes or practices: Royal Dutch Shell/Shell Oil (Nigeria), Sony Corporation (Mexico), Philipp Holzmann AG (China), and Total SA (Burma) (Burch and Smith 1998). However, it should be noted that most socially screened international funds—like their agnostic counterparts—invest primarily in Europe and perhaps East Asia rather than true "emerging markets" (Johansson 2000), thus limiting the scope for regime conditionality.

Although the majority of socially screened investment is concentrated in the dominant U.S. financial market, there are over 40 screened funds in Britain, 20 in Sweden, and several in other European markets (James 2000: 33). Britain's funds comprise around 2 billion pounds and are growing rapidly (Avery 2000). Fourteen Canadian funds invest $3.8 billion, German screened funds comprise $2.2 billion, and France hosts 30 screened funds (Neuberger/Berman Newsletter, "Visions," 11/99). Calvert and six partners launched an Association for Sustainable and Responsible Investment in Asia in November 2001 (Calvert Impact, Winter 2002).

Investment guided by social principles now encompasses a wide range of participants pursuing principled goals, from environmentalists to Muslims to antiabortion activists to gay rights advocates. However, the preponderance of funding and investment vehicles are oriented toward a classic progressive agenda of environmental responsibility, humane labor conditions, and respect for human rights at home and abroad. Recent conferences have focused on a "triple bottom line"—screening and auditing companies' performance in financial, social, and environmental sustainability. Industry leader Domini Social Equity Fund employs typical social screens.[7] Domini "does not invest in companies that manufacture tobacco, alcohol, nuclear power, supply services to gambling operations, or derive more than 2 percent of gross revenues from the production of military weapons" and seeks "companies which pay fair wages, support human rights and protect the environment where they operate in less developed countries. We also look for companies that enforce a code of conduct in choosing where and with whom they will do business"—as well as a good record on employee relations, diversity, and product safety (www.domini.com). Domini links its investment screens with proxy voting guidelines, which specify global standards of human rights conduct, labor relations with offshore vendors, justice for indigenous peoples, and political and labor conditions in Burma, China, Indonesia, Mexico, Nigeria, Northern Ireland, Tibet, and (reinvestment in) South Africa. The Calvert Group screens are constructed by an advisory council that includes issue experts and representatives of NGOs. Bridgeway deepens the level of grassroots investor involvement by allowing participants to pick the investment screens through a survey and point system; the top corporate characteristics chosen have been environmental impact, family benefits, and charitable contributions ("Tiny Five-Star Fund Is One To Watch," *Business Ethics*, March/April 1999).

Even fairly comprehensive customary social screens for environmental, health, and human rights issues exclude about half of the U.S. exchange but leave in major multinationals such as ARCO, Merck, and Microsoft. In Britain, a weak human rights screen based on involvement with at least five repressive regimes excluded eight companies, 14 percent of the FT-SE All Share index, and a more specific screen for active cases of abuse regardless of regime type raised the exclusions to 11 companies, or 20 percent of the FT-SE 350 (Mansley 2000: 218). Another impact of social screening is a shift in sectoral balance that mirrors market trends and thus boosts returns; socially responsible investment generally favors high-technology and service over extractive and some manufacturing sectors. At a financial managers' roundtable, one portfolio manager explained, "Social concerns have kept us out of the commodities industries and the energy sector, and those stocks have been poor performers," and another affirmed that "Technology, financials, and health care tend to pass social screens easily, and they've done well lately ... other social issues of importance are tobacco, guns, maybe alcohol. Social investors stay away from those, and that's starting to look financially smart" (Social Investing Roundtable 1999).

Few of the major funds absolutely exclude investments on the basis of human rights violations and other "qualitative screens"—as they may with more delimited and measurable activities such as tobacco—but rather try to tilt toward companies with better records on balance and dialogue with those in questionable situations.[8] Human rights evaluation of companies operating overseas is complicated by analyzing the relationship between a particular company's activities and a repressive regime, regional integration of "host governments" (Kinder et al. 1993), as well as geographic diffusion of corporate operations. On the other hand, companies' global reach sometimes enables social funds to promote transnational dialogue regarding the practices of a sector or industry across various regimes, such as Calvert's exchange with its pharmaceutical holdings on AIDS drug access (Calvert Impact, Fall 2002)—this issue is further discussed in the next chapter.

Socially responsible investment is an initiative of civil society. One survey of public attitudes toward multinationals showed that 56 percent of respondents objected to companies operating in oppressive regimes (Mansley 2000: 217). Socially responsible investors tend to be younger and better educated than average but unwilling to sacrifice financial returns to pursue their values. For most, socially responsible investment is an extension of other forms of political activism rather than a substitute for charitable giving. Their values center first on environment and labor issues, and such investors are more concerned with avoiding negative investments than pursuing affirmative policies or opportunities (Rosen, Sandler, and Shani 1991)

Religious activists often provide the impetus, normative basis, private resources, and transnational networks for socially responsible investment. For example, France's first ethical investment funds were started by Sister Nicole Rielle of the Order of Notre Dame in 1983. Her funds have now attracted investment from 80 religious orders in France, and she is moving to Rome to advise religious orders headquartered there (Simons 2003).

Several key organizations provide the information, rationale, and constituency for socially responsible investment. The Interfaith Center on Corporate Responsibility (ICCR) is a coalition of 275 religious institutional investors established in 1971 that controls about $90 billion in investments and engages in both social screening and shareholder activism. The ICCR, along with its British and Canadian counterparts, has issued an 80-page set of widely referenced standards, "Principles for Global Corporate Responsibility: Bench Marks for Measuring Business Performance." The Council on Economic Priorities has pioneered a rating system for corporations (the Social Accountability 8000 based on International Labor Organization conventions), and the 1,400-member Business For Social Responsibility includes industry leaders such as Levi Strauss, Reebok, General Motors, and Johnson & Johnson.

But even this purely private conditionality is regulated and mediated by the state. In 1983, the U.S. Securities and Exchange Commission limited the scope of shareholder activism by restricting shareholder resolutions to those holding $1,000 or 1 percent of the company's stock for at least 18 months prior to filing (Brill and Reder 1992). Different patterns of shareholding and corporate governance regulation generally make shareholder activism more difficult outside the United States; in Canada, activists are campaigning to repeal legislation that prohibits political or social shareholder resolutions. On the other hand, some states have provided a supportive regulatory environment for socially responsible investment: as of July 2000, British pension funds must disclose the social considerations that govern their investments and provide contributors with some form of voting rights over investment criteria (Mansley 2000).

Numerous studies confirm that socially screened investments thus far equal or even outperform conventional funds. A review of 21 studies conducted during the 1990s concludes that "the balance of evidence suggests a discernibly positive impact on financial performance from superior environmental performance [which almost always overlaps with human rights in screened funds]" (Mansley 2000: Appendix 1). The nonprofit Social Investment Forum confirms that 12 of 17 major screened funds earn high ratings from the industry tracking sources, Morningstar and Lipper. The Domini 400 alternative index exceeded the Standard & Poor's 500 for much of the 1990s (Sauser 1997)—although it trailed for the first time in 2000. Even during 2001 to 2003 market declines, leading socially responsible funds such as Neuberger lost less than their peers (Gould 2003). One recent study does sound a cautionary note, warning that the concentration on technology stocks may have artificially inflated social funds—and predicting that the restrictions inherent in social screening will inevitably reduce returns in the longer term (Hulbert 2003).

Activists debate the rationale and projected impact of socially responsible investment. Although early enthusiasts hoped that massive disinvestment would affect stock prices, this has generally not occurred. Even in two "best cases" of social impact via disinvestment—tobacco and South Africa—share prices never measurably changed. One analyst estimates that it would take 60 to 70 percent disinvestment to affect prices. Rather, "divestment works because it helps create a climate of opinion of social disapproval, and companies are very sensitive to this kind of disapproval. That's why they spend tens of millions of dollars every year on public relations and philanthropic activities: because they know that a well-regarded company will find every part of doing business easier. . . ." (Kelly 2000). And disinvestment can influence individual corporate decisions and *anticipated* risk even before it reaches the bottom line: one chief executive officer (CEO) explained that the company withdrew from South Africa because "we didn't want to sit by and watch while our stock was being dumped all around the country because of our South Africa ties" (Smith 1992). Two of the founders of the socially responsible investing movement, fund managers and creators of the benchmark Domini 400 Social Index, argue that "Most investors apply screens out of a need for personal or institutional consistency. No one involved in SRI would argue that it has as its objective increasing a company's cost of capital . . . [The objective is] the communication of a judgment both to the corporation and the world at large" (Kinder and Domini 1997: 14).[9]

In specific cases of isolated investments in highly vulnerable pariah regimes, financial accountability through social investment pressures may have a more marked impact. Sudan has been widely criticized for a 17-year civil war claiming millions of victims, "ethnic cleansing" by its fundamentalist Islamic regime, torture, political prisoners, slavery, abysmal treatment of women and girls, state-sponsored famine, and harboring terrorists. The connection to foreign investment is the use of oil revenues to sustain the Khartoum government; "proceeds from oil production have allowed the government to nearly double its military spending over the last three years."

One of the major investors was Talisman Energy, a Canadian oil company operating in southern Sudan in a consortium with Chinese, Malaysian, and Sudanese state oil companies. Talisman CEO James Buckee countered human rights critics by arguing that Talisman had adopted a code of ethics and human rights monitoring in its operations, provided human rights training to its security staff, constructed hospitals and schools in the oil concession area, and had "taken on an advocacy role at the highest levels of the government of Sudan, where we have discussed numerous issues, including the protection of human rights, the peace process and the equitable distribution of oil revenue. . . . While business interests cannot fix the problems inherent in many parts of the developing world, under most circumstances, ethical companies can help change society for the better" (Simon 2001). But socially responsible investors rejected these arguments. Following the Sudan controversy and $60 million of related divestments, Talisman's stock declined from $33 to $25 per share (Pike and Booysen 2000). The states of New York, California, New Jersey, Texas, and Wisconsin in various ways restricted government purchases of Talisman. Meanwhile, a U.S. congressional bill sought to exclude foreign companies operating in Sudan from trading on U.S. stock exchanges.[10] By November 2002, Talisman had agreed to sell its holdings in Sudan (Baue 2002).

Although corporate responses are often delayed and indirect, there are several visible areas of change—especially when investment pressures are combined with state sanctions or other types of information campaigns. When Burma was identified as a human rights pariah through boycott campaigns, shareholder resolutions, local selective purchasing sanctions, and investor dialogues during the 1990s, Levi's, Motorola, Eddie Bauer, Liz Claiborne, Pepsi, and eventually Atlantic Richfield all discontinued operations in that country. Between June 2000 and July 2003, an additional 39 companies have refused to sell goods made in Burma because of concerns about labor rights and human rights conditions (www.free-burmacoalition.org). Antisweatshop initiatives culminating in the five-year campaign against Nike resulted in the formation of the Apparel Industry Partnership, an industry-wide code of conduct and monitoring scheme for transnational apparel producers. Individual companies have gone further to identify themselves as "socially responsible" to investors and consumers: Levi's has drafted Global Sourcing Guidelines mandating country and contractor respect for rights, and Reebok shifted its outsourcing of soccer balls in Pakistan in an attempt to avoid child labor (Schoenberg 2000). Similarly, socially responsible investment pressure persuaded Wal-Mart in 1992 to adopt guidelines for vendors that barred the use of child labor (Kelly 2000). Reebok helped to secure the release of an imprisoned Indonesian labor leader whose case had been highlighted by Amnesty International (www.coopamerica.org/sweatshops/ssvictories.htm). TRW Inc. sold their Northern Ireland operation rather than go through a proxy battle over the MacBride Principles, which mandate specific workplace protections for religious minorities (Kinder et al. 1993: 242). Even oft-targeted Shell modified its policies in Nigeria after widespread negative publicity surrounding the execution of Ken Saro-Wiwa—and a 1997 shareholder action at its annual meeting. After a Colombian Indian leader from an area endangered by oil development visited a series of U.S. investors, Fidelity Investments sold more than $400 million of Occidental stock—and eventually Occidental suspended drilling in the disputed area (Rivera Brooks 2002).

The case of Conflict diamonds is probably the most systematic, multi-lateral, proactive case of private sector accountability to date. By 1999, UN reports combined with NGO publicity campaigns had revealed the illicit sale of diamonds from Sierra Leone, Angola, and Congo as a key source of finance for bloody insurgencies generating vast violations in those battered regions. The diamond industry is unusually concentrated in a single firm (DeBeers controls about half of global trade), the tainted gems constitute only an estimated 3 percent of that trade, and newly democratic South Africa worried that public castigation of conflict diamonds would spill over into a wider boycott that would harm their large legitimate industry. Therefore, the global private industry association—the World Diamond Council—collaborated actively with NGOs and trading states to set up a certification system, and DeBeers voluntarily withdrew from Angola. Meanwhile, UN embargoes on Angola's UNITA and Sierra Leone were followed by the 48-state Kimberley Process of regulation and monitoring. The United States passed the Clean Diamond Act of 2001. The Angolan government signed a direct agreement for certification with Belgium's Diamond High Council, which combines importers and the Ministry of Economy. And the British government blocked a diamond company linked to Congo exports (via Zimbabwe) from a seat on the London stock exchange (Tamm 2002). When the issue is clear and concentrated, the stakes are small, and coalitions of nongovernmental, intergovernmental, and transnational bodies collaborate, the flow of blood money can be stanched.

Systematic study seems to show that in the post–Cold War world, multinationals are "risk minimizers" who pursue pragmatic investment policies based on the relative size and profitability of their stake compared with potential costs at home from disinvestment, boycotts, negative publicity, and government sanctions (Rodman 2001). When the International Council of Mining and Metals—the world's 15 largest mining companies—along with Shell Oil pledged to forgo exploring in United Nations World Heritage sites, an investment firm leader explained that the companies "decided there is more shareholder value to their reputation than the resources" (Timmons 2003).

Cutting off Capital: Harnessing State Sanctions

As asset control has emerged as a tool of foreign policy, it has also become a potential pathway for the pursuit of financial accountability for human rights violations. Although asset control is generated by states and generally applied to state violators, it plays a role complementary to that of the private pathways profiled earlier. Government sanctions against repressive regimes are usually sought by global civil society activists as part of a multi-faceted campaign of boycotts, disinvestment, and legal action against both repressive regimes and their financial supporters. Sanctions often include state bans on private trade or investment, above and beyond interstate freezing of leaders' assets. This subtype of state sanctions on business also relies—and sometimes founders—on the private power of business to influence target regimes' policies and survival. The recent extension of asset control from deposed dictators to terrorists further intertwines public accountability, private flows, and private violators. Thus, state sanctions bear further examination as a distinct but related mechanism of human rights conditionality.

Guarantees of the sanctity of transnational financial property have always been subject to one significant exception: state security. Although the developed countries condemn economically based asset freezes and seizures (such as postrevolutionary nationalization of foreign investment), the U.S. and European banking centers have retained an arsenal of tools for asset control on security grounds. In response to evolving security threats and understandings, such mechanisms have expanded in range, frequency, and multilateralism. At the same time, by the 1980s human rights campaigns had moved from foreign aid conditionality to a recognition of the direct investor or purchasing role of northern governments in repressive regimes or exploitative multinationals. Thus, they began to scrutinize or suggest state sanctions. Sanctions may include bans on direct interstate economic transactions, government prohibition of trade or exchange by its citizens with a foreign government, national regulation of multinationals operating overseas, attempts to penalize foreign governments or firms for trading with a targeted regime, or participation in a multilateral prohibition or limitation of trade or investment in a specific country or region.

Unlike reparations or socially responsible investment, sanctions were designed not to promote human rights accountability but rather to punish regimes. But the promotion of human rights has periodically been served by the availability of local, national, and multilateral cutoffs of capital, even when such measures were adopted for unrelated or mixed purposes. Even symbolic state sanctions send a message to pariah regimes and third parties that may inform their long-term relationships. State sanctions can also have a multiplier effect on grassroots disinvestment or boycotts, as they seemed to do in South Africa (Rodman 2001). Government asset seizures may provide the funds to satisfy reparations judgments—as in the Marcos case discussed later. However, in some situations, unilateral state sanctions based on security may actually undermine human rights practices, multilateral institutions, and civic campaigns, as was widely alleged in Iraq during the 1990s. The coercive cutoff of capital is a blunt instrument, which must be carefully analyzed for appropriateness and effectiveness in particular cases, especially when private actors are implicated in the human rights violations.

The U.S. assets control regime is probably the most comprehensive and frequently employed. It began with direct interstate freezes on enemy property in wartime, as the United States did to Japan and Germany during World War II (under a doctrine called "custodian of enemy property"). This practice was extended to other warlike security situations, such as Iran's seizure of American diplomats as hostages in 1979. Assets have also been frozen as a response to foreign uncompensated expropriation, as in Cuba.[11] Most of this activity has fallen under the Trading with the Enemy Act or the president's International Emergency Economic Powers. As the asset control regime developed broader applications, the United States also increasingly cited the United Nations Participation Act and United Nations Security Council resolutions relevant to specific countries. Sanctions with a human rights basis or potential impact were usually adopted only when strong domestic or transnational constituencies combined with highly affective symbolic leaders and issues: the charisma of Aung San Suu Kyi in Burma and the Free Burma Coalition, the revulsion against slavery, and the U.S. network of religious activists in the case of Sudan.

The U.S. Treasury Department has established an Office of Foreign Assets Control to institutionalize and coordinate asset freezes and trade embargoes. OFAC administers 21 economic sanctions programs, including abusive regimes in Burma, North Korea, Sierra Leone, and Sudan in addition to the ongoing cases cited previously (such as Cuba). Afghanistan was added to the list in 1999, after the attacks on American embassies in Kenya and Tanzania; the Taliban regime also garnered UN sanctions. Human rights concerns are cited in the executive orders for sanctions against Burma, Cuba, Iraq, and Sudan (www.ustreas.gov/offices/eotffc/ofac). These asset control programs block thousands of transactions each year and refer hundreds of cases for prosecution (Statement of R. Richard Newcomb, Director of the Office of Foreign Assets Control, Senate Appropriations Subcommittee, May 10, 2001).

Country-specific sanctions on investment in Burma, trade with Sudan, and diamonds from Sierra Leone have responded directly to human rights campaigns. For example, imprisoned Burmese opposition leader Aung San Suu Kyi directly proposed sanctions on investment, and the director of the Free Burma Coalition testified at the 2003 Senate hearings preceding congressional expansion of sanctions from investment to trade. In response to 2003 physical attacks and the subsequent incommunicado detention of Aung San Suu Kyi, the United States has imposed a complete range of sanctions including a freeze on government assets and import ban (Bonner 2003).

Parallel developments concerning the regulation of assets have become relevant to the financial prosecution of foreign leaders. Measures adopted in response to tax evasion and later money laundering also became tools to locate and freeze the U.S. assets of corrupt fallen dictators. The (misnamed) 1970 Banking Secrecy Act requires U.S. banks to report certain transactions. The U.S. government may also secure a "financial search warrant" in both civil and criminal cases. Although criminal forfeiture of assets requires a conviction and link between the seized assets and underlying crime, the government can and does also seize assets via civil forfeiture—which merely requires the state to show probable cause that the property is unlawfully acquired or the instrumentality of a crime (Ferguson 1998). One of the Clinton administration's last acts was the introduction of voluntary intensified monitoring and reporting guidelines for the U.S. financial activities of foreign leaders, their families, and known business associates by U.S. banks and brokerages. The new guidelines were modeled on recent Swiss initiatives to monitor money laundering, in anticipation of future legal action (Kahn 2001).

During the post–Cold War era of democratization, the United States began financially prosecuting foreign leaders who were both opposing U.S. policy and violating the human rights of their own people. In a precursor of the trend, the United States froze the assets of deposed Haitian dictator Jean-Claude Duvalier in 1986 via an executive order responding to a congressional provision. During the Gulf War, the Allies froze Saddam Hussein's assets. But then, in 1992, Iraqi assets were seized by the UN on humanitarian grounds—to provide relief to starving Kurds and pay reparations to Kuwait. In 1993, the United States froze the assets of Haiti's ruling generals and several dozen associates, in response to their ouster of the elected president Jean-Bertrand Aristide. In this case, the justification mixed security and human rights sanctions—although the generals were not an enemy power and had not interfered with U.S. citizens or property (Hufbauer, Schott, and Elliott 1990; Lopez and Cortright 1995).

The first cases of financial freezes based *primarily* on human rights concerns involved former Philippine dictator Ferdinand Marcos (U.S.-Switzerland) and then Serbian President Slobodan Milosevic (Switzerland, see later). After Marcos was overthrown and exiled to Hawaii in 1986, a group of 10,000 human rights victims filed suit against the dictator in U.S. court. Meanwhile, the new Philippine government requested a freeze on Marcos' assets in Swiss banks, alleging massive corruption and plunder of the national treasury. The two cases came together when the torture victims received a $2 billion civil judgment in U.S. court against Marcos in 1995 but were unable to fulfill it—so they approached the Swiss banks, seeking access to the dictator's $500 million in frozen assets. The U.S. judge ordered the Swiss banks to forfeit Marcos' accounts to the victims but was refused by the Swiss government with the support of the U.S. State Department. Instead, the banks repatriated the dictator's funds to the Philippines, in an unprecedented move, while simultaneously urging the successor Aquino government to provide relief to the plaintiffs (Ramasastry 1998).

From the mid-1990s onward, terrorism came to represent a newly salient form of private sector human rights violation subject to growing financial conditionality. Terrorism combines all three historical bases of asset controls: security threat, opposition to U.S. foreign policy goals, and human rights violations. The Clinton administration laid the groundwork for the current financial campaign against Osama bin Laden in 1995. Following a dramatic suicide bombing in Israel, Clinton ordered the Treasury Department to freeze the assets of domestic Middle Eastern groups believed to support terrorism such as Hamas and Islamic Jihad—under the rubric of disrupting the Mideast peace process. In the same year, the president invoked the International Emergency Economic Powers Act to block assets of large-scale narcotics dealers based in Colombia. These moves marked a development in the targets of asset control from enemy states to illegitimate leaders to threatening individuals and organizations. Prior to September 11, 29 foreign terrorist organizations were already subject to OFAC sanctions (Newcomb 2001). The potential for private sector human rights accountability beyond U.S. security interests is further illustrated by a case in Colombia, where authorities have begun to trace the financial network of right-wing paramilitaries—responsible for the majority of that country's hundreds of massacres—to a Miami bank. Colombia has requested U.S. Treasury Department assistance to investigate (Weekly News Update on the Americas, #612, October 21, 2001).

The U.S. financial response to the September 11 terrorist attacks represents an expansion of kind as well as degree of asset controls, as well as a deepening of multilateral cooperation. By November 15, the United States had frozen the assets of 150 people or groups suspected of terrorist links (Wells 2001). Within the Department of the Treasury, a new Terrorist Asset Tracking Center has been created, and the Customs Service has activated Operation Green Quest. The United Nations has drafted a Convention on the Suppression of the Financing of Terrorism that requires signatories to freeze and seize the assets of organizations that support terrorism. After September 11, the UN Security Council adopted an unusually clear and sweeping resolution (1373) declaring that "States should prohibit their nationals or persons or entities in their territories from making funds, financial assets, economic resources, financial or other related services available to persons who commit or attempt to commit, facilitate or participate in the commission of terrorist acts" (Security Council, 4385th Meeting, SC/1758, September 28, 2001).

Meanwhile, at the local-global level, dozens of U.S. states and cities have enacted standards or preferences that limit their purchases in response to apartheid, human rights violations in Burma, forced labor, religious discrimination in Northern Ireland, claims by Holocaust survivors, and environmental impact (Stumberg and Waren 1999). At the peak of the anti-apartheid campaign in 1985, 58 U.S. cities, 14 states, and nine counties refused to deposit funds in banks that extended loans to South Africa.

Twenty U.S. states and 164 municipalities directly disinvested their funds from South Africa. A decade later, human rights advocates for Burma persuaded the state of Massachusetts and 21 major cities to ban procurement from companies doing business in Burma. These bans apparently influenced key investors, such as Apple Computers and Motorola, who withdrew from Burma to maintain more lucrative contracts with Massachusetts and San Francisco (Rodman 2001).[12] These municipal and state-level sanctions usually target financial actors rather than foreign leaders, so they are closer to the transnational civic model.

Although the United States has been the main exporter of financial conditionality, other major banking centers have also participated, and conditionality has grown increasingly multilateralized. Swiss measures are particularly significant because Switzerland is estimated to control about one third of the $2.2 trillion private international banking industry (Cowell 2003), and the Swiss tradition of banking secrecy historically sheltered a certain proportion of ill-gotten gains. Switzerland, in response to U.S. pressure, has passed a series of measures progressively limiting banking secrecy and increasing cooperation in prosecutions for financial and criminal offenses. In 1977, Switzerland and the United States signed a major treaty mandating information, freezing, and forfeiture of Swiss accounts in accordance with a U.S. government request, covering 35 offenses—including embezzlement and organized crime but not political offenses or tax evasion (Ferguson 1998). The 1981 Law on International Judicial Assistance in Criminal Matters and a 1983 Swiss banking law expanded this cooperation to all states requesting assistance (this formed the basis for the Marcos asset repatriation). In 1992, Switzerland prohibited truly anonymous accounts and expanded banks' due diligence requirements. A 1998 law on money laundering requires all financial intermediaries to ascertain the identity of (formerly secret) account holders and requires banks and brokerages to report and temporarily block suspicious transactions (Aubert 1997).

The human rights application of this escalating financial conditionality was a series of Swiss freezes on the assets of deposed dictators throughout the 1990s, including Ferdinand Marcos, Romania's Nicolai Ceausescu, Haiti's Jean Claude "Baby Doc" Duvalier, Zaire/Congo's Mobutu Sese Seku, Panama's Manuel Noriega, and Pakistan's Benazir Bhutto (Ramasastry 1998). In 1999, Switzerland also seized and partially repatriated the accounts of Nigeria's former leader Sani Abacha. All of these dictators had been accused, and in some cases convicted, of violations of fundamental rights such as murder and torture as well as looting their state's treasury.[13] Asset controls were also implemented by other banking centers relevant to each dictator: Britain froze Bhutto's holdings, Belgium blocked Mobutu's accounts, France investigated Duvalier, Liechtenstein and Luxembourg froze Abacha's accounts, and Cyprus cut off Yugoslav companies and banks associated with Slobodan Milosevic.

The Milosevic case was unique in that it resulted from a request by a multilateral legal tribunal, the International Criminal Tribunal for the former Yugoslavia (ICTY), which indicted the then-president for war crimes. In 1999, the ICTY issued an order to member countries of the UN to freeze assets, then a separate request to Switzerland (not a UN member). It was the first time that Switzerland had frozen the assets of an acting head of state, further diminishing sovereign immunity for human rights violations. The action against Milosevic is also cited to "indicate that increasingly war crimes are furnishing a predicate offense for international asset freezes" (International Enforcement Law Reporter, August 1999, v. 15, n. 8). In a related interjurisdictional case, in 1997 Switzerland agreed to freeze the bank accounts of four Argentine military officers charged by Spain with "disappearing" Spanish nationals during Argentina's 1976 to 1983 military dictatorship—asserting transnational jurisdiction over the objections of the Argentine government (Simons 1997).

There has been a convergence of mechanisms created for enemy states, illegitimate foreign leaders, and money laundering to sanction a growing class of human rights violations by transnational networks of private individuals. NGOs that developed to monitor corruption, such as Transparency International and Global Witness, provide complementary information on politics to human rights campaigns. And emerging mechanisms of global governance, such as the 32-state Financial Action Task Force on Money Laundering, have shrunk illicit fund havens to seven jurisdictions (Cowell 2004). The power of a panoply of new multilateral pressures for financial accountability on private actors and even banking haven states is illustrated by the head of Panama's newly active financial analysis unit, as she cooperated with American investigators: "Panama cannot afford to have a bad reputation. We are a service economy. You have to give service but with adequate controls" (Gonzalez 2001).

The Invisible Handcuff: From Profit to Principle

The cases discussed to this point reveal a clear emergence of growing channels for financial sector accountability for human rights violations. The establishment of new norms does seem to result in changes in behavior by transnational actors as well as states (Vayrynen 1999). Moreover, the proliferation of pressures for accountability seems to be producing a preemptive consciousness of social responsibility among leading corporate sectors. On July 26, 2000, 50 multinationals signed a UN-sponsored "global compact" on human rights and the environment, along with a dozen nongovernmental watchdog groups. The Global Social Compact with business includes the UN Human Rights Commission and has been adopted by hundreds of large international corporations—including

Bayer, DuPont, and Nike (variously targeted by socially responsible investment and Holocaust reparations campaigns discussed before). The compact is a voluntary code of conduct, legitimated by the UN and monitored by NGOs (Kahn 2000).

However, the scope and limits of financial accountability and these specific mechanisms vary widely. Although socially responsible investment is the most widespread, longstanding, and autonomous practice, its agenda is diffuse and its effectiveness seems limited to causes célèbre. By contrast, more clearly effective financial reparations have thus far been limited to a single (albeit massive and complex) case. Asset seizures are the most authoritative, but wholly dependent on state power, and thus generally subsumed in wider agendas of national security or economic malfeasance. And overall, the fungibility of markets may still weaken the power of shifts in resources to reduce repression. Disinvestment and sanctions may be evaded by diffuse market linkages or merely shift from more accountable multinationals and financiers to more local or less visible investors and bankers. For example, multinationals pulling out of South Africa often simply shifted control to white South African partners but continued to license technology or other parts of the production process (Rodman 2001).

To the extent that markets are regulated, the power and nature of the state become another potential barrier to financial accountability. Although human rights and victims' organizations have developed comparative skills in influencing legislatures and judiciaries—especially in the United States, executive and regulatory agencies exercise important influence over financial accountability. Socially responsible investment depends on the U.S. Securities and Exchange Commission, financial reparations depend on banking commissions and the State Department, and asset controls involve the president, State Department, and Treasury. These agencies' reduced transparency and responsiveness to civil society constitute challenges and potential limits for future campaigns.

Although all of these attempts to govern financial flows originated in the United States, initiatives for financial accountability have globalized through diffusion and hegemony. Socially responsible investment has spread by example to Europe and beyond. Financial reparations using the leverage (or mere threat) of U.S. political and commercial power motivated settlements in half a dozen countries. In the most multilateral arena, common interests in combating money laundering and security threats have inspired the developed countries to coordinate asset freezes pioneered by the United States, with the side effect of facilitating sanctions and suits against dictators across the major banking centers. Although these changes have spread, they have not yet truly *institutionalized*, and they stand mostly as intriguing precedents or "best practices."

As a short-run solution to governance of globalization, some suggest a combination of liberal free markets for economic gain with structured escape clauses for political accountability (Rodrik 2000). Although this model was postulated to explain state-based political struggles over the social welfare impacts of globalization, it also seems to fit the emerging pattern of integrating global finance with escape clauses for human rights. This "invisible handcuff" of loose, multifaceted sanctions on financial complicity in gross violations is a far cry from systematic transnational accountability. But it is a giant step beyond business as usual.

5

New Rights: "Our Bodies, Ourselves"

Big Science. Hallelujah. Every man, every man for himself.

Laurie Anderson

The globalization of science and medicine has introduced new challenges for human rights as new technologies create new boundaries for the body and governance strives to define corresponding boundaries of the person. New diseases, medicines, procedures, and research modalities push human rights beyond the defense of the bodily integrity of individuals from state coercion. The source of both boundary violations and putative duties is usually private, whether physicians, firms, or academic institutions. Medical phenomena such as the transmission of communicable disease or the transplantation of organs are public issues not reducible to an individual's relationship with a physician or scientist, and states struggle to regulate them but cannot fully encompass their transnational dimension. New procedures and research to address health problems often have collective implications, whether for families consenting to organ donations or entire ethnic groups affected by genetic privacy. Although new practices are often experienced as threats to human dignity, it is sometimes unclear exactly which rights are affected—or how to evaluate competing rights of patients versus society, donors versus recipients, or privacy versus freedom of inquiry.

Debates on medical and research rights represent a deep political challenge of the knowledge professions. Challengers carry a double burden: first, to demonstrate that the private is political, then, to show that rational expertise carries interests and bears consequences. As one analyst put it, after a broad survey of the role of scientists in human rights:

89

> Has politics entered the house of science, and if so, what is it doing there? In a dynamic society, it is impossible to draw a strict line between science and the tides of social change. They overlap, and if it is argued that science is value-free the same cannot be said of scientists. If scientific freedom is half the operative equation, responsibility is the other half. (Claude 2002: 145)

Each of the issues profiled here illustrates a different set of rights dilemmas for globalized medicine in a knowledge economy. Patients' access to patented pharmaceuticals pits intellectual property rights against health access and resource rights. In this case, multinational firms are the addressees of rights claims and both states and international organizations such as the WTO serve as the mediators.

Transplant trafficking embodies a multiple dilemma, partially dependent on the genre of practices: state sponsored or private, living donors or dead. The combinations of claims to self-determination and freedom from economic coercion echo debates over bonded labor, and state-sponsored organ trafficking raises familiar questions of government violation of bodily integrity. At a minimum, organ transplantation involves the rights of donors to be free of state coercion, the right to full informed consent for living donors, the right to full and fair compensation if donation is permitted, the right to protection of bodily integrity from commodification if donation is prohibited, the health rights of recipients to access life-sustaining technologies and resources, and the rights of families to decision making for their dead. These rights are controlled by states, markets, doctors, and brokers.

Finally, genetic research seems to counterpoise the right to knowledge and the right to privacy. But additional elements of identity and group rights complicate the picture and introduce collective subjects. And some claims actually mix the right to medical self-determination with the property rights of patients to their own bodies. The targets of genetic rights claims include academic researchers, affiliated physicians, transnational biotechnology firms, and states that license genetic databases.

Globalization and Medicine at the Human Rights Frontier

International human rights clearly encompass health, as a direct entitlement, a source of enabling agency, and an arena for self-determination. The Universal Declaration of Human Rights cites a right to "a standard of living adequate for the health and well-being of himself and of his family, including . . . medical care. . . ." (Article 25), everyone's right to access to the advances of science (Article 27), and an international order that permits the transfer of technology (Article 28). The binding International Covenant on Economic and Social Rights reiterates a right to the "highest attainable standard" of health and charges states to create "conditions which would assure to all medical service" (Article 12). Meanwhile, Article 7 of the International Covenant on Civil and Political Rights forbids medical or scientific experimentation without consent (Claude 2002). Like other rights, these standards are difficult to implement. But far more than other rights norms, in the generations since these definitions, their meaning is difficult to define and their source difficult to capture (Leary 1993). A "right to health" might mean a right to access to health services, a right to resources necessary to achieve health, a right to medical self-determination, a right to resist conditions or policies that endanger health, a right to health information and transparency, a right to informed consent, or even a right to decision making and accountability for health programs and policies.

Medical abuse has been a global concern since the Nuremberg trials' revelation of Holocaust medical experiments, which resulted in the widely referenced Nuremberg Code mandating informed consent and full disclosure of medical research (Annas and Grodin 1992). The World Medical Association, representing eight million physicians in 70 countries through memberships in national medical associations, adopted similar guidelines in its 1964 Helsinki Declaration and 1975 Declaration of Tokyo. The latter document was partially inspired by the revelation of physicians' participation in torture under the Pinochet regime that had recently taken power in Chile (Claude 2002: 188–89). In these codes as well as cross-cultural tradition, physicians as a special class of private individuals have a unique duty to safeguard the welfare and dignity of another group of individuals: their patients. The postwar Tuskegee experiments, in which U.S. Public Health Service physicians studied untreated syphilis in uninformed black males after treatment was available, highlighted the possibility of "routine" medical abuse in a democratic society in peacetime (Jones 1993). A widespread response was the creation of national human subjects standards and ethics review committees at hospitals and universities. But this regulatory regime could not address three kinds of situations that became increasingly salient with globalization: private control of public health resources, transnational trafficking in health procedures, and biotechnology transcending the boundaries of the individual patient.

Several strands of theory attempt to analyze the global politics of science and medicine. Feminist theory introduced the contemporary critique of the power relations of Western medicine, countering with a call for self-determination and democratization of knowledge rooted in a rediscovery of the body: "our bodies, ourselves" (Elshtain and Cloyd 1995). Sociological institutionalism charted the global diffusion of Western scientific norms and institutions and the resulting creation of transnational networks of governance (Boli and Thomas 1999). In a related vein, research on such transnational networks of experts has shown the power of knowledge-based interest groups to frame, lobby, and often influence states' or international organizations' treatment of a scientific issue (Haas 1992).

Beyond the power of scientists themselves, science also undergirds or participates in other forms of power. Critics of imperialism show how the knowledge professions contributed to the construction of empire (Anderson 1996), and postcolonial analysts decry the contribution of science to "biopiracy" and market domination of the developing world (Shiva 2001). In a more generic and global political economy critique, scientific and medical practices are subject to a spreading logic of commodification worldwide. Scholars of law debate the boundaries and desirability of property rights in human bodies and practices associated with personal identity (Radin 1996).

The deepest reading of scientific and medical knowledge as power comes from postmodern depictions of micropower and biopolitics (Foucault 1970, 1979, 1994). In this analysis, daily practices of modernist social control, exercised through homologous institutions that blur the boundary between public and private, such as hospitals, go beyond externally structuring health to penetrate our identities and understanding of our own needs and interests. For postmodernists, previous prescriptions of increased access to knowledge by individuals, definition of legal rights and decision making, or greater autonomy of science from coercion and commodification may not be sufficient to address this deeper process. Local resistance, subversive diversity, and deconstruction of liberal norms would be more appropriate responses.

Yet what this chapter shows has actually occurred is a slippery but familiar process of reframing new medical phenomena as human rights issues. Transnational networks have introduced new standards of accountability for private actors, although such standards are difficult to implement (Weissbrodt 2002). The standard human rights repertoires—diffusion of knowledge, legal regulation, and periodic protest—have been the key vehicles for progress on medical rights. Although the political *process* of reframing of medicine has followed the general patterns of liberal agenda reconstruction, the *content* has introduced some elements of the postmodern perspective of identity politics. Conventional knowledge campaigns are delivering some unconventional messages about the boundaries of the body and questioning the scientific imperative to maximize manipulation and control of health.

This new wave of human rights issues also differs from previous struggles in two additional ways: the source of challenge and the need to expand the central discourse of human rights. Professional associations rather than conventional human rights organizations lead the struggle to define new standards for practices such as pharmaceutical access, organ transplants, and genetic research. As one practitioner and scholar of medical campaigns for human rights puts it, "Medicine and public health benefit from an extraordinary symbolic capital that is, so far, sadly underutilized in human rights work" (Farmer 2003: 234). In addition, a new kind of group identity—the disease-affected community, clustered around disease organizations and advocacy groups—often emerges through struggles for medical rights (Greely 1997).

In terms of rights discourse, emerging medical practices often push human rights claims from the first generation of individual protection from coercion to the second generation of economic rights and even the third generation of group rights. In order to save lives threatened by deadly diseases that can be controlled with privately held medicines, physicians are brought to question an institutional order that denies the resources necessary to secure the right to life to millions by accident of birth. Widespread and socially sanctioned violations of the health rights of the poor illuminate "structural violence" and the dependence of civil and political rights on the fulfillment of social and economic rights (Farmer 2003). Similarly, transplant trafficking subjects individuals lacking economic rights to the deconstruction of bodily integrity and conditions the health rights of recipients on the resources and will to exploit structural inequalities (Pogge 2002). In general, international law now supports a broader "right to health." Although the right to health is usually conceived as state-sponsored equality of access, lack of interference, and provision of services and conditions, it may also imply regulatory or delegation relationships between the state and private parties (Toebes 1999). In the third generation of group rights, genetic research may entail the privacy, property, or persecution of an entire family, ethnic group, or nation (Lyons and Mayall 2003).

Many medical struggles also highlight property rights to one's own body or knowledge. Human rights advocates preoccupied with economic rights to public goods such as health care often slight property rights as a luxury for the rich, who generally live in capitalist societies that protect property rights in any case. But property rights are an integral part of the Universal Declaration and the International Covenants and may be important vehicles for social justice as well as fundamental freedoms. For example, state usurpation of peasant plots has been an important contributor to poverty and catalyst for physical abuse in both authoritarian capitalist and state socialist regimes in Africa, Asia, and Latin America. On the affirmative side, some strategies for poverty alleviation seek to foster the recognition and reward of property rights to traditional knowledge, unclaimed lands, unregistered businesses, or cultural production. These rest on some regime of intellectual property rights, which may be just as important to the poor as to a pharmaceutical company, particularly in group rights to genetic information. Where controlled commodification is deemed preferable to uncontrolled trafficking, as some advocates for organ donors now argue, a generalizable and enforceable system of property rights may be a key component of the protection of human dignity (Kass 1995; Blumstein 1995).

Evolving challenges to the human condition, along with the application of universal yet unique human capacities to those challenges, thus inspire the extension of existing rights to new fields, the creation of new rights, and the search for new forms of transnational governance. Like children's migration, struggles over globalized medicine have expanded the *agenda* of health rights, as well as *information* transparency and awareness. Health rights similarly lack *leverage* over private actors—although more successful cases of reform such as increased access to AIDS pharmaceuticals show the pattern of *transnational* governance shared by financial campaigns, with a convergence of transnational activism, national legal systems, and international organizations.

AIDS Pharmaceuticals: "Human Rights Not Property Rights"[1]

"An estimated 36.1 million people are living with HIV. In 2000, about 5.3 million people around the world became infected, 600,000 of them children. Since the epidemic began, AIDS has killed a total of 21.8 million people—almost three times the population of Switzerland. In 2000 alone, AIDS claimed three million lives" (www.unaids.org).

But what makes this global pandemic unique in the annals of public health scourges is that medical knowledge can bring relief—for some. A decade after immunosuppressant drugs revolutionized organ transplants (see later), the introduction of antiretroviral drugs that can forestall fatality from AIDS raised urgent questions about the rights of patients and the commodification of health care. Ninety-five percent of AIDS victims live in countries with annual per capita incomes in the hundreds of dollars, but the package of antiretrovirals that could keep them alive costs around $10,000 to $15,000 per year per patient (www.msf.org). Initially, these treatments were available only from the multinational pharmaceutical companies that had patented them. But Third World competitors in India and Brazil soon produced generic versions at a fraction of the cost. In 2001, Indian generic manufacturer Cipla announced that it would sell a triple therapy combination to Médecins Sans Frontières (MSF; Doctors Without Borders) for $350 per patient per year, and $600 per year for governments (Macan-Markar 2001). Patients, their advocates, and their governments thus struggled to gain access to affordable medicines for a deadly disease, while multinationals and their home governments strove to safeguard their property rights and international trade law.

Who owns knowledge, and under what conditions may the common good transcend private ownership of scarce resources? During the period in which the new AIDS medications were discovered, intellectual property rights were being globally coordinated and consolidated under the World Trade Organization. The majority of the world's nations belong to the WTO, and membership and compliance govern access to a wide range of necessary goods in a globalized world economy. The WTO's 1994 Trade-Related Aspects of Intellectual Property Rights Agreement grants unconditional patent protection to pharmaceuticals but permits limited exceptions for essential products not introduced in a given market and for "national emergencies." Thus, in certain situations a government could be permitted to grant an alternative license to a local manufacturer or import from an alternative source if normal patented production were insufficient for a public health emergency (these practices are known as "compulsory licensing" and "parallel importing"). Scholars of political economy point out that the TRIPS agreement was virtually drafted by a coalition of a dozen CEOs—including pharmaceutical giants Bristol-Myers, Merck, and Pfizer—backed by U.S. structural power. This "latter-day enclosure movement" avoided the more multilateral World Intellectual Property Association, where the developing country majority of intellectual property importers have greater influence (Sell 2000). A few countries have exceptional patent regimes that affect this picture; India has become a major source of generics in part because India permits patenting of pharmaceutical production *processes* only—no one can own the "recipe" for medicine in that country. But in general, countries seek to conform to WTO guidelines—or they may face both multilateral sanctions from that body and bilateral punishment from major trading states such as the United States.

The World Health Organization creates an "essential drug list" of medications deemed necessary to meet basic public health needs. The WHO also certifies that certain drugs meet international standards of safety and effectiveness and are thus recommended for adoption by national health agencies and international programs. Over 90 countries have adopted the WHO list as a guideline for their national health programs, and in this case UNAIDS supplies a substantial component of treatment in the least developed countries in accordance with the WHO list. This international expert approval also substitutes for the weak or absent regulatory agencies for quality control of other providers: NGOs such as Doctors Without Borders and poor governments experiencing an AIDS emergency. Beyond serving as a set of standards for this specialized area of global trade, some have argued that drugs on the WHO essential drug list should be more amenable to alternative production or importing than others because they address basic public health conditions with global implications.

South Africa has one of the highest rates of HIV infection in the world, a national income wholly insufficient to permit commercial purchase of anti-retrovirals, and a newly democratic government committed to expanding social rights for its historically excluded black majority. The 1996 South African Constitution states that "everyone has the right to have access to health care services. . . . The state must take reasonable legislative and other measures, within its available resources, to achieve the progressive realization of each of these rights." But one of the legacies of apartheid was the development of two separate and unequal health care systems, with especially high drug prices and resulting shortages. This system was particularly ill equipped to cope with the AIDS epidemic, and the historic roots of health care economic inequalities in racial discrimination bridged two generations of human rights. Thus, in 1997 South Africa modified its Medicines and

Related Substances Act to permit compulsory and parallel importing of generic AIDS medication. Shortly thereafter, the Pharmaceutical Manufacturers Association comprising 39 northern-based multinationals sued the South African government, alleging that the reforms were vague and could disrupt future patent protection. A representative of GlaxoSmithKline stated their concern that the law could empower governments to relax patent protection for any drug; "this industry requires patents," she told United Press International (UPI) (Samson 2001). The United States initially supported this action by placing South Africa on a U.S. trade representative "watch list" (Heywood 2001).

A massive coalition engaged in a combined campaign of public information, symbolic protest, and legal action that eventually led the companies to withdraw the suit in 2001. The Clinton administration also removed South Africa from the watch list, with an executive order recognizing the rights of African countries to pass specific legislation for health care under the TRIPS emergency provisions. The coalition was spearheaded by MSF, which provided expert advice and extensive publicity, and lobbied the World Health Organization. MSF doctors also directly approached pharmaceutical companies; after MSF targeted Pfizer in South Africa in March 2000, that country agreed to provide its exclusive drug free to South Africans with AIDS. Doctors Without Borders joined with the transnational development NGO Oxfam to reframe the debate internationally as a human rights and public health issue. They circulated a "Drop the Case" petition that garnered more than 250,000 signatures from 130 countries and persuaded the European Union to adopt a resolution (MSF, TAC, Oxfam press release, http://lists.essential.org/pipermail/pharm-policy/2001-April/000944.html). U.S.-based AIDS advocacy groups such as the AIDS Coalition to Unleash Power (ACT UP) organized worldwide protests in 30 cities on a March 5, 2001 Global Day of Action against the pharmaceutical companies (Heywood 2001). ACT UP Paris even blockaded Pfizer's Viagra factory (South Africa 2000).

Meanwhile, South African advocacy and treatment groups formed the Treatment Action Campaign (TAC), which protested the pharmaceuticals' actions at U.S. consulates and filed affidavits in the legal suit as a "friend of the court." These affidavits were supported by South Africa's largest trade union federation, COSATU, a nationally powerful political force with millions of members. The legal case combined plentiful scientific information on the epidemic and treatments with poignant and symbolic personal testimonies by people with HIV and their doctors. They explicitly appealed to the South African government's constitutional duties to provide health care access. Working with students at the University of Minnesota and Yale, TAC showed how some retroviral drugs were developed with public funds at these universities and only subsequently licensed to Bristol-Myers Squibb and Burroughs Wellcome—undercutting the companies' claim that high prices reflected research and development costs and that patents were a necessary incentive for further discoveries (Claude 2002: 152–3). TAC also engaged in acts of civil disobedience—labeled the "patent abuse defiance campaign"—by publicly importing and distributing mass quantities of generic drugs from Thailand on several occasions. "TAC's main arguments were that access to health is a human right that trumps rights to private property" (Heywood 2001). By 2003, Britain's GlaxoSmithKline and German pharmaceutical Boehringer Ingelheim agreed to expand licensing of several key antiretroviral drugs to generic manufacturers, in response to a price-gouging inquiry by South African regulators (Wines 2003b).

In Brazil, which had one of the highest AIDS rates in the Americas, the government had taken an even stronger role in trying to meet the health needs of its citizens. By the mid-1990s, Brazil was both aggressively distributing antiretrovirals through its national health agencies and producing its own generic medications for over 100,000 people. These programs were linked to lowering hospitalizations, reducing mother-to-child transmission, and halving the death rate from AIDS in Brazil. Brazil has also signed medical cooperation agreements with five heavily affected African nations, including technology transfer for production of medications (Kyodo News, December 15, 2002; home.kyodo.co.jp) Local NGOs played an important role as service providers and community advocates in Brazil's AIDS program, designated under a World Bank loan (Mowjee 2003).

But Brazil also had a history of trade disputes with its giant northern neighbor, including other intellectual property issues related to computers and medicines. In 1987, the U.S. Pharmaceutical Manufacturers' Association had requested and received U.S. retaliatory tariffs on Brazilian products, forcing a 1990 change in Brazil's patent legislation. Yet by 2001, the United States filed a complaint with the World Trade Organization alleging Brazilian unfair trading practices, specifically citing a Brazilian law permitting parallel domestic production of patented products not introduced to Brazil within three years of discovery (Mowjee 2003). Merck and Roche also threatened to sue Brazil for specific patent violations of their products (Yamey 2001; "Drug Companies vs. Brazil," www.oxfam.org.uk).

Nevertheless, Brazil benefited from the transnational wave of publicity and norm change coming "out of Africa" at just this moment. In April 2001, the United Nations' Human Rights Commission voted 52–0 in support of Brazil's program (Capdevila 2001), strengthening the human rights frame and the right to health (Claude 2002). The European Union also endorsed Brazil's position. ACT UP protested in the United States. Oxfam issued a special report, "Drug Companies vs. Brazil: The Threat to Public Health." A chastened Clinton administration withdrew the complaint in favor of bilateral trade negotiations that exempted the HIV drugs (Darlington 2001, Crossette 2001)—at the beginning of a UN Special Session on AIDS (Mowjee 2003).

A similar dynamic of foreign policy implementation of the international intellectual property rights regime occurred in Thailand. Like Brazil,

Thailand had a regionally notable infection rate (about one million citizens), an active health administration, a developing local pharmaceutical industry, and preexisting trade disputes with the United States. By 1998, the Thai government began to seek a compulsory license for a single important AIDS drug manufactured by Bristol-Myers Squibb. U.S. government trade representatives questioned Thailand's claim to exemption from patent law under the TRIPS provision for national emergencies and threatened to block Thai exports in retaliation. During 1999, the evolving coalition of transnational NGOs publicized Thailand's plight and lobbied U.S. officials. Doctors Without Borders (MSF) was joined by U.S. AIDS advocacy groups such as ACT UP and trade critics such as Public Citizen (Wilson et al. 1999). Thai activists and AIDS patients demonstrated at the U.S. Embassy in Bangkok, gaining coverage in the business-oriented *Far Eastern Economic Review* headlined "Drug Patents vs. Human Rights." Similarly, the *Straits Times* of Singapore editorialized, "The U.S. government must realize that what is at stake here is not intellectual property rights, but human rights" (Ching 2000).

In January 2000, shortly before the Brazilian withdrawal, the U.S. trade representative outlined a more conciliatory approach, endorsing the WTO standards Thailand had originally cited. A legal challenge filed later that year in Thailand's Central Intellectual Property and International Trade Court by Thai NGOs resulted in a 2002 limitation of the scope of Bristol-Myers Squibb's patent claims and a ruling that the AIDS Access Foundation and HIV-infected plaintiffs have standing as injured parties deprived of important elements of human survival (list.essential.org/pipermail/ip-health/2002-October/003536.html; Inter Press Service, October 18, 2002; Agence France Presse October 2, 2002). A follow-up lawsuit by Thai consumer and AIDS groups challenges the broader patent process (Coday 2002).

Although the resolution of conflicts in South Africa, Brazil, and Thailand did improve health care access, negotiated compromises case by case initially changed policy without necessarily establishing new rights. Along similar lines, following these controversies several major pharmaceutical companies began offering extensive discount programs for AIDS medications to African governments under the Accelerating Access Initiative introduced in 2000—a humanitarian gesture in markets with miniscule profit potential, modeled on previous discount programs for vaccines and oral contraceptives. UNAIDS and the WHO have served as intermediaries to negotiate reduced prices between developing countries and pharmaceutical producers, although this program lacks consistency and transparency.

Major international donors have also created a Global Fund to Fight AIDS, Tuberculosis and Malaria that is mandated to provide additional resources for access to medications, research new medications and vaccines, and target additional fatal contagious developing world epidemics. But the Global Fund is severely underfunded, at an estimated 20 percent of its estimated budget. Even a newly approved $15 billion U.S. fund to combat AIDS will provide less than half for treatment and is also under-subscribed. Furthermore, the Bush administration has thus far purchased only drugs still under patent, reducing the buying power and treatment reach of the U.S. fund. As a result of the shortfalls in these two major sources, the World Health Organization estimates that only about 300,000 patients in the developing world are receiving antiretrovirals, whereas six million need them (McNeil 2004).

Nevertheless, recent changes in international standards do seem to be building toward a right to health—at least in principle. First, at the 2001 Doha conference of the World Trade Organization, there were substantial concessions on interpretations of the conditions for compulsory licensing and production of generics as well as a separate declaration on TRIPS and public health that granted significant latitude to member states to deter-mine a "national emergency" of health conditions. This agreement was extended in August 2003 to permit parallel importing from midlevel pro-ducers of generics, with stringent certification, by poor countries with insufficient domestic capacity to produce their own, potentially overcom-ing a lingering barrier to drug access (Becker 2003). Moving from the trade to the health regimes, the World Health Organization in March 2002 included four generic AIDS drugs on its list of safe medicines approved for purchase by UN programs. This approval is anticipated to create greater competition and thereby lower the price of multinational commercial products (McNeil 2002). An MSF study shows that between May 2000 and July 2002, "originator prices" for a three-drug AIDS treatment package fell from $10,000 to $700 per person per year in response to the introduction of competitive generic drugs (www.msf.org, "Equitable Access"). Bringing international standards into domestic practice, once South African activ-ists overcame the lack of international access to AIDS drugs, they success-fully sued their own government to force it to provide a key medication that reduces mother-to-child transmission to expectant mothers nation-wide (Kraft 2001).

Meanwhile, MSF/Doctors Without Borders has generalized an "Equita-ble Access" initiative for *all* essential medicines (www.msf.org, "Equitable Access: Scaling up HIV/AIDS Treatment in Developing Countries"). For example, MSF and WHO negotiated with Eli Lilly to discount its medi-cines for drug-resistant tuberculosis. Similarly, MSF lobbied Novartis to provide lower cost malaria drugs to South Africa. The organization has also pressed drug companies to retain or develop unprofitable treatments for critical diseases. Negotiations with Bayer in 2000 resulted in continua-tion of two commercially unpromising drugs for African trypanosomiasis (www.accessmed-msf.org, "Campaign Accomplishments for 2000"). Oxfam has been involved in lobbying for such changes under its global campaign—Cut the Cost—to modify trade rules to permit poor countries greater access to medicines across the board. In 2002–2003, WTO negotiations foundered on implementing alternative exporting of generic pharmaceuticals by midlevel producers to supply the smallest, poorest, and sickest nations. Pharmaceutical company and U.S./EU resistance to expansion of the Doha agreement to nonepidemic diseases underlines both the potential of and barriers to a true universal right to medicine.[2]

Through a combination of symbolic reframing, dense and diverse transnational networks, information politics, and global institutions, the campaign for access to AIDS drugs began to map a new right to health care—including the responsibility of nonstate transnational actors. "The ambassador from Norway [to the UN Commission on Human Rights] stated that the question of access to low-cost medications goes beyond HIV/AIDS and extends to all diseases. "Access to drugs carries the features of what we now refer to as 'global public goods.' Yet, drugs are largely manufactured and marketed as 'global private goods' by large multinational companies," said the Norwegian delegate (Capdevila 2001). As South Africa's Health Minister concluded, ". . . [I]nternational markets, which play an increasingly important role in all our lives, have no inbuilt conscience. But governments and ordinary people acting collectively have a precious responsibility to make the huge companies that dominate the markets accountable for how they respond to the most critical issues of our times" (Heywood 2001).

Transplant Trafficking: The Boundaries of Bodily Integrity

New discussions of the commodification of health care have revealed without significantly ameliorating a new genre of human rights abuse. Advances in surgical techniques and the advent of a new class of immunosuppressant drugs during the 1980s have made it possible for large numbers of people with failing hearts, livers, and kidneys to benefit from transplants. In the case of kidneys, living donors can safely donate one of the pair and continue a relatively normal life, with only some increased risk of long-term complications. But only patients with ample income and access to highly developed medical systems are in a position to receive transplants, and there are severe shortages of transplant organs in almost every country. This has led to a growing global trade in organ transplants, in which poor donors from developing countries supply transplant organs to wealthy, desperately ill foreigners. Sometimes the donors or their families are paid for their body parts, but sometimes they may be coerced or deceived by abusive states and/or transplant brokers.

Some argue that commodification of body parts may be the only way to secure the health rights of patients who need transplants. In the United States, which does not allow payments for organ donations (living or posthumous), there are almost 50,000 people on the kidney waiting list (Finkel 2001). In the United States alone, it is estimated that 6,000 people die each year waiting for a transplant (Kristof 2002). But the costs to donors are high, informed consent is problematic, and monetary compensation may not protect the donor's health or economic rights. A 2001 follow-up study of kidney donors in India shows that most experienced declines in family incomes and health following the surgery, and the payments did not release them from debt as planned (Madhav et al. 2002).

Certain countries seem to have specialized in this new form of trafficking because of some combination of a large desperate population, sufficient medical resources to perform the surgery, and lax regulation or even state encouragement. Through the 1990s, the United Nations identified India as a leading source country. One source estimated over 2,000 organ sales in 1991 and at least 4,000 transplants in Bombay alone during the 1980s—involving at least $7.8 million (Chandra 1991, *Los Angeles Times* 1989). Many recipients came from the small oil-rich Gulf states. After publicity and trafficking scandals, including "kidney tours" in the mid-1990s, India passed an Organ Transplantation Act forbidding the sale of organs in 1994. However, the legislation has been unevenly adopted by Indian states, and even where adopted a substantial clandestine market continues (Moore and Anderson 1995).

Turkey, Iraq, and Russia have also been reported to play an especially active role in hosting transplants (Finkel 2001). South Africa has emerged as a site for medical tourism including transplants in its highly developed private sector, with special connections to white ex-colonials from neighboring African states (www.organswatch.org). South Africa was recently highlighted as the nexus for a "trans-Atlantic organ peddling scheme," involving poor Brazilians flown to South Africa as donors by Israeli brokers. Fourteen people were arrested in South Africa and Brazil, and police in several countries are investigating the involvement of doctors and a South African hospital (Wines 2003c).

Testimony in reports and hearings indicates that some brokers are doctors or nurses, and some even have Internet home pages. For example, an untitled Web site consulted on June 25, 2003 promises transplants in Manila in as little as 10 days with physicians licensed in the United States, United Kingdom, or Philippines. Kidneys run $35,000 to $85,000 and the site states that both cadaveric and live donors are available (www.liver4you.org).

Although Thailand has become a center for medical tourism for plastic surgery, gender reassignment, and more routine procedures (Mydans 2001), Thailand forbids commercial organ transplants. A leading Thai surgeon stated that Thailand's laws were drafted with the advice of Thai physicians trained in the United States, in emulation of U.S. standards. Although Thailand has a kidney shortfall of thousands per year, Thai physicians discourage their patients from going to China. Yet one Thai physician testified that he had treated over 40 patients returning with transplanted organs in the previous seven years (U.S. Congressional Hearing 1998).

Advanced states that limit transplants for legal or cultural reasons tend to export their demand, and even moderately developed countries begin to enter medical tourism as a market niche. Because of a combination of religious norms and adherence to international standards, Israel has one of the strictest bans on nonrelative transplants, yet a high standard of medical care and expectations, creating a large demand proportional to a relatively small population. Several Israeli surgeons have openly defied their country's strictures and accompanied patients to perform overseas operations, with attendant debate about their humanitarian or profit-seeking motives. Yet Israel's national health insurance program will cover part of the cost of transplants without investigating the source as the surgery is cheaper than years of dialysis treatment. At one Israeli hospital, about one quarter of post-transplant patients had purchased their kidney from a stranger (probably overseas) (Finkel 2001). On the other side of the exchange, the head doctor of one of Estonia's leading hospitals—where transplant operations were performed on Israelis—stated that the law on patient protection applies only to Estonian citizens. He added that, "As to foreigners, I can only say that Estonia is a land of endless opportunities" (Ivanov 1998).

In China, the problem is not state neglect but rather state sponsorship. The vast majority of transplant organs in China come from executed prisoners. China covertly but systematically sells the organs of executed prisoners to foreign "medical visitors" (and a few members of the Chinese elite). Exiled Chinese physicians have testified to their role in extracting livers, hearts, and kidneys from recently executed prisoners—even some not yet dead—and rushing them to military hospitals where transplant patients were waiting (U.S. Congressional Hearing 2001). It is believed that such transactions average $30,000, with large numbers of patients from Hong Kong, Taiwan, Singapore, and even the United States. China has performed more than 35,000 kidney transplants (Smith 2001). China executes about 6,000 prisoners each year and performs an estimated 2,000 organ transplants annually. Prisoners slated for execution are given anticoagulants to facilitate organ removal, and a former Chinese Judicial Police officer testified that he had orders to shoot prisoners in the head in order to preserve their organs—for which he received payment from the hospital. In addition, in 1997 China introduced execution by lethal injection for some prisoners, a practice that one medical expert believes was adopted to facilitate transplants. A Thai transplant recipient dealt directly with the Chinese hospital, where he witnessed five foreign transplants occurring in the same hospital on the same day as his own. Paying foreigners are given preference for transplants over needy Chinese citizens (U.S. Congressional Hearing 1998).

An additional concern beyond the direct violation of bodily integrity is that transplant trafficking in China may create an economic incentive for increased use of the death penalty. China now prescribes the death penalty for 68 offenses. China executes more people than all other countries combined. Transplant patients are screened and matched to prisoners and informed of the execution schedule to plan their travel and hospital stay. A U.S. surgeon refused to perform a transplant in China that was timed around an execution. Some evidence suggests that prisoners are chosen for execution on the basis of organ compatibility rather than the severity of their crime or potential threat to society (Rothman 1997). As a Japanese medical researcher concluded after 10 years of trips to China, "The thorough utilization and commodification of human body parts has been progressing in the world, as a result of 'life-utilitarianism.' Transplant medicine is one of the driving forces of this" (U.S. Congressional Hearing 1998).

Finally, in the shadow zone between voluntary private trafficking and coercive state corruption, rumors abound in Latin America and parts of Africa of kidnapping for organ removal. Such widespread coercive covert transplant activity has never been documented and is unlikely because of the medical requirements—although not impossible in isolated cases.[3] The rumors of organ stealing have caused so much friction that the U.S. government appointed an information team to quash reports in Latin American periodicals—without success (Lippman 1996).

Although the widespread practice of organ transplantation depends on technology developed in the last generation, norms have developed rapidly through professional associations and international organizations. In 1970, the Ethics Committee of the Transplantation Society forbade "the sale of organs by donors living or dead." In 1985, the same body required that the transplant team ascertain the altruistic motives of donors. The WHO Guiding Principles on Human Organ Transplants (1991) ask physicians not to transplant organs if they believe they have been sold or trafficked. By 1985, the World Medical Association had condemned the purchase and sale of human organs for transplantation, at its 37th Congress in Brussels. Comprehensive guidelines were issued by the WMA in 2000, which state that physicians' primary obligation is to their patients—whether donors or recipients—but that paid donations should be rejected and that "the physician has an independent responsibility to ensure that organs to be used for transplantation have been procured in a legal and ethical manner." To avoid conflicts of interest separate physicians must certify donors' deaths, remove donor organs, and care for recipients (World Medical Association 2000, www.wma.net). The Council of Europe's Convention on Human Rights and Biomedicine (2000) forbids all organ commercialization or trafficking and requires that doctors certifying the death of a donor must be separate from transplant physicians. A European Additional Protocol on Organ Transplants introduced in 2002 additionally states that donation from a living person may be carried out only where there is no organ available from a dead person or alternative therapy and requires a donor's informed consent in writing or before an official body (ETS No.186, January 24, 2002).

Prior to this time, before the introduction of immunosuppressants that made widespread transplantation feasible, a 1977 Protocol to the Geneva Conventions had already banned the use of organs from prisoners of war—presuming that they could not give informed consent. Similarly, the UN's Principles of Medical Ethics state that health personnel should not be "involved in any professional relationship with prisoners or detainees the purpose of which is not solely to evaluate, protect or improve their physical and mental health" (UN GA 37/194, December 1982). In 1994, the WMA also condemned the transplantation of organs from executed prisoners without prior consent and exhorted national medical associations to discipline physicians involved. In its 2000 revision, the World Medical Association deems prisoners incapable of informed consent and thus ineligible as donors (www.wma.net).

As revelations of organ trafficking and prisoner transplants surfaced during the 1990s, concerned researchers, physicians, ethicists, and activists set up a working group at Columbia University to draft additional standards. The resulting Bellagio Task Force on Transplantation, Bodily Integrity and the International Traffic in Organs met in 1997 and proposed a two-pronged policy—a continued ban on the sale of organs from live donors, but closely supervised programs to allow rewards for the families of cadaver organ donors. The Task Force based their rejection of more transparent and regulated commodification with the argument that "inequities in political power and social well-being remain so profound and the poverty and deprivation so extreme, that the voluntary character of a sale of an organ remains in doubt." Moreover, the group concludes that executed prisoners should not be allowed as sources of cadaver organs because they cannot give full free consent and the donation is veiled from monitoring. Furthermore, the required participation of physicians in managing the execution to meet organ donation requirements "subverts the ethical integrity of the medical profession" (Rothman et al. 1997).

Within the medical profession participating in the practice, these norms have a very mixed impact. One Brazilian doctor claimed, "I don't want to know what kinds of private exchanges have taken place between my [kidney] patients and their [living] donors" (Scheper-Hughes 1998b). A lawyer for an Israeli transplant surgeon accused of participating in hundreds of overseas transplants says this doctor "doesn't feel as though he is bound by national laws if these laws do not suit him. He arrived at the conclusion that if he didn't do something to stop people from dying on dialysis, then nobody would. It's unclear, she adds, which laws Shapira has broken, what the potential punishment might be and where he might be subject to jurisdiction" (Finkel 2001).

On the other hand, several U.S. physicians presented with patients returning from China with transplanted organs have expressed ethical quandaries and consulted ethics boards of their hospitals and professional associations. Most conclude that their ethical condemnation of transplants from executed prisoners is outweighed by their duty to provide care to their living patients, just as they would not deny care to any other patient on the basis of previous behavior (Smith 2001). The Asian Society of Transplant Agents has pressured the Chinese Transplant Society regarding transplants from executed prisoners and at one point barred Chinese physicians from the Asian Society's Congress and journal (U.S. Congressional Hearing 1998).

In addition to professional networks, traditional human rights organizations, international bodies, and developed states have challenged transplant abuses. Amnesty International issued a special report in 1996, and Human Rights Watch Asia's 1994 study stressed the involvement of medical personnel in China. The U.S. Congress has held hearings three times on China's coercive transplants, most recently in 2001. These hearings have included Chinese refugee doctors and officials, transplant physicians and researchers from several Asian countries, transplant recipients, and U.S. human rights activists. The European Parliament passed a 1998 resolution condemning organ trafficking. China's practices have been challenged in the UN Committee Against Torture in 1993 (48th Session, General Assembly, Supplement No.44, A/48/44, 1993) and in the UN Human Rights Commission in 1997. And a specialized new organization, Organs Watch, has been formed to monitor and condemn these new forms of abuse. Based at the University of California, Berkeley, Organs Watch conducts ongoing research, including a special investigation by an official of the International Red Cross (www.organswatch.org).

On the commercial trafficking side, one response to reduce demand is a growing trend by states to mandate "presumed consent" to transplant organs at death. Under legislation in Brazil, Italy, Poland, Switzerland, Spain, and Singapore, organs can be removed without explicit permission at death—unless the patient has recorded objections during his or her lifetime. However, this seemingly sensible policy may have ironic consequences for human rights. Although it is questionable whether any rights continue after death (except of course property rights), presumed consent practices may also color the rights of the living poor. Many Brazilian doctors object to presumed consent because of the lack of safeguards in that country's legal and medical systems. As one woman choosing to opt out put it, "This is Brazil, my dear—doctors will take out your organs while you're still alive just to make money." Another reported, "Now we have to worry about ambulance workers who may be paid on the side to declare us 'dead' before our time is really up" (McDaniels 1998; Scheper-Hughes 1998b).

Bilateral pressure has been the main influence on China, albeit thus far quite limited in scope and impact. After the U.S. State Department explicitly raised the issue of coerced transplants with China in 1996, that country issued and publicized new regulations tightening the requirements for consent—although testimony and numbers of transplants suggest that these regulations have been ignored. Similarly, in 1998 the Federal Bureau of Investigation (FBI) arrested two Chinese citizens in New York for organ trafficking, including one former official; but the case was subsequently dropped when a key witness disappeared (1998 Congressional Hearing). In 2001, U.S. legislators introduced a bill to bar the entry of Chinese doctors coming to the United States for training in transplant techniques (Samson 2001b). Finally, by 2001 the slow liberalization of China's press produced some scattered reports at home revealing this practice, which seem to have produced some local pressure in a few cases (Pomfret 2001).

New forms of medical care and global commodification have stimulated the development of new standards of medical ethics and new forms of the right to bodily integrity. New international standards and awareness have led to several forms of policy change, including regulation in India, presumed consent in Brazil and Singapore, and U.S. attempts to pressure China via law and diplomacy. But state regulation of this private global flow is less effective than official trade in AIDS pharmaceuticals. Widespread change will depend on two factors: deep structural inequalities between economically desperate donors and medically desperate recipients and the participation of expert physicians in an ethically murky practice. Transnational professional communities are thus the best hope for implementing new rights in an age of body barter across borders.

Genetic Research: Knowledge, Privacy, and Identity

New trends in genetic research also pose dilemmas that propose the articulation of new rights related to control of knowledge and the body. Whereas access to pharmaceuticals assigns new responsibilities for an existing right to health and transplant trafficking expands the right to bodily integrity and medical self-determination, genetic research seems to call for a new type of rights to deal with an evolving politics of knowledge. In this case, the research process does not generally violate bodily integrity or influence access to health care. Instead, the knowledge that results may violate rights to privacy, identity, and control of one's own bodily "property."

"The study of DNA is an industry with high visibility, a claim on the public purse, the legitimacy of a science, and the appeal that it will alleviate individual and social suffering" (Lewontin 1995: 59). Analysis of genetic material from groups of families, disease victims, or ethnic groups has the potential to produce knowledge concerning genetic causes of health conditions. Genetic material from an individual with exceptional characteristics can be used to produce a cell line, which may contribute to the development of pharmaceuticals or gene therapy. Comparison of genetic material from groups with a known characteristic may be analyzed for genetic variations potentially associated with that outcome. Most significantly, creation of large-scale genetic data banks associated with well-developed medical records may allow tracing of genetic determinants of disease in delimited populations with similar environmental conditions.

Genetic analysis can also provide individual proof of paternity or grandpaternity, as well as groups' historical patterns of origin. Finally, DNA identification can link suspects to crimes.

How could this contribute to human rights violations—and what rights are at issue? First, those who equate a person's genetic sequence with her personal identity may apply a right to privacy to the knowledge of an individual's genetic code—or even to the revelation of group information with implications for discrimination against all members of the group. Second, others may focus on the right to control and benefit from intellectual property rights in information derived from one's personal identity. The history of medical abuse of vulnerable groups may inspire fears that genetic information could contribute to direct violations such as biological warfare, genocide, or eugenics schemes. Or genetic research could have more diffuse and indirect pernicious effects on policy by building inaccurate but politically powerful public images of race as an essential, eternal form of biological variation that determines behavior. Finally, genetic information could be used by governments to impose a genetic test on group membership and attendant policy costs or benefits; more specifically, for indigenous peoples genetic tracing of ancestry could be used to challenge land rights (Greely, 2000a; Cavalli-Sforza, Menozzi, and Piazza 1994). Each kind of use of genetic information could contribute in different ways to these types of violations, and researchers and their critics debate the technological feasibility and likelihood of these threats.

It is also important to note that genetic research has contributed to safeguarding human rights in some situations. Perhaps the best known case is the use of genetic testing for grandpaternity to locate children of the "disappeared" in Argentina, which has served as the basis for legal action to reassign custody from illicit adoptive parents to surviving biological families. On this basis, Argentina created a National Genetic Data Bank for forensic purposes unrelated to medical research (Brysk 1994).[4] In a similar vein, Howard University plans to create an African-American DNA repository to ensure that blacks can benefit from the new wave of genetic research—promoting equal attention to diseases more prevalent in the black community and equal understanding of possible differential responses to treatments (Pollack 2003). The Innocence Project at Yeshiva University uses DNA evidence to reverse false convictions (Wade 2003).

Overall, the regulation of genetic research raises the larger question of knowledge processors' social responsibility for the use as well as the production of information. Medical codes of "informed consent" purport to deal with the human rights of research subjects as producers of knowledge, although some debate the adequacy of existing models of consent for genetic research. In particular, because genetic research is usually meaningful only for groups and has implications for all members of the group, how and to what extent should informed consent be obtained from an entire family, disease community, or ethnic group? Once knowledge is created, what rights govern its use? The default mode of the "marketplace of ideas" is already limited when information or images may contribute to unacceptable social harm—for example, recipes for chemical weapons. How much and in what way does genetic information fall into this category? Can and should we limit the collection, revelation, or exchange of genetic research because it may violate someone's religious beliefs, contribute to discrimination in employment or health care, provide the potential to infect them with a deadly disease, or market their most personal property without their benefit?

Genetic research is a transnationalized enterprise, sponsored by universities, biotechnology firms, and public agencies, but somewhat regulated by states in key countries such as the United States. As in children's migration issues, the preponderance of U.S. participation in the transnational flow gives U.S. standards significant influence. The EU hosts 1,570 biotechnology firms with 61,000 employees generating $5 billion euros; the United States employs 162,000 at 1,273 firms producing $11.4 billion euros (europa.eu.int/comm./biotechnology). But the field is dominated by about a dozen companies that have patented hundreds of genes for tens of millions of dollars in partnership with major pharmaceutical manufacturers; prominent names include Celera, Incyte, Myriad, Asys, and Icelandic émigré Kari Stefanson's U.S.-based deCODE (see later). Most of these companies share personnel and/or data with major research universities, some publicly funded. For example, Myriad Genetics draws on Rockefeller University, the University of Texas, and the University of Utah—and provides data to Germany's Bayer and Schering, Switzerland's Novartis, and U.S. Monsanto (www.etcgroup.org). Any researchers or research institutions funded by the U.S. government must be reviewed by special boards to ensure that human subjects are not subjected to undue risk and that fully informed consent is obtained. But in addition, any research supporting an application for licensing of drugs by the Food and Drug Administration (FDA), regardless of its country of origin, must satisfy U.S. human subjects regulations (Greely 1997, Houston Law Review).

International standards have evolved significantly but with the most diffuse linkages and leverages of any issue area. In 1997, the United Nations Educational, Scientific, and Cultural Organization (UNESCO) adopted a Universal Declaration on the Human Genome and Human Rights unanimously, which was endorsed by the UN General Assembly in December 1998. UNESCO's Declaration on the Human Genome views the genome as the common heritage of humanity, eschewing property rights to genetic research. Yet it cites both the full range of human rights instruments and those concerning intellectual property, as well as the Convention on Biological Diversity. Above all, it affirms "rights regardless of their genetic characteristics" and exhorts us "not to reduce individuals to their genetic characteristics" (www.unesco.org). A follow-up International Declaration on Human Genetic Data drafted by the International Bioethics Committee in 2002–2003 envisions monitoring by that body and regular reports by states on policies adopted in conformity with these principles. The more detailed document affirms that human genetic data have a special status, in part because of their implication for families and groups, and calls for state regulation of transborder flows of genetic data and samples. It specifies that archived biological samples may be used to derive genetic data without explicit consent if the data have medical significance and the process is approved by an ethics committee. But the draft declaration explicitly bans cross-matching of medical data with forensic data (SIIS/EST/03/CIB-10/3, Paris, April 23, 2003). The European Convention on Human Rights and Biomedicine follows similar principles, with the additional element of possible interpretation by the European Court of Human Rights at the request of either states parties or a Steering Committee on Bioethics (ETS 164, 4.IV.1997). The Human Genome Organization Ethics Committee in 1996 published a set of general principled guidelines for human genetic research that reiterates informed consent, confidentiality, avoidance of conflicts of interest, and monitoring of research (Greely, 1998b).

In the major individual legal case to date, Moore v. Regents of the University of California, a patient was deemed to have no property rights to a cell line developed from his surgically removed tissue. In a similar group level case, British patients who had contributed genetic material to a study that resulted in the patenting of a test for a gene predisposing individuals to breast cancer protested. Although the United States granted the patent, the European Parliament somewhat limited commercial status (Claude 2002: 165–168). As noted previously, developing cell lines from individuals' tissue, DNA sampling of individuals, DNA sampling of populations, and associated access to medical records are technically and legally related yet distinct activities. The United States has issued an Executive Order to Prohibit Discrimination in Federal Employment Based on Genetic Information (February 2000), and legislation has been introduced at both federal and state levels to improve genetic privacy and prevent genetic discrimination in insurance and employment (www.genome.gov).

Campaigns on knowledge issues are based in transnational networks and target transnational actors. Indigenous groups have evinced a special concern and selectively stronger focus on genetic research, and other challengers combine concerns across a range of biotechnology issues, from genetically modified organisms in agriculture to reproductive cloning. Opponents of genetic research generally combine a suspicion of globalization, resistance to commodification, and concern with privacy and increased opportunities for state and corporate control of individuals. For example, in a 2001 statement the Erosion, Technology and Conservation group projects that the next wave of genetic research will promote "human performance enhancement" which will "control dissent and 'eradicate the different'" (www.etcgroup.org, "The New Genomics Agenda," October 23, 2001). Greenpeace explains that life patents grant the genetic engineering industry monopoly control over the food chain, may deter public and independent scientific research and medicine, and divert funds from understanding of environmental health factors and resultant preventative measures (http://greenpeace.org/international_en). Biotechnology opponent Jeremy Rifkin of the Foundation for Economic Trends has filed briefs and joined court cases against the patenting of genetically engineered life forms, animal and human genes. His foundation has created an international coalition of over 350 NGOs from 52 countries calling for an international treaty to declare the gene pool a global commons, which includes environmental groups such as the Rainforest Action Network and Green Party of South Africa and Italy, development groups such as Food First, consumer advocates Public Citizen, and the Indigenous Peoples' Biodiversity Network (www.foet.org; Rifkin 1998—The Biotech Century).

For indigenous peoples, the issue of genetic research became inextricably linked to wider debates on control of botanical and cultural knowledge and identity politics (Brysk 2000a). Indigenous peoples' particular sensitivity to genetic research can be traced to a dual legacy of "biopiracy"—usurpation of traditional products and practices for commercial gain by outsiders—and medical abuse, including genocidal germ warfare by settlers on several continents. More practically, indigenous activists fear that the genetic data could be sold, manipulated to produce racially specific biological weapons, or simply used to substitute a genetic museum for the preservation of living endangered communities (Acosta 1994). North American native activists founded the Indigenous Peoples' Biodiversity Network now headed by Peruvian Quechua Alejandro Argumendo, with offices in Ecuador, Panama, and Peru. The advocacy groups Cultural Survival and SAIIC both produced special issues of their journals on research in indigenous communities. The pan-Amazon Basin COICA organized a 1994 regional conference on "Biodiversity and Intellectual Property," under the auspices of the UN Development Program (Cultural Survival 1991, Abya Yala 1994). In November 1996, indigenous groups staged a parallel forum to the World Congress on Biodiversity in Buenos Aires, insisting on the recognition of indigenous knowledge. The Canadian development NGO RAFI (Rural Advancement Foundation International—later the ETC group) and Swissaid regularly monitored public patent applications for their potential impact on indigenous communities throughout the 1990s (Posey and Dutfield 1996: 80). A more specific concern with genetic research has been highlighted by the Indigenous Peoples' Council on Biocolonialism, which has prepared briefings questioning the participation of native communities in such research. As Hopi geneticist Frank Dukepoo explains on the IPCB Web site, the current regime of genetic research violates indigenous beliefs as it promotes genetic determinism regarding human identity and a mechanistic world view in which atomized elements of life are subject to amoral human manipulation. Indigenous peoples are disproportionately the subjects but rarely the beneficiaries of such research, and transnational exchange of data is very difficult to monitor or control (www.ipcb.org).

Indigenous activists' fear of appropriation of genetic data received some confirmation in a series of patent disputes regarding cell lines that were blocked by network protest. The National Institutes of Health has applied to patent more than 2,800 genes and DNA fragments "discovered" in its research on human subjects. In a widely debated case, a Panamanian Guaymi woman infected with a retrovirus thought possibly to cause leukemia had a blood sample taken from which a cell line was produced for research in 1991. Her cells were sent to the U.S. Centers for Disease Control for study. In 1993, U.S. researchers applied for a patent on the Guaymi woman's cell line. Only after protests by the Guaymi Congress, World Council of Churches, Worldwide Fund for Nature, and Swissaid, including appeals to the General Agreement on Tariffs and Trade (GATT) and intergovernmental Biodiversity Conference, was the patent application dropped (Brysk 2000a). At the same time, a similar patent application based on a cell line from a Solomon Islands resident was also dropped. Several years later, a similar scenario arose with a member of Papua New Guinea's Hagahai tribe. In this case, the tribe's anthropologist intermediary actually favored the patent for the potential commercial benefits to the group, but the patent was abandoned after protest from RAFI (Greely 2000a). Indigenous advocates remain concerned about possible misuse or commercial appropriation of academic genetic diversity studies available on the Internet, such as Yale University's Allele Frequency Database, which includes dozens of indigenous populations (www.etcgroup.org).

The most developed group level genetic research plan implemented to date has been instituted in Iceland. Iceland is particularly fertile ground for genetic research because it is relatively homogeneous and historically isolated, is small enough to sample thoroughly yet large enough to have some genetic variation, and has had a comprehensive national health service with excellent records for almost a century. In that democratic, highly developed country, the government authorized a private company to conduct proprietary genetic research on the entire population in 1998. The multinational research firm, deCODE, was founded by an Icelandic émigré physician now resident in the United States and controlled by a combination of international investors, Icelanders, and U.S. venture capital funds. DeCODE has licensed access for 12 years to the national health service records—including disease patterns, existing genetic tests, and genealogical information (Greely 2000b). In addition, Iceland has approved a "presumed consent" regime for genetic research on existing tissue samples collected by the health service for other purposes (Greely 2001a). Beyond this, deCODE's Web site states that the firm has now collected DNA samples from 80,000 volunteer participants, approximately one third of the adult population of Iceland. By combining this information with "anonymized, encrypted data" from patients' records, the firm claims to have genetically mapped 25 common diseases and identified seven specific presumed disease-associated genes—including a gene believed to contribute to osteoporosis. In order to apply this research to the development of genetic tests and pharmaceuticals, DeCODE has created an "alliance" with around a dozen biotech firms, including Roche and Merck pharmaceuticals, IBM for informatics, and Emory University School of Medicine (www.decode.com).

Although Iceland's national genetic research plan was approved by its government, there has been significant opposition and debate. The Iceland Medical Association has argued against the agreement and invoked the disapproval of the World Medical Association in 1999. Some doctors have pledged not to supply data on their patients that their national health service employer has contracted to provide to deCODE. A new social movement was formed specifically to contest the plan; Mannvernd—the Association of Icelanders for Ethics in Science and Medicine. This movement has sponsored international publicity and petitions, domestic legal challenges, and filed a complaint on privacy grounds with Iceland's subregional European trading group, the EEA. In addition, by December 2002 more than 20,000 Icelanders had opted out of the database (www.mannvernd.org). After controversy, deCODE granted a limited share of its profits to Iceland's national health system. In addition, pharmaceutical partner Roche will provide any products developed on the basis of its Icelandic database free to citizens of Iceland during the period of patent protection. The enterprise is estimated to create around 400 new jobs but may also interfere with public genetic research in Icelandic institutions (Greely 2000b, 2001a).

Furthermore, similar national population databases have been proposed for Estonia, Newfoundland, and Tonga (Frank 1999, Greenwood 2000, Skene 2001). Biobanks and/or health records genetic research programs are pending in Sweden, the United Kingdom, and the United States. Several private commercial biobanks in the United States house data and samples from over 100,000 people, operating with basic informed consent and confidentiality but numerous unregulated areas, such as permitted uses of data by successor companies that acquire the original collectors. The nonprofit Estonian Genome Foundation began a pilot project in fall 2002 with funding from U.S.-based company Egeen, collecting DNA samples and a health questionnaire from 10,000 donors. The Estonian project, which will eventually encompass 1 million of its 1.4 million population, utilizes more affirmative informed consent rather than Iceland's presumed consent. But the renewal of informed consent for studying different conditions—including controversial behavioral links to genetic information—is not provided. In Estonia, doctors were included in the planning process, and genetic profiles are returned to donors. The British BioBank will be the largest population database in the world when complete, with 500,000 samples. It will track volunteers and their medical records longitudinally, and the results will be open to researchers rather than proprietary (Uehling 2003; Kaiser 2002). But an Australian academic institute database of psychiatric studies of twins was acquired in 1998 by a British commercial firm, raising numerous questions of renewed consent, confidentiality, and intellectual property (www.gemini-research.co.uk).

A broader transnational academic enterprise, the Human Genome Diversity Project (HGDP), attempted to raise $25 million to explore the genetic variation of the entire species. The Diversity Project is a separate intellectual spin-off from the $3 billion Human Genome Project (sponsored by the U.S., Japanese, and European governments), which seeks to map the DNA sequence. Genetic material is extracted from human subjects and analyzed for patterns; the Diversity Project hoped to sample 400 to 500 world populations. The research received planning support from the National Science Foundation (NSF), the European Community, the National Institutes of Health, and the U.S. Department of Energy. The physical diversity and genetic isolation of indigenous peoples would seem to make their genetic information especially interesting data for the project to balance previous collections. Advocates claim that the project will produce new knowledge of human origins, perhaps shed light on genetic diseases, and address basic research questions (Posey and Dutfield 1996: 162–172).

Although the Diversity Project has not yet begun collection on a global scale, a 1993 project workshop approved the inclusion of genetic samples previously collected by participating scientists under previous research protocols (Posey and Dutfield 1996: 165). And in 1999 the project arranged with a French institute to store existing cell lines and grant access to qualified researchers (Greely 2000a). A complicating factor is the project's two-tiered structure at global and regional levels, which effectively collapsed into regional groupings during the mid-1990s. The Ethics Committee of the North American Committee of the HGDP developed and published a Model Ethical Protocol that requires group as well as individual consent and mandates sharing of any potential commercial benefits—which are deemed unlikely. But this protocol has been adopted by the North American Committee only. Some collections did commence in China and Southwest Asia, under the auspices of their regional committees. The South American committee disbanded. In the meantime, the overall Diversity Project itself has stalled because of lack of funding, based largely on an ambivalent evaluation by the National Academy of Sciences in 1997, and the simultaneous appearance of rival research programs (which do not involve indigenous peoples). The NSF report reflected ethical concerns about the project but concluded that the federal government could fund U.S. researchers who would be subject to U.S. rules on the protection of human subjects (Greely 2000a, 2001b).

In contrast, many Indian rights movements in the Americas see the project as a violation of indigenous identity at the deepest level. In 1995,

Indian leaders from the United States, Panama, Ecuador, Peru, Bolivia, and Argentina met in the United States to debate and denounce what they dubbed "Project Vampire." A 1997 "Heart of the Peoples" Declaration states that "We oppose biological engineering and manipulation of the natural world and life forms through biological prospecting, genetic research, cloning, organ harvesting and human experimentation." The movement calls for a moratorium on the patenting of life forms, UNESCO global standards, and return of previous samples obtained without "full prior informed consent" (also Declaration of Indigenous Peoples of the Western Hemisphere, International Indian Treaty Council 1995). Along these lines, in 1997–1998 Colombian indigenous organizations demanded a return of blood samples that had been collected by the Universidad Javeriana and exported to the NIH years earlier, fearing their subsequent use for DNA research (www.etcgroup.org). When the Human Genome Diversity Project's originator, Stanford scientist Luigi Cavalli-Sforza, requested UNESCO's International Bioethics Commission to monitor the project in 1994, indigenous opposition at the UN led UNESCO to issue a mixed report and eschew further involvement (Interview, August 14, 1997). The Washington, D.C.-based Foundation on Economic Trends threatened suit against the Diversity Project on behalf of several indigenous organizations (Abya Yala News, Spring 1995: 30). The International Indian Treaty Council also substantially influenced a 1997 resolution by the UN's Sub-Commission on Prevention of Discrimination on bioethics and indigenous rights. Responding to these concerns, the MacArthur Foundation provided funds to develop model ethical protocols for genetic research (Cultural Survival Quarterly Summer 1996: 24), and the NSF sponsored a series of pilot projects to improve methods of informed consent and information storage that respect both scientists' access and donors' privacy (Fourth World Bulletin, Summer 1998, p.80). ETC group has proposed increased standard setting by the UN Convention on Biological Diversity, the WHO, the UN Human Rights Commission, and the Biological and Toxic Weapons Collection (www.etcgroup.org).

Above all, genetic research has been reframed and shifted to a new *agenda*: from a neutral search for knowledge in the pursuit of progress to a potential threat to human rights. The human rights critique asserts that human information is more than data. The challenge to genetic research simultaneously draws on autonomy, property, and identity. Native peoples and other national groups seek sovereign regulation of researchers' entry into their communities. At the same time, communities and individuals assert property rights to control, use, and benefit from the information produced by research. Finally, Indians and some opponents of globalization claim the right to determine which knowledge is a secular subject of science and which is an inalienable source of identity or belief.

Potential leverage via state control of research funds and facilities has not been realized overall thus far. Although the patent claims on cell lines derived from indigenous people were dropped, Iceland's national genetic research program has expanded, and genetic databases are in process in half a dozen additional countries. At a normative level, the debate on genetic research has stimulated one of the most serious and concrete discussions of the "third generation" of *group rights*. Following the HGDP's Model Ethical Protocol mandating group consent for genetic research, subsequent proposals extend the notion of group consent from the special case of indigenous peoples to families, disease organizations, and ethnic communities (Greely 1997, 2001). This proposal has been debated in a series of law and scientific journals but in many cases founders on the determination of the relevant group boundaries (Weijer, Goldsand, and Emanuel 1999, Sharp and Foster 2000, Juengst 1998, Reilly 1998).

Genetic research has also been reframed from a matter of updating individual medical ethics to insertion in a broader debate on biotechnologies that are potential vehicles for social engineering by states and markets. Wider campaigns on related issues such as genetically modified organisms and cloning have implanted in public discourse the "precautionary principle"—the idea that the burden of proof is on science to demonstrate that the benefit of innovations outweighs the potential harm. Diverse transnational communities now share the concern of the Indigenous Project on Bio-colonialism that "Tampering with genetic materials in any life form, which developed over generations in response to years of environmental influence, creates a risk of throwing everything else out of balance as well" (www.icpb.org). Although still lacking leverage, this debate has bridged from Icelandic doctors to Brazilian Greens to North American Native Americans—to build toward a new understanding of the requisites of self-determination.

Habeas Corpus: From Tuskegee to TRIPS

Resistance to free markets in organs, medicines, and genes has established new boundaries for debates on human dignity. At the same time, transnational campaigns assign accountability to private firms, physicians, and researchers for the human rights standards developed for states: denying access to essential resources, violating bodily integrity, and breaching privacy. Through a politics of communicative action, international institutions have crafted new standards, some states have stepped in to regulate or mediate, and activists have vastly increased monitoring and awareness of potentially problematic medical practices.

Although this process has not yet secured significant leverage or institutionalization, it has shaped agendas, forged new coalitions, and mobilized collective identities. The AIDS drugs campaigns brought together transnational physicians, gay advocates, grassroots development activists, and local patients' groups and women's organizations on three continents. For local patients, the campaigns for pharmaceutical access seem to have increased collective identity, helped to overcome stigma, and stimulated further action against local governments. Concern with organ trafficking and prisoner donors brought together human rights organizations, an overlapping but distinct set of physicians, and critics of China's record and mobilized a specific new organization—Organs Watch. On genetic research, the burgeoning "red-green" coalition of indigenous peoples and environmentalists was joined by still more physicians and researchers. In countries debating databases and biobanks, genetic research has catalyzed a renewed sense of national identity and corresponding genetic patrimony. In all of these cases, physicians' professional norms and identities have been transformed from individual Hippocratic restraint to engaged expertise, attempts at self-regulation, and sometimes a broader structural critique of global medical markets.

Where these campaigns have achieved leverage, they have done so through diffusion of international standards and/or hegemonic influence of the United States. International campaigns rapidly influence standards, and standards rapidly diffuse through "international regimes" in the WHO, WMA, UNESCO, and EU. The AIDS drug issue had the additional leverage of regulation under the WTO, as well as hegemonic U.S. defense of private violators as a channel for foreign policy lobbying. Chinese organ abuses are potentially subject to slowly growing U.S. leverage, but more widespread commercial organ trafficking would require something like an international certification regime. However, the hospitals and research facilities that support organ transplantation and genetic research are dependent on public funding, so any concerned OECD (Western) government could exercise greater power of the purse—as the United States has chosen to do on abortion and stem cell research.

The cumulative impact of these types of struggles has been to begin to reclaim the body from the ideological hegemony of science. The ultimate promise of science was to remove human survival and suffering from the vagaries of nature, granting greater control and justice to human agency. Although human rights originates in modern medicine's Western liberal package of freedom, equality, protection, and progress, unregulated markets in modern medical practices may come to be seen to threaten all but the last of these values. Under these circumstances, science loses its taken for granted status, and social groups mobilize to contest "progress at any price." Once these campaigns subject science and medicine to scrutiny as political processes with winners and losers, respect for human rights demands more than scientists' private morality or noncomplicity in state abuses. Medical patients and research subjects have a right to self-determination, access to the fruit of collective inquiry, and freedom from coercion, deception, and alienation of personal identity. One of the founding doctrines of human rights against the state was defense of the body from obliteration by force: *habeas corpus*. Now, the agenda has been set for defense of the body from its students, healers, and merchants.

6

Conclusion: Private Authority and Global Governance

Have human rights come to govern private power? Like state violations, human rights abuse by private actors continues—but is increasingly challenged and intermittently checked. A new wave of global consciousness and transnational struggle has introduced new norms and strategies that chart possibilities for safeguarding human dignity across public-private borders. Such possibilities for global governance still founder too often over lack of resources, inconsistent institutionalization, or diffuse responsibility. Nevertheless, human rights are slowly and unevenly constructing global civil society: setting new agendas, empowering new agents, and crafting new tools.

What Has Changed

Human rights challenges have provided elements to reconstruct some of the norms underlying the liberal global social order. The slogans and claims of campaigns against private wrongs have been adopted by wider circles of international organizations, leading state officials, and public opinion, as we have seen. Overall, worldwide movements on women's issues, children's rights, ethnic and racial discrimination, corporate responsibility, religious issues, and medical ethics have fostered a widespread understanding that—at least for some issues—"the personal is political." A corollary emerging in international law is the notion that *power* carries responsibility—not just juridical sovereignty (Frey 1996, Romany 1994, Weissbrodt 2002).

117

At the same time, conflicts over commodification are threaded through transnational contests over the terms and pace of globalization. The controversies profiled here over children, organs, and genes all resist the marketing of people. When the private wrongs campaigns assert that some things should not be for sale, they draw from and contribute to the broader critique of market mores shared by "IMF riots" and antiglobalization protests worldwide (Broad 2002, O'Brien et al. 2000).

New human rights movements have also constructed norms on specific issues—the previous discussion shows that these principles are not always accepted, but they set the agenda for future discourse. Children's rights advocates have established that "best interests of the child" may theoretically trump state sovereignty in international standards and liberal state policy, even at a time when broader regimes of citizenship rights have narrowed (albeit with severe gaps in implementation). Campaigns for financial reparations and socially responsible investing have expanded the notion of "dirty money" across time and space—a global and historical vision of white-collar crime. Movements for medical ethics and public health access begin to build the idea that health care is a right, not a privilege.

Human rights also help to construct new agents of global civil society. New messages are carried by new movements, networks, and coalitions—although the mainstream human rights organizations usually get involved at some point, they are not necessarily the originators or critical actors in struggles against private wrongs. Doctors Without Borders exemplifies a combined broader shift from professional associations and humanitarian relief groups to the activist projection of a professional ethos. Entirely new types of issue-specific organizations arise in response to unprecedented problems, such as Organs Watch or the Icelandic Mannsverd movement challenging genetic mapping. Meanwhile, issues such as children's rights and socially responsible investment forge coalitions among existing networks of religious, environmental, labor, human rights, and country campaigns. These coalitions may then form the basis for new movements; for example, medical ethics concerns have led to the establishment of the new group Global Lawyers and Physicians Working Together for Human Rights (www.glphr.org).

These new types of activists use new strategies and introduce new repertoires. The conventional civil rights strategy of litigation becomes transnational litigation. Grassroots disinvestment and shareholders' resolutions join the financial leverage of government and international organization sanctions. Medical activists target international regulatory bodies such as the WHO and the WTO. Professional organizations become a focus for standard setting and conditionality, as when physicians' groups attempt to limit access to journals, conferences, and training by their professional peers suspected to be complicit in organ trafficking.[1]

New norms, actors, and strategies have produced some policy change to limit private wrongs—although far less than needed, and not on equally urgent issues beyond the scope of this study. The rights of child migrants in the United States have been improved through INS reforms regarding juvenile custody conditions and increased scrutiny of transnational adoptions, as well as the Victims of Trafficking legislation. Financial accountability for past abuses has secured Holocaust settlement funds and encouraged several parallel suits still pending. Socially responsible investment shifts have inspired manufacturer codes of conduct and selected withdrawals of multinationals and may have contributed to negotiations in pariah states Burma and Sudan. Medical campaigns resulted in the elimination of legal barriers to pharmaceutical access for AIDS, changes in organ transplant regulation in a number of countries, and dropping of patent claims on indigenous peoples' genetic material. None of these changes is sufficient to address the abuses in question, but each offers some relief and some precedent.

How has change come about? In contrast to the liberal vision of convergence and end of history, globalization has produced new arenas of power and conflict. Moreover, some of these realms spill across public-private as well as national boundaries; they are not just international, but transnational. Within these new transnational arenas, the same dynamic of communicative action prevails that we have previously seen as a source of change when transnational networks target states and/or international institutions. Campaigns that combine symbolic politics, information politics, leverage, and institutionalization have the capacity to confront private power across borders (Keck and Sikkink 1998). An intermediary step, generally prior to institutionalization, is social learning.

Symbolic politics involves the creation and projection of compelling subjects and narratives in the global public sphere (Brysk 1995). Children's rights activism has benefited from the generic resonance of children's vulnerability and innocence, as well as specific causes célèbre of immigration. Financial accountability claims are often more difficult to tie to human impact—the most successful cases are those with testimonials, such as Holocaust survivors or Colombian Indians protesting Occidental Petroleum. Labor rights and environmental campaigns have introduced broader narratives of sweatshops and ecological plunder that are invoked to frame investors' understandings of more distant situations. On the medical front, the highly visible, vulnerable victims of lack of access to antiretroviral medications inspired an affective response. Poor and dying men, women, and children aroused compassion as well as a sense of "David versus Goliath" confronting well-heeled pharmaceutical firms. Organ trafficking has a visceral impact by nature—this helps explain why general opponents of China's human rights policies have focused on this genre of abuse more than equally serious forms of medical denial or exploitation in that impoverished and repressive country. Genetic research, by contrast, has suffered diminished responsiveness because of its more abstract and even arcane quality.

The discovery and publicity of *information* are also especially important in revealing private power, elucidating global reach, and contesting expertise. Monitoring of hidden practices is a traditional human rights strategy extended to new domains such as transnational adoption or organ transplants. But uncovering and analyzing data itself is an important component of many struggles against private wrongs: annual reports, bank statements, drug formulas, genetic sequences. Activists may also produce independent information that influences a struggle, such as social responsibility screens and lists of best practice companies.

Like other human rights campaigns, attempts to limit private wrongs often begin by setting standards. Standard setting may have greater weight in these conflicts because it concerns areas previously ungoverned or even unknown. In this sense, standard setting may be intertwined with social *learning*. What is a reasonable standard of informed consent for a medical procedure or a transnational adoption that crosses cultures and jurisdictions? What resources and practices are necessary for diverse countries to manage various threats to public health? How much responsibility does a company have for the actions of a host government? For its predecessor firm? Struggles against private wrongs often force international institutions, courts, and professional associations to establish new guidelines in these areas, with implications for future debates.

The state still matters as a key source of *leverage*—even for issues that arise above, below, or across governments. Private wrongs often demand public solutions, as the state moves from human rights target to regulator and mediator of private transnational action. This means that lobbying and litigation of governments must be maintained alongside information politics, symbolic appeals, grassroots campaigns, and standard-setting strategies. And it means that some states matter more than others; notably host states for transnational flows and hegemonic states that shape international institutions. Because the United States is both host and hegemon, it is not surprising that the U.S. government was a source of leverage on each of the issues examined. U.S. reforms directly regulated child migrants, and the United States brokered the Holocaust settlements. The United States initially impeded but later facilitated AIDS drug access through the WTO. U.S. congressional hearings on organ trafficking and subsequent pressure on China are virtually the only pressure brought to bear on this aspect of the issue.

Finally, *institutionalization* must solidify reforms into replicable shifts in authority relations and new rules and roles. This level of change has been uneven and elusive for private wrongs, but there are a few promising developments. For children's migration, the creation of intergovernmental consortia to combat trafficking is the outstanding achievement. Transnational coordination for child refugees is sometimes helpful but more ad hoc, and more general economic migration represents a poorly institutionalized area of global governance. Similarly, although legal precedents grow in financial reparations cases, economic sanctions are increasingly bilateral rather than global, and socially responsible investment is periodically coordinated but not institutionalized through an ongoing system of rules and roles. Medical rights have emerged so recently and are so diffused through transnational actors that it is difficult to identify any institutional pattern, except possibly escape clauses in international trade agreements for intellectual property rights in health emergencies.

This study has tried to map a broader process of change, exemplified in these issue-areas. How can these changes be deepened and expanded to other types of private wrongs?

What Is to Be Done?

At the level of policy, what additional elements should be brought to bear to correct private wrongs based on the experience chronicled here? First, we will consider policy initiatives specific to the issues discussed and then more general recommendations for global governance.

In order to safeguard the rights of child migrants, additional measures would be helpful at the national and international levels. Within dominant host countries such as the United States, unaccompanied migrant children should be assigned an automatic advocate to represent them to legal authorities and bureaucracies. This follows a practice increasingly adopted in juvenile courts and foster care systems in the United States for child citizens and proposed in one form by the Unaccompanied Alien Child Protection Act. Such advocates should be nongovernmental professionals, ideally with some training in relevant fields such as law and social work. Recent reports of the confusions, delays, and inefficiencies resulting from the reorganization of U.S. migration agencies make coordinated advocacy an urgent priority for child migrants—who because of sheer bureaucratic incompetence are increasingly detained for long periods without evaluation or deported because they exhaust juvenile status while their cases are being glacially considered (Bernstein 2004a, 2004b).

At the multilateral level, international institutions need to develop a true regime for transnational adoption that transcends and coordinates the patchwork of bilateral policies. Based on the Convention on the Rights of the Child and Hague Convention on Transnational Adoption, an adoption regime might be located in UNICEF. It would serve to set standards, register national and private agencies, and monitor practice.

But in addition, reductions in trafficking of persons will ultimately require addressing supply and demand factors. All industrialized states must increase enforcement and intensify sanctions against traffickers and sex tourists—as the United States has done for the former and France along with a dozen peers for the latter (Vargas Llosa 2001). Measures must be sought to encourage greater enforcement in developing source countries, which will often be tied to larger problems of underdevelopment, corruption, and ineffective policing. Until such structural problems can be addressed, international policies can also help on the supply side. Educational campaigns for parents and children about the nature of trafficking in regions and social sectors at risk and shaming publicity of participants in trafficking may be helpful short-term adjuncts to weaken local linkages in smuggling networks. Aid programs should incorporate education credits designed to raise the value of a child at home and in school over the family yield from a migrant worker, expanding on the types of interventions the United Nations has sponsored in Cambodia and similar programs to combat domestic child labor in Brazil. Social services to educate law enforcement and reintegrate victims, such as the U.S. NGO Polaris project, can also provide critical support.

Turning to the area of finance, financial accountability may be increased with new strategies building on the pioneering practices of socially responsible investment. To facilitate historical accountability, activists should push regulators to require a corporate history in the annual reports filed with the U.S. Securities and Exchange Commission (although this would affect only publicly held companies). Although socially responsible investing has multiplied its impact by increasingly targeting institutional investors such as pension funds, facilitating shareholder resolutions opens the funding allocation process to other sorts of interest group politics and even concerns inimical to human rights. For example, a recent proposed resolution to TIAA-CREF specified that the fund *not* invest in concerns promoting gun control. An alternative strategy that avoids selective single-issue politics is to tie investment to corporate adherence to national legislation (such as the U.S. Corrupt Practices Act), international treaties, and existing codes of conduct.

Sanctions remain a powerful tool, but one difficult to target and easily subsumed in bilateral security agendas. Only multilateralism, universal criteria, and private sector participation can overcome these problems—as in the case of conflict diamonds. A parallel proposal by Thomas Pogge would condition multilateral and private lending on the maintenance of democracy, as assessed by an international board with universal scope and criteria (Pogge 2002). Sanctions could incorporate the democracy assessment board as a screen, with additional human rights monitoring by designated universal organizations, and provide complementary capital flows to reward change.

Reparations are a sporadic and retrospective form of leverage. But reparations can be expanded through more systematic linkage to post-transition judicial processes. Following the model of Nuremberg, war crimes tribunals and the International Criminal Court can and should prosecute complicit financial actors. Beyond this, transnational civil tribunals should be created to systematize the accountability for global financial actors currently being pursued through diverse national legal systems. Until such mechanisms can be crafted, the complaint mechanisms of the WTO, EU, and other regional trade organizations can be bridged to attempt transnational leverage for financial complicity—slave labor or repression of labor organizers are not just violations of human rights; they are also unfair trade practices.

The cluster of medical issues discussed earlier could also be ameliorated through better global coordination. The world's ailing poor would be better served by a comprehensive concessionary medicine regime rather than permission for privately manufacturing generic pharmaceuticals combined with sporadic charitable efforts. Such an undertaking could be administered through the World Health Organization.

Organ trafficking could be better controlled by an international organ certification program, with participation from physicians' associations and the World Medical Association. A minimal version would simply seek to ensure informed consent by donors. A more comprehensive system could create an international organ registry, with coordinated standards for consent and compensation and guarantees of adequate medical treatment of donors.

Finally, genetic research could be better managed through patent conditionality. Patent conditionality would require that researchers provide a demonstration of informed consent from any human subjects involved in the research—including the filing of an impact statement including anticipated applications and disclosing financial relationships, in order to receive intellectual property certification. Although patent conditionality would not resolve the problems of group rights or privacy, the impact statement would permit those potentially affected to be notified and pursue their rights in an appropriate venue. Despite efforts by UNESCO and the EU, the only plausible source of enforcement for the foreseeable future is the WTO, under the rubric of intellectual property rights.

These measures would help to solve problems and expand rights in specific areas, but we must also consider the wider field of private wrongs as a challenge for global governance. Families, firms, religions, professions, and other social institutions will continue to exercise power in abusive ways at times, and that power will be increasingly projected across borders. There is no global government to restrain these forces, national governments often lack the will or capacity, and atomized individuals are relatively helpless in the face of organized authoritative institutions and their collective resources. What we may see instead is a replication of the small victories described in the chapters and a proliferation of the modest suggestions made earlier across many issue-areas.[2]

At some point, such changes in expectations, institutions, incentives, and enforcement will begin to cumulate, to form a web of global governance. This is precisely the pattern of development of multilevel measures for controlling state-sponsored human rights violations, a pattern of slow and checkered change that is now so persistent and widespread that we call it an "international regime." The elements of such a regime include:

- Increased monitoring and the production of information
- The establishment of standards, codes, and legal instruments
- Creation and maintenance of ongoing transnational networks and coalitions
- National regulation and conditionality, especially in hosts and hegemons
- Expansion of international certification, administration, and allocation in accordance with new norms in existing issue-areas
- The occasional creation of new international bodies to promote and eventually enforce the most consolidated norms, usually with some initial help from states

Although the weakness of private wrongs is their control by unaccountable "estates," this characteristic may sometimes supplement global governance through self-regulation or normative projection by a profession, religion, or other transnational community—even business, through measures such as industry-wide codes of conduct.[3]

However, it is difficult to conceive of a private rights regime that could accommodate even the variety of actors and authority relationships sketched here, let alone the full range of private wrongs and social authority. A more plausible and appropriate goal would be the construction of sectoral modes of governance for areas such as religion as well as the broadening and deepening of existing sectoral regimes around issues such as labor. The interlinked and overlapping nature of such private authority sectors would necessitate a complex architecture of relationships between linked and nested regimes, which would doubtless generate its own struggles. The construction of such "neo-medievalism (Bull 2002) with a human face" is a mind-boggling and imperfect project, but it seems the best interim option for global governance of private wrongs.

This raises the question of participation *by* global civil society in global governance *of* global civil society. If private authority is the source of the problem, and sometimes part of the solution, would more systematic representation in international organizations permit greater accountability? Advocates of cosmopolitan democracy generally propose a global Peoples' Parliament, United Nations NGO Assembly, or sometimes a permanent parallel flow of social movements around the institutions and opportunities for international decision making (Held 1995, Falk 2002)—although their general goal is the governance of states rather than private authority. Beyond the intense problems of determining representation in such groups, there is no guarantee that increased representation would promote human rights goals rather than self-interest, ideology, or even majoritarian oppression.

More issue-specific representation of relevant social authority groups, along with representatives of affected sectors, within existing international regimes has greater potential to promote human rights within global civil society. This ILO-style, issue-specific representation has been proposed as a halfway house to global governance to close the global citizenship gap by providing a venue for transnational or subnational groups (Brysk and Shafir 2004). In order to ensure that such global quasi-corporatist representation does not itself contribute to private wrongs, participation of civic groups would be conditioned on civility: adherence to the Universal Declaration of Human Rights and relevant treaties as a condition for entry.

However, even this humanistic form of limited global corporatism still does not address the realities and responsibilities of the relationship between peak organizations and their branches and members. Much abuse by private actors may still occur at the grassroots level. Nor would such limited corporatism be appropriate for the most diffuse, widespread, and often most powerful private authority: the family.

Despite these and other limitations, pluralistic global governance can evolve to weave a greater web of accountability for private wrongs, as human rights becomes a growing norm of international relations. Stronger standards and monitoring, creative insertion of leverage mechanisms in multiple venues, establishment of institutions for ungoverned areas, and systematic representation of affected groups can help to begin to realize a broader vision of human rights for all.

What Next?

What trends can we project for the construction of human rights, based on the experience chronicled in this book? As we have seen, private governance and human rights accountability will continue to increase. But private power and transnational struggle will grow unevenly, in response to developments in states, markets, technology—and ideas of human rights. Those ideas will develop in three interconnected ways: new bearers of rights, new strategies for leverage and accountability, and new rights for new realms of social life and human endeavor.

Who will be the *new bearers* of rights? Although struggles will intensify in this generation to include all forms of biological variation within the rubric of human rights, ascriptive diversity will eventually achieve maximal coverage under the human rights regime. Unresolved areas for inclusion by identity that are likely to evoke intense controversies revolve around reproduction: gender, sexual orientation, children, and their precursors.

Even as the "human" is expanded to include all identities, we are challenged to include all human *conditions*—above all, the condition of poverty. Truly universal rights must provide the necessary conditions for human survival and dignity for the majority of the world's population, and this inevitably requires rethinking the linkages between economic and civil rights. As Farmer articulates the next rights agenda:

> Do the invisible poor come into view only when they become research subjects or immigrants, or is the next step the inclusion of everyone under the rubric of "everybody?" The inclusion of all humans under the rubric "human?" The inclusion of social and economic rights under the rubric "human rights?" (2003: 202)

The next horizon will be behavioral characteristics and choices—already guaranteed for public expression and political contestation, but later applied to private and social nonpolitical behavior. Contrary to the fears of some advocates, increasing linkages between behavior and biology may ironically strengthen the claim to behavioral rights—if difference is asserted to be ascriptive. For example, some educators now speak of "neurodevelopmental diversity" as a human right within schools (Levine 2002).

In a parallel move, the "third generation" of community rights will acquire increasing content, controversy, and a double-edged dimension. Rights *of* the community will expand to include rights *in* the community of diverse kinds of members. This is already a trend at the national level, in the resolution of ethnic conflict and postconflict nation building. Community participation rights will include not just the right to be different but also the right to behave differently.

The ultimate extension of new bearers of human rights is when the human community becomes identified with the planetary community and rights are extended to all living beings. Many Buddhists, animal rights advocates, some ecofeminists, and partisans of "deep ecology" already argue for this position (Rasmussen 1996). But the transition from *human* rights to *life* rights is difficult to conceive, let alone enforce, and may strain the concept to the breaking point.

New strategies within the existing regime have more straightforward implications, based on the trends toward rules and information. The judicialization of all realms and venues of human existence will continue, albeit unevenly, with some regions and issues more densely legally contested than others. National, regional, hybrid, and international courts will intensify their activities for classical human rights, such as war crimes and crimes against humanity. But international legal venues will also selectively increase coverage of second- and third-generation issues, such as workers' rights and the right to a life-sustaining environment. For example, Ecuadorian residents of the Amazon have sued Texaco for environmental damages incurred in oil production (Aguinda v. Texaco 1993). Financial complicity will especially lend itself to transnational litigation at all levels.

In parallel fashion, in an increasingly information-based political economy, the production and publicity of data and analysis will be ever more relevant to human rights struggles. This means that demands for transparency and struggles against censorship will provide enabling rights for monitoring, debating, and regulating both state-based and private abuses.

It also means that expertise and professional certification of both practices and reforms will play a growing role in human rights debates.

As a metastrategic question, with the normalization of human rights as a discourse, human rights institutions may face the ironic challenge of "mainstreaming." As respect for human rights comes to be seen as a desirable dimension of all social life, some will argue that human rights guidelines and conditions should be incorporated into governance of war, trade, and other international interactions rather than set aside in specific treaties, commissions, and courts. Although human rights should not be ghettoized, experience in other areas suggests that *both* separate institutions with a deep focus and expertise *and* human rights clauses woven through global governance are necessary, desirable, and complementary.

Finally, *new rights* will continue to emerge in response to changing life conditions, which are largely driven by new technologies and patterns of economic development. Access to natural resources and distributions of production become ever more critical determinants of the right to a meaningful and sustainable life with expanding population and sharpening environmental constraints, extending the palette of second- and third-generation rights. Meanwhile, growing transnationalism, dependence, and surveillance technology diffuse the forms of authority and potential for abuse adumbrated by Foucault's "governmentality." New patterns of public-private hegemony will evoke new claims to defend human dignity from "Leviathan.com," with an emphasis on privacy.

Furthermore, new rights claims will increasingly articulate identities that respond to global science. As knowledge claims seek to define or reshape the boundaries of the body, new rights to privacy and self-determination will reassert the dignity of the person. But with increasing social insertion of new technologies, the scope of such new rights to personal autonomy will increasingly conflict with that of other persons or groups: transplant recipients versus donors, genetic patients versus research subjects, or unborn fetuses versus ailing seekers of stem cells. The specific forms and impact of new conditions generated by scientific knowledge and technology will be unpredictable, but struggles over their boundaries are especially important to monitor—because these rights claims will reveal the counterhegemony of an era.

Human rights is a powerful and persuasive ideology because it represents a progressive program for the realization of universal human dignity. From its emergence out of the ashes of human agency, human rights has grown to construct a compelling challenge to state sovereignty and a modest scaffolding of global governance to limit states' repression of their own citizens. While pursuing the core concerns of genocide, war crimes, political prisoners, and torture, human rights activists have also come to recognize and resist the other forms of suffering that states wreak—from mass hunger to cultural destruction.

Now, the world community has turned from many directions inward and outward: to the private sphere and the global arena. At the human rights frontiers, new groups and old are constructing an enhanced vision of the human condition. This vision is based on articulating a set of deep questions under changing social circumstances and across domains: who counts as human, what are rights, and who is responsible?

This book has tried to show that asking such questions and acting upon the new visions that result can contribute to the relief of human suffering. Struggles against private wrongs can help an abused child in a foreign land, a dying patient, a torture survivor, or an exploited laborer. Change will come slowly and unevenly, but the best hope for these and many others is the steady, creative expansion of the human rights frontier.

Notes

Notes for Chapter 1

1. The U.S. occupation of Iraq has utilized private security contractors to an unprecedented degree, comprising approximately fifteen thousand personnel in roles that include armed combat. All such private holders of delegated armed authority lack accountability under international law. Furthermore, some transnational security contractors have recruited human rights violators from deposed dictatorships to serve as security forces in combat zones and occupied territories. In Iraq, security contractors have deployed South African death squad members with documented crimes granted amnesty by that country's Truth Commission, as well as former security guards for Chilean ex-dictator Augusto Pinochet (Singer 2004a, 2004b, http://marketplace.publicradio.org [4/19/04, Steve Henn]).
2. In this study, the term "human rights" refers to a normative discourse and resulting struggles to change political behavior and institutions. It does *not* mean legal rights or justiciable norms or imply that the emergence of new human rights establishes their legal status or necessarily provides for their enforcement. What is new about new rights is a new set of claims, new campaigns or coalitions to pursue these claims, and some increased response to claims from audiences and/or targets—ranging from mere acknowledgement to isolated behavior change to broader policy reform to full institutionalization (which may include legalization).
3. Even organized crime may be part of a system of delegated social authority, enabled or subcontracted by state power and the globalized economy. See Friman and Andreas (1999).
4. Although religious and cultural beliefs are often cited as the motive for these behaviors, they are not usually performed or directly ordered by religious authorities. Religious groups, however, may provide authorized but unaccountable surrogate family services, such as health care, education, and shelter for the socially displaced. It is in these roles that religious personnel have the greatest opportunity to violate children's rights.
5. Traditional slavery is still found in parts of Africa, state-sponsored forced labor in Burma and North Korea, and debt bondage in India and Brazil (Bales 1999, Rohter 2002). Debt bondage may have the additional element of children's sale by families and/or trafficking and sexual exploitation.

Notes for Chapter 2

1. Many thanks to Bill Maurer for stimulating reflection on this point.

Notes for Chapter 3

1. In an echo of this type of patrilineal resettlement, when the United States withdrew from Vietnam in 1975, "Operation Babylift" transported 2,800 (mostly mixed-race) Vietnamese children to the United States for adoption.
2. This fear of loss of children may help to explain the persistent but unsubstantiated rumors in Latin America that adopted children have been secretly kidnapped for organ transplants (Pahz 1988: 16, Scheper-Hughes 1998a). Although illicit international traffic in organ transplants has developed, it overwhelmingly involves adults who could not medically benefit from children's organs. Although isolated cases of illicit local medical experimentation on street children have been documented in Latin America, there is no evidence of transnational trafficking of children to the United States for medical purposes.
3. Comparative and international law distinguishes between two forms of adoption. A "simple" adoption transfers guardianship to adoptive parents without severing the legal relationship to the biological family. By contrast, a "full" adoption completely transforms the child's legal identity to the natural child of the adoptive parents and extinguishes all claims to or from the birth parents.
4. General characteristics of the legal institution that differ among states are whether adoption requires a court order or a simple contract, whether it cuts off the relationship to the biological family (full adoption), whether adoption gives the child full equal status vis-à-vis the adoptive parents, and whether adoption is revocable. Although most states are moving toward court-ordered, full, equal status, irrevocable adoption, there are significant exceptions—such as Brazil's prohibition of full adoption to foreigners (Loon 1992: 138–139).
5. It is interesting to contemplate how many domestic biological parents could satisfy these criteria—and whether they should.

Notes for Chapter 4

1. Other challenges include alternative banking in Islamic or local U.S. communities, environmental impact assessment of global finance, protest of financial institutions on equity grounds, and shareholder governance initiatives. For a fascinating account, see Maurer forthcoming.
2. International financial regulations and conventions are analogous to and sometimes affected by private international trade law, analyzed as a form of private authority by Cutler (1999).
3. Factual material and chronologies of lawsuits, settlements, and related events are available from Web sites of the U.S. State Department (www.state.gov, especially see www.state.gov/www/regions/eur/holocausthp.html), Presidential Commission on Holocaust Assets (www.pcha.gov/), Swiss Bankers' Association, International Commission on Holocaust Insurance Claims (www.icheic.org), Conference on Jewish Material Claims Against Germany (www.claimscon.org), Claim Resolution Tribunal (www.dormantaccounts.ch), www.swissbankclaims.com, International Organization for Migration (www.iom.int), German Economy Foundation Initiative Steering Group, "Remembrance, Responsibility, and the Future" (stiftungsinitiative.de/eindex.html), the New York State Banking Commission (www.claims.state.ny.us), the Geneva Financial Center (www.geneva-finance.ch/e/measures.htm), and the extremely comprehensive independent Web resource "Switzerland and the Holocaust Assets," edited by Swiss journalist and Internet entrepreneur Bruno Giussani (www.giussani.com/holocaust-assets). The following account represents a digest of these sources.
4. Refugee and financial accountability claims were sometimes mixed. In response to the refugee claims, the Swiss government commissioned the Bergier report, released in December 1999. The report estimates that about 25,000 Jewish refugees were refused admission to Switzerland, about half of the total accepted. Swiss courts initially rejected several cases in which children who survived the family's deportation to concentration camps sued for the death of their parents, but in May 2000 the Swiss government paid its first refugee-related settlement to the surviving Sonabend siblings.

5. The 1946 Swiss reparations agreement was part of a larger settlement between the Allies and the three neutral countries holding Nazi assets (Switzerland, Sweden, and Portugal). Reclaimed funds were earmarked for stateless Holocaust victims unable to claim government assistance. However, Switzerland did not even fulfill its minimal settlement—after further negotiations, in 1952 the Swiss transferred only $34 million to the Allies (Ramasastry 1998: 13–14).
6. Although a 1999 California law extending the statute of limitations to permit these suits to proceed was struck down by an appeals court in January 2003, that decision has been appealed and the cases themselves remain in the courts.
7. It is virtually impossible—and practically unnecessary—to separate human rights screens from allied concerns, especially the ubiquitous environmental sustainability. On the ground, repressive regimes and exploitative companies generally also have poor environmental records. Furthermore, activists in the environmental and human rights movements have identified a growing pattern of human rights persecution based on environmental activism and consequently formed collaborations such as the Sierra Club–Amnesty International Alliance. Nevertheless, it is important to recognize that socially responsible investment is not necessarily primarily or exclusively focused on human rights and could theoretically ignore human rights problems in an investment situation that maximized more widespread environmental goals.
8. Alternative mechanisms for social screening include exclusionary screening of investments with negative impacts, weighting or limitations on such investments within the portfolio, a positive tilt toward companies with good records, the incorporation of social scores in performance rankings of prospective investments, the use of ethical factors as a "tie breaker" among investments, exclusion of selected unethical activities based on argued linkage to performance, positive selection of firms with "best-in-class" records within a given sector, use of a prepared social responsibility index or index fund, a sectoral approach concentrating on "sunrise industries," and a concentration of social screening on international holdings (Mansley 2000).
9. A California lawsuit against Nike for "false advertising" concerning its labor record highlights the power of this dimension of corporate communications. Domini Social Investments is one of the plaintiffs, along with 17 U.S. states and various antiglobalization groups. Because of the implications for "corporate free speech," Nike is being supported by the ACLU and the New York Times as well as the expected Business Roundtable (Greenhouse, S. 2003).
10. The Sudan Peace Act was approved by Congress, but the provision regarding access to U.S. capital markets was dropped in order to secure President Bush's signature. This mechanism had been adopted at the suggestion of an NGO, the U.S. Committee on International Religious Freedom. (Information is available at the Web site of the Washington Office on Africa, www.woa.org.)
11. "But for the United States, the Castro government seizures represent the largest confiscation without compensation by a foreign government in its history. Registered claims of its citizens and corporations—assumed by the U.S. government—total $1.8 billion, amounting to over $5.2 billion in 1993 ... In March 1996, the Helms-Burton law was enacted giving U.S. citizens with valid claims the right of action in U.S. courts against investors who knowingly traffic in their confiscated properties, enabling restitution procedures against those investors who also hold assets in the United States" (Werlau 1997).
12. However, the Massachusetts selective purchasing law was struck down by the U.S. Supreme Court in 2000, with unclear implications for the future of autonomous state and local sanctions.
13. The Marcos conviction in U.S. courts was discussed previously, and Ceausescu was convicted of abuses by the successor government. Benazir Bhutto's husband, also a target of asset freezes, has been accused of murdering her brother. And Switzerland finally froze Abacha's accounts when his son and heir was charged by the new government with the murder of an opposing politician's wife (Xinhua News Agency, October 15, 1999).

Notes for Chapter 5

1. This slogan appeared on signs held by protestors against pharmaceutical companies' legal case in South Africa.
2. In January 2003, the EU proposed a compromise draft of implementing language that would delimit compulsory licenses and exporting to the following list of epidemic contagious diseases to the exclusion of chronic diseases: "This covers at least HIV/AIDS, malaria, tuberculosis, yellow fever, plague, cholera, meningococcal disease, African trypanosomiasis, dengue, influenza, leishmaniasis, hepatitis, leptospirosis, pertussis, poliomyelitis, schistosomiasis, typhoid fever, typhus, measles, shigellosis, haemorrhagic fevers and arboviruses. When requested by a Member, the World Health Organization shall give its advice as to the occurrence in an importing Member, or the likelihood thereof, of any other public health problem." Debate on the implementation of the Doha document is covered extensively on the Web site of the Consumer Project on Technology, www.cptech.org. Similarly, a pioneering global program for cancer drug donations by Novartis has been critiqued as an inadequate effort whose real purpose is to provide leverage to block the production of generics in midlevel markets such as India (Strom and Fleischer-Black 2003).
3. One person can perform less complex procedures (such as a back-alley abortion) with a few simple tools, but transplants require two surgical teams, access to sophisticated equipment and antirejection drugs, and proximity to the recipient. Furthermore, many allegations specify that Latin American *children* are kidnapped for organ extraction and that some children released for transnational adoption are actually being sold for parts. This is even less plausible; although a small proportion of adopted children may be exploited in other ways, the vast majority of organ recipients are adults who could not use children's organs. Foreigners do not usually travel for transplants to the children's countries of origin, and U.S. hospitals are subject to fairly extensive monitoring and scrutiny of transplants. Knowledgeable investigators conclude that these rumors do seem to reflect and project real problems with other aspects of medical care and commodification for Latin America's urban poor (Scheper-Hughes 1998). But the rumors have led to conflicts such as a 1994 lynching of two North American women in Guatemala who were seeking adoption but accused of organ trafficking (Adams 1998).
4. An outstanding illustration of the multivalent debates on genetic research is the role of geneticist Mary-Claire King, who helped create the genetic test for grandpaternity at the behest of Argentina's Grandmothers of the Disappeared—King was later one of the founders of the Human Genome Diversity Project, which was challenged by Indian rights organizations as a violation of their information and medical rights.

Notes for Chapter 6

1. A very similar dynamic is present in the World Psychiatric Association's criticism of forcible psychiatric commitment of dissidents in China. The transnational body has mandated an inspection visit and received cooperation from the Chinese Society of Psychiatry—although not from China's state authorities (*New York Times*, May 21, 2003).
2. For example, the increased attention to the rights of socially vulnerable migrants has extended to some types of women. The Victims of Trafficking legislation covers and has been used by adults as well as children. And a bill has been introduced in the U.S. Congress to protect "mail-order brides" from domestic abuse (*New York Times*, July 6, 2003).
3. In August 2003, the United Nations Sub-Commission for the Promotion and Protection of Human Rights approved "Draft Norms on the Responsibilities of Transnational Corporations and Other Business Enterprises with Regard to Human Rights." These are the most comprehensive and universal standards to date and encompass both transnational and local business enterprises in all sectors.

References

"A Rape Victim in Pakistan Sees Justice for Attackers," *New York Times*, September 2, 2002.

Abraham, David. 2001. "Asylum . . . ," *American Journal of International Law*, 95 (January), 204–212.

Acosta, I. 1994. "The Guaymi Patent Claim." pp. 44–50 in *Voices of the Earth*, ed. Leo van der Vlist. Amsterdam: Netherlands Center for Indigenous People.

Adams, Abigail E. 1998. "'Gringas', Ghouls and Guatemala: The 1994 Attacks on North American Women Accused of Body Organ Trafficking," *Journal of Latin American Anthropology*, 4, 1: 112–134.

Alston, Philip (ed.). 1994. *The Best Interests of the Child: Reconciling Culture and Human Rights*. Oxford: Clarendon Press.

Altstein, Howard, and Rita J. Simon (eds.). 1991. *Intercountry Adoption: A Multinational Perspective*. New York: Praeger.

Alvarez, Lizette. 2003. "Helping Retrieve Muslim Children, Including Her Own," *New York Times*, June 16.

Amnesty International. 1997. *Arming the Torturers*.

_____. *Interact: A Bulletin About Women's Human Rights*.

_____. 2003. *Amnesty Now*, 29 (Summer).

Amon, Elizabeth. 2001. "Access Denied: Children in INS Custody Have No Right to a Lawyer," *National Law Journal*, 23 (April 16).

Anaya, James. 1996. *Indigenous Peoples and International Law*. New York: Oxford University Press.

Anderson, Benedict. 1996. "Census, Map, Museum." Pp. 243–259 in *Becoming National*, ed. G. Eley and Ronald Grigor Suny. Oxford: Oxford University Press.

Anderson, Bridget. 2000. *Doing the Dirty Work? The Global Politics of Domestic Labour*. London: Zed Books.

Andersson, Gunilla. 1986. "The Adopting and Adopted Swedes and Their Contemporary Society." Pp. 23–36 in *Adoption in Worldwide Perspective: A Review of Programs, Policies and Legislation in 14 Countries*, ed. R. A. C. Hoksbergen. Lisse: Swets and Zeitlinger.

Annas, George J., and Michael A. Grodin (eds.). 1992. *The Nazi Doctors and the Nuremberg Code: Human Rights in Human Experimentation*. New York: Oxford University Press.

Archard, David William. 2003. *Children, Family and the State*. Burlington, VT: Ashgate Publishing.

Archard, David William, and Colin M. MacLeod (eds.). 2002. *The Moral and Political Status of Children*. Oxford: Oxford University Press.

Arendt, Hannah. 1958. *The Origins of Totalitarianism*. New York: Meridian.

Armas, Genaro. 2003. "Census Finds Americans Looking Overseas to Adopt Children," Associated Press, *North County Times*, August 22.

Armony, Ariel. 2001. "The Serpent's Egg: Civil Society's Dark Side," paper delivered at the 2001 Annual Meeting of the American Political Science Association, San Francisco.

Aubert, Maurice. 1997. "Swiss Banking Secrecy: General Extent and Recent Developments," Geneva Financial Center Foundation.

Avery, C./Amnesty International United Kingdom. 2000. *Business and Human Rights in a Time of Change*. London: Amnesty International UK, February.

Baard, Erik, and Rebecca Cooney. 2001. "China's Execution, Inc.," *Village Voice*, May 2–8.

Baer, Ingrid. 1986. "The Development of Adoptions in the Federal Republic of Germany." Pp. 169–188 in *Adoption in Worldwide Perspective: A Review of Programs, Policies and Legislation in 14 Countries*, ed. R. A. C. Hoksbergen.. Lisse: Swets and Zeitlinger.

Bagley, Christopher. 1986. "The Institution of Adoption: A Canadian Case Study." Pp. 221–238 in *Adoption in Worldwide Perspective: A Review of Programs, Policies and Legislation in 14 Countries*, ed. R. A. C. Hoksbergen.. Lisse: Swets and Zeitlinger.

Bagley, Christopher, with Loretta Young and Anne Scully. 1993. *International and Transracial Adoptions: A Mental Health Perspective*. Aldershot, England: Avebury.

Bales, Kevin. 1999. *Disposable People*. Berkeley: University of California Press.

Barboza, David. 2003. "A Chinese Hotel, Full of Proud American Parents," *New York Times*, March 31.

Baue, William. 2002. "Talisman Leaves Sudan But Remains on Social Investment Nix List," SocialFunds.com, November 19.

Becker, Elizabeth. 2003. "Poor Nations Can Purchase Cheap Drugs Under Accord," *New York Times*, August 31.

Bedont, Barbara, and Katherine Hall Martinez 1999. "Ending Impunity for Gender Crimes under the International Criminal Court," *Brown Journal of World Affairs*, I, 1: 65–85.

Bennett, Margaret. 1992. "Latest Developments in Intercountry Adoption," *International Legal Practitioner*, 17, 1, 10–13.

Bennetto, Jason. 2001. "War on Terrorism: Investigation," *The Independent (London)*, October 4, p. 5.

Berman, Sheri. 1997. "Civil Society and the Collapse of the Weimar Republic," *World Politics*, April.

Bernstein, Nina. 2004. "Children Alone and Scared, Fighting Deportation," *New York Times*, March 28.

———. 2004. "Out of Repression, into Jail," *New York Times*, January 15.

Bertone, Andrea. 2000. "Sexual Trafficking in Women: International Political Economy and the Politics of Sex," *Gender Issues*, Winter, 4–21.

Bhabha, Jacqueline. 1998. "Enforcing the Human Rights of Citizens and Non-Citizens in the Era of Maastricht: Some Reflections on the Importance of States," *Development and Change*, 29, 697–724.

Bibler Coutin, Susan, Bill Maurer, and Barbara Yngvesson. 2002. "In the Mirror: The Legitimation Work of Globalization," 27 *Law and Social Inquiry*, 801 (Fall), 701–742.

Biersteker, Thomas J., and Rodney Bruce Hall. 2002. "Private Authority as Global Governance." Pp. 203–222, in *The Emergence of Private Authority in Global Governance*, ed. Rodney Hall and Thomas J. Biersteker. Cambridge, UK: Cambridge University Press.

Binder, David. 2003. "12 Nations in Southeast Europe Pursue Traffickers in Sex Trade," *New York Times*, October 18.

Bluestone, Barry. 1986. "The Social Reform of Business: Market Goods, Human Rights, and Social Externalities." Pp. 127–133 in *Socially Responsible Investing and Economic Development*, ed. Jemadari Kamara. University of Michigan, Michigan Business Paper #68.

Blumstein, James F. 1995. "The Case for Commerce in Organ Transplantation." Pp. 176–192 in *Politics and the Human Body: Assault on Dignity*, ed. Jean Bethke Elshtain and J. Timothy Cloyd. Nashville, TN: Vanderbilt University Press.

Bob, Clifford. 2002. "Globalization and the Social Construction of Human Rights Campaigns." In *Globalization and Human Rights*, ed. Alison Brysk. Berkeley: University of California Press, 2002.

Bogdanich, Walt, and Eric Koli. 2003. "2 Paths of Bayer Drug in 80's: Riskier Type Went Overseas," *New York Times*, May 22.

Boli, John, and George Thomas. 1999. *Constructing World Culture*. Stanford: Stanford University Press.

Bonner, Raymond. 2002. "Pakistani Gang Said to Kidnap Children to be Sold Abroad," *New York Times*, March 17.

_____. 2003a. "A Challenge in India Snarls Foreign Adoptions," *New York Times*, June 23.

_____. 2003b. "Burmese Defy U.S. Demands for Release of Activist," *New York Times*, September 14.

Borkin, Joseph. 1978. *The Crime and Punishment of I.G. Farben*. New York: Free Press.

Bower, Tom. 1997. *Nazi Gold*. New York: HarperCollins.

Braillard, Phillippe. 2000. *Switzerland and the Crisis of Dormant Assets and Nazi Gold*. New York: Columbia University Press.

Brighouse, Hamm. 2002. "What Rights (if any) Do Children Have?" In David Archard and Colin M. MacLeod (eds.) *The Moral & Political Status of Children*. Oxford, UK: Oxford University Press. pp. 31–52.

_____. 1995. "Hearts and Minds: Bringing Symbolic Politics Back. In *Polity*, vol. xxvii, No. 4, Summer, 559–585.

Brill, Jack A., and Alan Reder. 1992. *Investing from the Heart: The Guide to Socially Responsible Investment and Money Management*. New York: Crown Publishers.

Broad, Robin. 2002. *Global Backlash: Citizen Initiatives for a Just World Economy*. Lanham, MD: Rowman and Littlefield.

Brysk, Alison. 1994. *The Politics of Human Rights in Argentina: Protest, Change, and Democratization*. Stanford: Stanford University Press.

_____. 1995. "Hearts and Minds: Bringing Symbolic Politics Back." In *Polity*, Vol. XXVII, No. 4, Summer, 559–585.

_____. 2000a. *From Tribal Village to Global Village: Indian Rights and International Relations in Latin America*. Stanford: Stanford University Press.

_____. 2000b. "Democratizing Civil Society in Latin America," *Journal of Democracy*, 11 (July), 3.

_____ (ed.). 2002. *Globalization and Human Rights*. Berkeley: University of California Press.

Brysk, Alison, and Gershon Shafir (eds.). 2004. *People out of Place: Rethinking Citizenship and Globalization*. New York: Routledge Press.

Buckley, Neil. 1997. "Belgium Probes Mobutu Assets," *The Financial Times (London)*, July 11.

Bull, Hedley. 2002. *The Anarchical Society*. New York: Columbia University Press.

Burch, Dana and Tim Smith. 1998. "Taking SRI Overseas," *Business Ethics*, September/October, 20.

Bushe, Andrew. 2003. "Major Crackdown on Minor Refugees," Sunday *Mirror* [Britain], March 18.

Capdevila, Gustavo. 2001. "Brazil Wins International Backing for Drugs Policy," *Third World Network/IPS*, April 23, www.twnside.org.sg.

Carothers, Thomas. 1999–2000. "Civil Society," *Foreign Policy*, Winter, 19–29.

Carpozi, George. 1999. *Nazi Gold*. Far Hills, NJ: New Horizon Press.

Cavalli-Sforza, L., P. Menozzi, and A. Piazza. 1994. *The History and Geography of Human Genes*. Princeton: Princeton University Press.

Cerny, Philip (ed.). 1993. *Finance and World Politics*. Cheltenham, UK: Edward Elgar.

Chandra, Prakash. 1991. "Kidneys for Sale," *World Press Review*, 38 (February), 53.

Chang, Iris. 2001. "Betrayed by the White House," *New York Times*, December 24.

Charlesworth, Hilary. 1994. "What Are 'Women's International Human Rights'?" In *Human Rights of Women: National and International Perspectives*, ed. Rebecca Cook. Philadelphia: University of Pennsylvania Press.

Charlesworth, Stephanie. 1993. "Ensuring the Rights of Children in Inter-Country Adoption: Australian Attitudes to Access to Adoption Information." Pp. 251–265 in *Parenthood in Modern Society*, ed. J. Eekelaar and P. Sarcevic. Dordrecht, The Netherlands: Martinus Nijhoff Publishers.

Chinen, Mark A. 1999. "Presidential Certifications in U.S. Foreign Policy Legislation," *New York University Journal of International Law and Politics*, 31 (Winter/Spring), 217.

Ching, Frank. 2000. "Drug Patents vs. Human Rights," *Far Eastern Economic Review*, February 17.

Clapham, Andrew. 1993. *Human Rights in the Private Sphere*. New York: Oxford University Press.

Clark, John (ed.). 2003. *Globalizing Civic Engagement: Civil Society and Transnational Action*. London: Earthscan.

Claude, Richard Pierre. 2002. *Science in the Service of Human Rights*. Philadelphia: University of Pennsylvania Press.

Coalition to Stop the Use of Child Soldiers. 2001. *Child Soldiers Global Report*.

Coday, Dennis. 2002. "Thai AIDS Activists Score Victory over Pharmaceutical Giant," *National Catholic Reporter*, November 29.

Cohen, Jean L., and Andrew Arato. 1992. *Civil Society and Political Theory*. Cambridge, MA: MIT Press.

Cook, Rebecca (ed.). 1994. *Human Rights of Women. National and International Perspectives*. Philadelphia: University of Pennsylvania Press.

Cowell, Alan. 2004. "Stealing May Be Easy, But Hiding Gets Harder," *New York Times*, April 18.

———. 2003. "Switzerland Is Odd Piece in the Continent's New Mosaic," *New York Times*, December 10.

Cox, R. W., and H. K. Jacobson (eds.). 1973. *The Anatomy of Influence*. New Haven, CT: Yale University Press.

Cox, Robert. 1996. *Approaches to World Order*. Cambridge, UK: Cambridge University Press.

Crary, David. "Mail-Order Bride Abuse Prompts Bill," *North County Times [Associated Press]*, July 6, 2003.

Crossette, Barbara. 2001. "U.S. Drops Case over AIDS Drugs in Brazil," *New York Times*, June 26.

———. 2002. "Survey Finds 'Extensive' Abuses of Refugee Children in Africa," *New York Times*, February 27.

Cushman, John. 2001. "Sierra Club Considers a Mutual Fund to Lure Investors," *New York Times*, July 20.

Cutler, A. Claire. 1999. "Locating 'Authority' in the Global Political Economy," *International Studies Quarterly*, 43 (March), 59–81.

Cutler, Claire, Virginia Haufler, and Tony Porter (eds.). 1999. *Private Authority and International Affairs*. Binghamton, NY: SUNY Press.

Damrosch, Lori Fisler. 1999. "Sanctions Against Perpetrators of Terrorism," *Houston Journal of International Law*, 22 (Fall), 63.

Darlington, Shasta. 2001. "Brazil to Violate Roche Patent on AIDS Drug," Reuters, August 22.

Day, Kathleen. 2001. "O'Neill Seeks Freedom to Trace Money to Sources," *The Washington Post*, October 4, E01.

Dharmaruksa, Darawan. 1986. "Adoption in Thailand." Pp. 115–142 in *Adoption in Worldwide Perspective: A Review of Programs, Policies and Legislation in 14 Countries*, ed. R. A. C. Hoksbergen. Lisse: Swets and Zeitlinger.

Diamond, Larry. 1999. *Developing Democracy: Toward Consolidation*. Baltimore: Johns Hopkins University Press.

Doek, Jaap, Hans van Loon, and Paul Vlaardingerbroek (eds.). 1996. *Children on the Move*. Dordrecht: Martinus Nijhoff Publishers.

Donnelly, Jack. 1986. "International Human Rights: A Regime Analysis," *International Organization* 40 (3), 599–642.

Dorsey, Ellen, and Paul Nelson. 2004. "New Rights Advocacy: Origins and Significance of a Partial Human Rights-Development Convergence," paper delivered at the International Studies Association, Montreal, March.

Drucker, Olga Levy. 1992. *Kindertransport*. New York: Holt.

Dubois, Josiah. 1953. *Generals in Grey Suits*. London: Bodley Head.

Duncan, Julianne. 2002. "Joint Testimony of Migration and Refugee Services/U.S. Conference of Catholic Bishops and Lutheran Immigration and Refugee Service on the Unaccompanied Alien Child Protection Act before the Senate Subcommittee on Immigration," February 28, http://www.usccb.org/mrs/duncantestimony.htm.

Einolf, Christopher. 2001. *The Mercy Factory: Refugees and the American Asylum System*. Chicago: Ivan R. Dee.

Elliott, Andrea. 2003. "For Some Adoptive Parents, SARS Brings a Heart-Rending Delay," *New York Times*, May 17.

Elshtain, Jean Bethke. 1981. *Public Man, Private Woman*. Princeton, NJ: Princeton University Press.

Elshtain, Jean Bethke, and J. Timothy Cloyd (eds.). 1995. *Politics and the Human Body: Assault on Dignity*. Nashville, TN: Vanderbilt University Press.

Enloe, Cynthia. 1989. *Bananas, Beaches, and Bases: Making Feminist Sense of International Relations*. London: Pandora Press.

"Experts Examine Nationality Laws Restricting Women's and Children's Rights in the Arab World," *Africa News Service*, July 30, 2003, p. 10082111u8459.

Falk, Richard. 2001. *Human Rights Horizons*. New York: Routledge Press.

Falk, Richard, and Richard Strauss. 2002. "Towards Global Parliament," *Foreign Affairs*, 80 (January–February), 212.

Farmer, Paul. 2003. *Pathologies of Power: Health, Human Rights, and the Poor*. Berkeley: University of California Press.

Felice, William F. 2002. *The Global New Deal: Economic and Social Human Rights in World Politics*. Lanham, MD: Rowman Littlefield.

Ferguson, John M. 1998. "Swiss Bank Account 'Secrecy' Today: More Holes Than Cheese," *Emory International Law Review*, Spring.

Files, John. 2004. "Black Groups Seeking Asylum for a Teenager from Guinea," *New York Times*, March 14.

Finder, Joseph. 1998. "Switzerland Postcard Unaccountable," *New Republic*, November 23.

Finkel, Michael. 2001. "This Little Kidney Went to Market," *New York Times Magazine*, May 27.

Finnemore, Martha. 1996. "Norms, Culture, and World Politics: Insights from Sociology's Institutionalism," *International Organization*, 50 (2), 325–47.

Finnemore, Martha, and Kathryn Sikkink. 1998. "International Norm Dynamics and Political Change," *International Organization*, 52 (Autumn), 887–917.

Florini, Ann (ed.). 2000. *The Third Force: The Rise of Transnational Civil Society*. Japan Center for International Exchange and Carnegie Endowment for International Peace.

Foley, Michael, and Bob Edwards. 1996. "The Paradox of Civil Society," *Journal of Democracy*, July.

Ford, Peter. 2001. "Tough Trail of Terror's Money," *The Christian Science Monitor*, October 19.

Forero, Juan. 2003. "Rights Groups Overseas Fight U.S. Concerns in U.S. Courts," *New York Times*, June 26.

———. 2004. "Private U.S. Operatives on Risky Missions in Colombia," *New York Times*, February 14.

Foucault, Michel. 1970. *The Order of Things: An Archeology of the Human Sciences*. New York: Random House.

———. 1979. *Discipline and Punishment: The Birth of the Prison*. New York: Random House.

———. 1994. *The Birth of the Clinic: An Archeology of Medical Perception*. New York: Vintage.

Fox, Anne, and Eva Abraham-Podietz. 1998. *Ten Thousand Children: True Stories Told by Children Who Escaped the Holocaust on the Kindertransport*. Springfield, NJ: Behrman House.

Frank, L. 1998. "Storm Brews over Gene Bank of Estonian Population," *Science*, 286, 162.

Freeman, Michael, and Philip Veerman. 1992. *The Ideologies of Children's Rights*. Boston: Kluwer Publishing.

French, Hilary. 2000. "The Greening of Wall Street," *Humanist*, 60, May: 9.

Freundlich, Madelyn. 1999. "Families Without Borders," *UN Chronicle*, 36 (Summer), 88.

Frey, B. A. 1996. "The Legal and Ethical Responsibility of Transnational Corporations in the Protection of International Human Rights," *Minnesota Journal of Global Trade*, 6, 1 (Winter).

Fried, Charles. 2000. "Markets, Law, and Democracy," *Journal of Democracy*, 11 (3), 5–18.

Friman, H. Richard, and Peter Andreas (eds.). 1999. *The Illicit Global Economy and State Power*. Lanham, MD: Rowman and Littlefield.

Fung, Archon, Dara O'Rourke, and Charles Sabel. 2001. *Can We Put an End to Sweatshops?* Boston: Beacon Press 1.

Gall, Carlotta. 2004. "With Child Kidnappings on Rise, Afghans Seek Help from Public," *New York Times*, April 30.

Galpin, Richard. 1998. "Court Freezes All Bhutto's Assets," *The Guardian (London)*, April 28.

"Ghana: Slave Boys Go Home," [World Briefing], *New York Times*, September 12, 2003.

Glaberson, William. 2002. "Judge Gives Children Voice in Deportation," *New York Times*, February 12.

———. 2004. "Putting a Price on Holocaust Survivors' Hopes," *New York Times*, March 13.

Goldhagen, Jonah. 1997. *Hitler's Willing Executioners: Ordinary Germans and the Holocaust*. New York: Vintage.

Goldstein, Judith, and Robert Keohane (eds.). 1993. *Ideas and Foreign Policy*. Ithaca, NY: Cornell University Press.

Gonzalez, David. 2001. "Changed Panama Banks Root out Terror Funds," *New York Times*, October 26, A6.

Goodstein, Laurie. 2002. "Suits Say Vatican and Pope Are Liable in Priest Scandal," *New York Times*, April 4.

Gootman, Elissa. 2002. "Visa Problems Snarl Adoptions in Vietnam," *New York Times*, January 29.

Gordon, Neve. 2003. "Strategic Violations: The Outsourcing of Human Rights Violations," *The Humanist*, September/October, 10–14.

Gould, Carole. 2003. "Investing with Janet Prindle and Arthur Moretti: Neuberger Berman Socially Responsive Fund," *New York Times*, February 23.

Greely, Henry T. 1997. "The Control of Genetic Research: Involving The 'Groups Between'," *Houston Law Review*, 33 (5), 1398–1430.

_____. 1998a. "Legal, Ethical, and Social Issues in Human Genome Research," *Annual Review Anthropology*, 27, 473–502.

_____. 1998b. "Informed Consent, Stored Tissue Samples, and the Human Genome Diversity Project: Protecting the Rights of Research Participants." In *Stored Tissue Samples: Ethical, Legal, and Public Policy Implications*, ed. Robert Weir. Iowa City: University of Iowa Press.

_____. 2000a. "Human Genome Diversity Project." pp. 552–566 In *Encyclopedia of Ethical, Legal, and Policy Issues in Biotechnology*, ed. Thomas J. Murray and Maxwell J. Mehlman. pp. 552–566. New York: John Wiley & Sons.

_____. 2000b. "Iceland's Plan for Genomics Research: Facts and Implications," *Jurimetrics*, 40 (Winter), 153–191.

_____. 2001a. "Informed Consent and Other Ethical Issues in Human Population Genetics," *Annual Review of Genetics*, 35, 785–800.

_____. 2001b. "Human Genome Diversity: What about the Other Human Genome Project?," *Nature*, 2 (March), 222–227.

Greenhouse, Linda. 2003. "Free Speech for Companies on Justices' Agenda," *New York Times*, April 20.

Greenhouse, Steven. 2001. "Report Outlines the Abuse of Foreign Domestic Workers," *New York Times*, June 14.

_____. 2003. "Capping the Cost of Atrocity," *New York Times*, November 19.

Greenwood, J. 2000. "The Business of Genes: Newfoundland Hopes to Reap the Benefits after Its Genetic Heritage Has Helped Decode the Human Genome," *National Post*, June 24.

Griffin, James. 2002. "Do Children Have Rights?" In David Archard and Colin M. MacLeod (eds.), *The Moral & Political Status of Children*, Oxford, UK: Oxford University Press, pp. 19–30.

Grossberg, Michael. 1985. *Governing The Hearth: Law and the Family in Nineteenth-Century America*. Chapel Hill: University of North Carolina Press.

Haas, Peter. 1992. "Epistemic Communities and International Policy Coordination," *International Organization*, 46 (1), 1–36.

Hakim, Danny. 2001. "On Wall St., More Investors Push Social Goals," *New York Times*, February 11, A1, 24.

Hall, Tony. 1986. "The Adoption Revolution in Britain." In *Adoption in Worldwide Perspective: A Review of Programs, Policies and Legislation in 14 Countries*, ed. R. A. C. Hoksbergen. pp. 57–78. Lisse: Swets and Zeitlinger.

Harris, Mark, and Deborah Oppenheimer (eds.). 2002. *Into the Arms of Strangers: Stories of the Kindertransport*. London: Bloomsbury.

Hartsock, Nancy. 1983. *Money, Sex, and Power: Towards a Feminist Historical Materialism*. Boston: Northeastern University Press.

Hayes, Peter. 2000. "Deterrents to Intercountry Adoption in Britain," *Family Relations*, 49 (October), 465–472.

Hechter, Michael, and Karl-Dieter Opp (eds.). 2001 *Social Norms*. New York: Russell Sage Foundation.

Held, David. 1995. *Democracy and Global Order: From the Modern State to Cosmopolitan Governance*. Stanford,: Stanford University Press.

_____. 2000. "Markets, Private Property, and the Possibility of Democracy." In *Principled World Politics: The Challenge of Normative International Relations*, ed. Paul Wapner and Lester Edwin J. Ruiz. pp. 151–165. Lanham, MD: Rowman and Littlefield.

Held, David, Anthony McGrew, David Goldblatt, and Jonathon Perraton. 1999. *Global Transformations*. Stanford: Stanford University Press.

Helleiner, Eric. 1994. *States and the Reemergence of Global Finance*. Ithaca, NY: Cornell University Press.

Helleiner, Eric, and Emily Gilbert (eds.). 1999. *Nation-States and Money*. New York: Routledge Press.

Henkin, Louis. 1999. *Human Rights*. New York: Foundation Press.

Hernandez, Raymond. 2001 "Children's Sexual Exploitation Underestimated, Study Finds," *New York Times*, September 10.

Heywood, Mark. 2001. "Debunking Conglomo-talk: A Case Study of the *Amicus Curiae* as an Instrument for Advocacy, Investigation and Mobilisation," paper presented at Health, Law and Human Rights, Philadelphia, October 1.

Hill, Patrice. 2001. "Bush Takes Big Bite of Terror's Assets." *The Washington Times*, November 8.

Himes, James R. 1994. "Preface." In *The Best Interests of the Child: Reconciling Culture and Human Rights*, ed. Philip Alston. Oxford: Clarendon Press, 1994.

Hoksbergen, R. A. C. (ed.). 1986. *Adoption in Worldwide Perspective: A Review of Programs, Policies and Legislation in 14 Countries*. Lisse: Swets and Zeitlinger.

Hoksbergen, Rene A.C. 1991. "Intercountry Adoption Coming of Age in the Netherlands: Basic Issues, Trends, and Developments." pp. 141–160 in *Intercountry Adoption: A Multinational Perspective*, ed. Howard Altstein and Rita J. Simon. New York: Praeger.

_____ and Lucile A. C. Bunjes. 1986. "Thirty Years of Adoption Practice in the Netherlands." Pp. 37–56 in *Adoption in Worldwide Perspective: A Review of Programs, Policies and Legislation in 14 Countries*, ed. R. A. C. Hoksbergen. Lisse: Swets and Zeitlinger.

"Holocaust Reparations: German CEOs Unlock Their Vaults," *Businessweek*, February 22, 1999.

"Holocaust Reparations: Watman v. Deutsche Bank," *Bank and Lender Liability Litigation Reporter*, January 11, 6 (10), 9.

Hufbauer, Gary Clyde, Jeffrey J. Schott, and Kimberly Ann Elliott. 1990. *Economic Sanctions Reconsidered*. Washington, DC: Institute for International Economics.

Hulbert, Mark. 2003. "Good for Your Conscience, If Not for Your Wallet," *New York Times*, July 20.

Human Rights Watch/Asia. 1994. *Organ Procurement and Judicial Execution in China*. New York.

_____. 1996. *Death by Default: A Policy of Fatal Neglect in China's State Orphanages*. New York.

Human Rights Watch. 1998. *United States: Detained and Deprived of Rights—Children in the Custody of the U.S. Immigration and Naturalization Service*. New York.

_____. 2001. *Hidden in the Home: Abuse of Domestic Workers with Special Visas in the United States*. New York.

"Human Trafficking May Result in U.S. Sanctions," Associated Press, June 12, 2003.

Hunter, Jane. 1995. "Critics Call Clinton's Ban on Funding to Middle East Groups Biased, Illegal," *National Catholic Reporter*, February 10, 31 (15).

Ignatieff, Michael. 2001. *Human Rights as Politics and Ideology*. Princeton, NJ: Princeton University Press.

"Illegal Guinea Immigrant Sues over Conditions in Detention," *New York Times*, November 2 2002.

Indonesian National Council on Social Welfare. 1986. "Adoption of Children in Indonesia." Pp. 107–114 in Hoksbergen, R.A.C. (ed.) *Adoption in Worldwide Perspective: A Review of Programs, Policies and Legislation in 14 Countries*, ed. R. A. C. Hoksbergen. Lisse: Swets and Zeitlinger.

Ingram, Helen, and Anne Schneider. 1993. "The Social Construction of Target Populations: Implications for Politics and Policy," *American Political Science Review* 87 (June), 334–47.

International Labor Organization. 2002. *International Programme on the Elimination of Child Labour (IPEC), Statistical Information and Monitoring Programme on Child Labour (SIMPOC), Every Child Counts: New Global Estimates on Child Labour*. Geneva, April (www.ilo.org).

International Organization for Migration. 2003. *World Migration Report*.

Ivanov, Andrei. 1998. "Health: Israeli Link in Estonian 'Human Kidneys For Sale' Scam," IPS, February 20.

Jaffe, Eliezer D. 1991. "Foreign Adoptions in Israel: Private Paths to Parenthood." Pp. 161–182 in *Intercountry Adoption: A Multinational Perspective*, ed. Howard Altstein and Rita J. Simon. New York: Praeger.

James, Jennie. 2000. "The Calculus of Conscience: Socially-Responsible Investing Can Be Both Profitable and Ethical," *Time International*, 156 (August 14), 33.

Jantera-Jareborg, Maarit. 1990. "The Procedural and Material Conditions for Intercountry Adoption in Sweden." In *Swedish National Reports to the XIIIth International Congress of Comparative Law*, Montreal, ed. Stig Stromholm and Carl Hemstrom. Stockholm: Almqvist and Wiksell International.

_____. 1994. "Convention on Protection of Children and Cooperation in Respect of Intercountry Adoption," *Nordic Journal of International Law*, 63, 185–203.

Jeungst, E. T. 1998. "Groups as Gate Keepers to Genomic Research: Conceptually Confusing, Morally Hazardous, and Practically Useless," *Kennedy Institute of Ethics Journal*, 8, 183–200.

Jochnik, Chris. 1999. "Confronting the Impunity of Non-State Actors: New Fields for the Promotion of Human Rights," *Human Rights Quarterly*, 56.

Johansen, Bruce. 1993. "Kidnapped by 'La Migra'," *Progressive*, 57 (April), 21.

Johansson, Philip. 2000. "25 Sizzling Funds that Beat a Tough Market," *Business Ethics*, July/August.

Jones, James H.1993. *Bad Blood: The Tuskegee Syphilis Experiment*. New York: Free Press.

Joppke, Christian. 1998. "Why Liberal States Accept Unwanted Immigration," *World Politics*, 52 (2), 266–293.

"Judge Refuses to Halt Suit Against ChevronTexaco Unit," *New York Times,* March 27, 2004.

Judge, Sharon Lesar. 1999. "Eastern European Adoptions: Current Status and Implications for Intervention," *Topics in Early Childhood Special Education*, 19 (Winter), 244.

Jungalwalla, Avi. 1986. "Adoption Policies and Experiences in India." Pp. 93–106 in *Adoption in Worldwide Perspective: A Review of Programs, Policies and Legislation in 14 Countries*, ed. R. A. C. Hoksbergen. Lisse: Swets and Zeitlinger.

Kabbany, Jennifer. 2004. "Leaders Discuss Ways of Fighting Prostitution Rings," *North County Times*, March 19.

Kahn, Joseph. 2000. "Multinationals Sign U.N. Pact on Rights and Environment," *New York Times*, July 27.

Kahn, Joseph. 2001. "Clinton Seeks to Keep Foreigner from Hiding Wealth in U.S." *New York Times,* January 16.

Kaiser, Jocelyn. 2002. "Population Databases Boom, from Iceland to the U.S.," *Science*, 298 (November 8), 1158–1161.

Kane, John. 2001. *The Politics of Moral Capital*. Cambridge, UK: Cambridge University Press.

Kane, June. 1998. *Sold for Sex*. Ashgate Publishing.

Kashiwazaki, Chikako. 1998. "Jus Sanguinis in Japan: The Origin of Citizenship in a Comparative Perspective," *International Journal of Comparative Sociology*, 39 (August),278.

Kass, Leon R. 1995. "Organs for Sale? Propriety, Property, and the Price of Progress." Pp. 153–175 in *Politics and the Human Body: Assault on Dignity*, ed. Jean Bethke Elshtain and J. Timothy Cloyd. Nashville, TN: Vanderbilt University Press.

Katzenstein, Peter (ed.). 1996. *The Culture of National Security*. New York: Columbia University Press.

Kaufman, Marc. 2001. "U.S. Froze $254 Million in Taliban Cash in 1999," *Washington Post*, October 13, A16.

Kaufman, Natalie Hevener, and Irene Rizzini (eds.). 2002. *Globalization and Children*. New York: Kluwer Academic Publishers.

Kaur, Hardev. 2001. "About-turn in U.S. Position," *New Straits Times (Malaysia)*. October 20.

Keane, John. 2003. *Global Civil Society?* Cambridge, UK: Cambridge University Press.

Keck, Margaret, and Kathryn Sikkink. 1998. *Activists Beyond Borders*. Ithaca, NY: Cornell University Press.

Kelly, Marjorie. 2000. "Does Social Investing Make a Difference?," *Hope Magazine*, Spring.

Kent, George. 1995. *Children in the International Political Economy*. New York: St. Martin's.

Keohane, Robert O., and Joseph S. Nye Jr. 2000. "Introduction." In, *Governance in a Globalizing World*, ed. Joseph S. Nye Jr. and John D. Donahue. Washington, DC: Brookings Institution Press.

Khagram, Sanjeev, James Riker, and Kathryn Sikkink (eds.). 2001. *Restructuring World Politics: Transnational Social Movements, Networks, and Norms*. Minneapolis: University of Minnesota Press.

Kinder, Peter, and Amy L. Domini. 1997. "Social Screening: Paradigms Old and New," *The Journal of Investing*. 6 (Winter), 12–19.

Kinder, Peter D., Steven D. Lydenberg, and Amy L. Domini. 1993. *Investing for Good: Making Money While Being Socially Responsible*. New York: HarperBusiness.

Kingsbury, Benedict. 2002. "The Democratic Accountability of Non-governmental Organizations," *Chicago Journal of International Law*, 3 (Spring).

Kiss, Alexandre. 1993. "Concept and Possible Implications of the Right to Environment." In *Human Rights in the Twenty-first Century: A Global Challenge*, ed. Kathleen Mahoney and Paul Mahoney. Dordrecht: Kluwer-Martinus Nijhoff Publishers.

Klotz, Audie. 1995. *Norms in International Relations: The Struggle Against Apartheid*. Ithaca, NY: Cornell University Press.

Klusmeyer, Douglas. 2000. "Four Dimensions of Membership in Germany," *SAIS Review*, 20 (1), 1–21.

Knestout, Brian P. 2000. "Value Times Two: Socially Responsible Investments Offered by Vanguard and TIAA-CREF," *Kiplinger's Personal Finance Magazine* 54 (March), 76.

Korey, William. 1998. *NGOs and the Universal Declaration of Human Rights: A Curious Grapevine*. New York: St. Martin's Press.

Kraft, Dina. 2001. "South Africa Loses AIDS Lawsuit," Associated Press, December 14.

Kristof, Nicholas. 2002. "Psst! Sell Your Kidney?," *New York Times*, September 12.

Kyle, David, and Rey Koslowski (eds.). 2001. *Global Human Smuggling*. Baltimore: Johns Hopkins University Press.

LaFraniere, Sharon. 2003. "Court Convicts 3 in 1994 Genocide Across Rwanda: Media Fomented Violence," *New York Times*, December 4.

Landesman, Peter. 2004 "The Girls Next Door," *New York Times Magazine*, January 25.

Laxer, Gordon, and Sandra Halperin (eds.). 2003. *Global Civil Society and Its Limits*. New York: Palgrave Macmillan.

Leary, Virginia. 1993. "Implications of a Right to Health." Pp. 481–493 in *Human Rights in the Twenty-first Century: A Global Challenge*, ed. Kathleen Mahoney and Paul Mahoney. Dordrecht: Kluwer-Martinus Nijhoff Publishers.

"Legal Battle Looms as Holocaust Survivors Ignore U.S.-Austria Deal," *Insurance Day*, June 21, 2001.

Lewis, Neil. 2002. "Agreement Sets Up Rules for Holocaust Claims," *New York Times*, May 19.

Levesque, Roger J.R. 1999 *Sexual Abuse of Children: A Human Rights Perspective*. Bloomington: Indiana University Press.

Levin, Itamar. 1999. *The Last Deposit: Swiss Banks and Holocaust Victims' Accounts*. Westport, CT: Praeger.

Levine, Melvin. 2002 *A Mind at a Time*. New York: Simon & Schuster.

Lewontin, Richard C. 1995. "The Dream of the Human Genome." Pp. 41–66 in *Politics and the Human Body: Assault on Dignity*, ed. Jean Bethke Elshtain and J. Timothy Cloyd. Nashville, TN: Vanderbilt University Press.

Lifton, Robert Jay. 1986 *The Nazi Doctors: Medical Killing and the Psychology of Genocide*. New York: Basic Books.

Lion, Aviva. 1986. "Adoption in Israel." Pp. 189–210 in *Adoption in Worldwide Perspective: A Review of Programs, Policies and Legislation in 14 Countries*, ed. R. A. C. Hoksbergen. Lisse: Swets and Zeitlinger.

Lipkin, David. 2001. "Tracking Down All the Holocaust Beneficiaries," *Insurance Day*, July 10.

Lippman, Thomas W. 1996. "U.S. Fails to Erase Sketchy Tale," *Washington Post*, March 19.

Lipschutz, R.D. 1992. "Reconstructing World Politics: The Emergence of Global Civil Society," *Millennium: Journal of International Studies*, 21 (3), 389–420.

Lipschutz, Ronnie D., and Cathleen Fogel. 2002. "Regulation for the Rest of Us? Global Civil Society and the Privatization of Transnational Regulation." Pp. 115–140 in *The Emergence of Private Authority in Global Governance*, ed. Rodney Hall and Thomas J. Biersteker. Cambridge, UK: Cambridge University Press.

Liptak, Adam. 2003. "Court Dismisses Claims of Slave Laborers." *New York Times*, January 22.

Loon, J. H. A. van. 1992. "Intercountry Adoption of Children: A Challenge for International Cooperation to Protect Children's Rights," *Hague Yearbook of International Law*, 5, 137–163.

Lopez, George A., and David Cortright (eds.). 1995. *Economic Sanctions*. Boulder, CO: Westview Press.

Los Angeles Times. 1989. "Kidney Sales Brokerage Is Flourishing in India," July 16.

Lucker-Babel, Marie-Francoise. 1991. "Inter-Country Adoption and Trafficking in Children: An Initial Assessment of the Adequacy of the International Protection of Children and Their Rights," *International Review of Penal Law*, 62 (3–4), 799–818.

Lyons, Gene M., and James Mayall (eds.). 2003. *International Human Rights in the 21st Century: Protecting the Rights of Groups*. Lanham, MD: Rowman and Littlefield.

Macan-Markar, Marwaan. 2001. "Generic Drug Makers Brace for Battle with Pharmaceuticals," *Third World Network*, February 11, IPS, www.twnside.org.sg.

MacFarquhar, Neil. 2001. "In Egypt, Law of Man Creates a Caste of Shunned Children," *New York Times*, May 14.

Madhav Goyal, Ravindra L. Mehta, Lawrence J. Schneiderman, and Ashwini R. Sehgal. 2002. "Economic and Health Consequences of Selling a Kidney in India," *JAMA*, 288, 1589–1593.

Maher, Kristen Hill. 2004. "The Globalization of Social Reproduction." In Alison Brysk and Gershon Shafir (eds.) *People Out of Place*, New York: Routledge.

Mann, Jonathan M., Sofia Gruskin, Michael A. Grodin, and George J. Annas (eds.). 1999. *Health and Human Rights*. New York: Routledge Press.

Mann, Michael, and Richard Wolffe. 2001. "US Accuses Africa Banks of Failing to Assist Search Al-Qaeda Assets," *Financial Times (London)*, October 3, 4.

Mansley, Mark. 2000. *Socially Responsible Investment: A Guide for Pension Funds and Institutional Investors*. Short Run Press.

Marbella, Jean. 2001. "Islamic Charities Under Scrutiny," *The Baltimore Sun*, October 7, 1A.

Marquis, Christopher. 2004. "New System Begins Rerouting U.S. Aid for Poor Countries," *New York Times*, February 22.

Marshall, Patricia. 1993. "Violence Against Women in Canada by Non-State Actors." Pp. 319–334 in *Human Rights in the Twenty-first Century: A Global Challenge*, ed. Kathleen Mahoney and Paul Mahoney. Dordrecht: Kluwer-Martinus Nijhoff Publishers.

Matthews, Jessica. 1997. "Power Shift," *Foreign Affairs*, January/February.

Matthews, Mark. 2001. "Hitting bin Laden in the Wallet Not Easy," *Baltimore Sun*, September 25, 9A.

McAdam, Doug, Sidney Tarrow, and Charles Tilly. 2001. *Dynamics of Contention*. Cambridge, UK: Cambridge University Press.

McDaniels, Andrea. 1998. "Brazil Mandates Organ 'Donation' for Transplants," *Christian Science Monitor International*, January 16.

McHenry, James R. 2002. "The Prosecution of Rape under International Law," *Vanderbilt Journal of Transnational Law*, 35 (October), 1278.

McNeil, Donald G. 2002. "New List of Safe AIDS Drugs, Despite Industry Lobby," *New York Times*, March 21.

———. 2004. "Plan to Battle AIDS Worldwide Is Falling Short," *New York Times*, March 28.

Melchior, Torben. 1986 "Adoption in Denmark." pp. 211–220 in *Adoption in Worldwide Perspective: A Review of Programs, Policies and Legislation in 14 Countries*, ed. R. A. C. Hoksbergen. Lisse: Swets and Zeitlinger.

Meyer, John W., John Boli, George M. Thomas, and Francisco Ramirez. 1997. "World Society and the Nation-State," *American Journal of Sociology*, 103 (1), 144–81.

Miller, Sara B. 2003. "Spain to Morocco's Child Migrants: Go Home," *Christian Science Monitor*, May 2.

Milotte, Mike. 1997. *Banished Babies: The Secret History of Ireland's Baby Export Business*. Dublin: New Island Books.

Moore, Molly, and John Ward Anderson. 1995. "Kidney Racket Riles Indians," *Washington Post*, 118, April 30.

Mowjee, Tasneem. 2003. "Campaigns to Increase Access to HIV/AIDS Drugs." Pp. 66–85 in *Globalizing Civic Engagement: Civil Society and Transnational Action*, ed. John Clark. London: Earthscan.

Muro, Diego. 2003 "Campaign for a 'Robin Hood Tax' for Foreign Exchange Markets." Pp. 150–163 in *Globalizing Civic Engagement: Civil Society and Transnational Action*, ed. John Clark. London: Earthscan.

Murphy, Craig. 1994. *International Organization and Industrial Change: Global Governance Since 1850*. New York: Oxford University Press.

Mydans, Seth. 2001. "U.S. Interrupts Cambodian Adoptions," *New York Times*, November 5.

———. 2002. "The Perfect Thai Vacation: Sun, Sea and Surgery," *New York Times*, September 9.

Nadelmann, Ethan. 1990. "Global Prohibition Regimes: The Evolution of Norms in International Society," *International Organization*, 44 (Autumn), 479–526.

Nazi Medicine: Doctors, Victims, and Medicine in Auschwitz. 1986. New York: Howard Fertig.

Nelson, Roy. 1999. "The Importance of the 'Democracy Variable' in Explaining Foreign Investment Decisions," *International Studies Notes*, 24 (3), 46–52.

O'Brien, Robert, Anne Marie Goetz, Jan Aart Scholte, and Marc Williams. 2000. *Contesting Global Governance: Multilateral Economic Institutions and Global Social Movements*. Cambridge, UK: Cambridge University Press.

OECD (Organization for Economic Cooperation and Development). 2000. *Trends in International Migration*. Paris.

Olson, Elizabeth. 2001a. "Swiss Find $10 Million from Nazi Era," *New York Times*, October 12.

_____. 2001b. "Swiss Were Part of Nazi Economic Lifeline, Historians Find," *New York Times*, December 2, A18.

_____. 2002a. "50 Million Children without a Nationality," *New York Times*, June 5.

_____. 2002b. "Swiss Compete Aid Payments to Nazi Victims," *New York Times*, May 5.

_____. 2003. "Commission Concludes That Swiss Policies Aided the Nazis," *New York Times*, March 22.

Oxfam Great Britain. 2001. *Drug Companies vs. Brazil: The Threat to Public Health*. Oxford; www.oxfam.org.uk; reprinted in *Pan American Journal of Public Health*, 9 (5), 331–337.

Pahz, James A. 1988. *Adopting from Latin America: An AGENCY Perspective*. Springfield, IL: Charles C Thomas.

Pandit, Nirmala. 1993. "Inter-Country Adoption: The Indian View." Pp. 267–275 in *Parenthood in Modern Society*, ed. J. Eekelaar and P. Sarcevic. Dordrecht, The Netherlands: Martinus Nijhoff Publishers.

Passy, Florence. 2001. "Political Altruism and the Solidarity Movement: An Introduction." Pp. 1–25 in *Political Altruism? Solidarity Movements in International Perspective*, ed. Marco Giugni and Florence Passy. Lanham, MD: Rowman and Littlefield.

Peel, Michael, and John Willman. 2001. "The Dirty Money That Is Hardest to Clean Up," *Financial Times (London)*, November 20.

Pettman, Jan Jindy. 1996. *Worlding Women: A Feminist International Politics*. New York: Routledge Press.

Picton, Cliff. 1986. "Adoption in Australia." Pp. 151–168 in *Adoption in Worldwide Perspective: A Review of Programs, Policies and Legislation in 14 Countries*, ed. R. A. C. Hoksbergen. Lisse: Swets and Zeitlinger.

Pike, David, and Reinie Booysen. 2000. "U.S. Rights Groups Target CNPC, Talisman," *Oil Daily*, 50, 14.

Pilotti, Francisco J. 1986. "Intercountry Adoption; a View from Latin America." Pp. 143–150 in *Adoption in Worldwide Perspective: A Review of Programs, Policies and Legislation in 14 Countries*, ed. R. A. C. Hoksbergen. Lisse: Swets and Zeitlinger.

Pogge, Thomas. 2002. *World Poverty and Human Rights: Cosmopolitan Responsibilities and Reforms*. Cambridge: Polity Press.

Polanyi, Karl. 1957. *The Great Transformation*. Boston: Beacon Press.

Pollack, Andrew. 2003. "Big DNA Files to Help Blacks Fight Diseases," *New York Times*. May 27.

Pomfret, John. 2001. "Rare Chinese Newspaper Expose Details Prisoner Organ Harvests," *Washington Post Foreign Service*, July 31.

Posey, D. A., and G. Dutfield. 1996. *Beyond Intellectual Property*. Ottawa: International Development Research Center.

Price, Richard. 1998. "Reversing the Gun Sights: Transnational Civil Society Targets Land Mines," *International Organization*, 52, (Summer), 613–44.

Price Cohen, Cynthia. 1990. "The Role of Non-Governmental Organizations in Drafting of the Convention on the Rights of the Child," *Human Rights Quarterly*, 12 (February), 137–147.

Pyne, Hnin Hnin. 1995. "AIDS and Gender Violence: The Enslavement of Burmese Women in the Thai Sex Industry." Pp. 215–223 in *Women's Rights, Human Rights*, ed. Julie Peters and Andrea Wolper. New York: Routledge Press.

Rabkin, Jeremy. 2000. "Children Adrift," *American Spectator*, 33 (March), 44.

Radin, Margaret Jane. 1996. *Contested Commodities*. Cambridge, MA: Harvard University Press.

Ramasastry, Anita. 1998. "Secrets and Lies? Swiss Banks and International Human Rights," *Vanderbilt Journal of Transnational Law*, 31 (March), 325–456.

Rasmussen, Larry. 1996. *Earth Community, Earth Ethics*. Maryknoll, NY: Orbis Press.

Reilly, P. R. 1998. "Rethinking Risks to Human Subjects in Genetic Research," *American Journal of Human Genetics*, 63, 682–685.

Rich, Ruby. 2000. "Ming Has Two Mommies," *Advocate*, July 18, 45.

Rifkin, Jeremy. *The Biotech Century*. New York: Jeremy P. Tarcher/Putnam.

Riles, Annelise. 2000. *The Network Inside Out*. Ann Arbor: University of Michigan Press.

Risse, Thomas. 2000. "Let's Argue! Communicative Action in World Politics," *International Organization*, 54 (1), 1–39.

Rivera Brooks, Nancy. 2002. "Occidental to Exit Colombia Drilling Site," *Los Angeles Times*, May 8.

Rodley, Nigel. 1993. "Can Armed Opposition Groups Violate Human Rights?" Pp. 297–318 in *Human Rights in the Twenty-first Century: A Global Challenge*, ed. Kathleen Mahoney and Paul Mahoney. Dordrecht: Kluwer-Martinus Nijhoff Publishers.

Rodman, Kenneth A. 2001. *Sanctions Beyond Borders: Multinational Corporations and U.S. Economic Statecraft*. New York: Rowman and Littlefield.

Rodrik, Dani. 2000. "Governance of Economic Globalization." Pp. 347–365 in *Governance in a Globalizing World*, ed. Joseph S. Nye Jr. and John D. Donahue. Washington, DC: Brookings Institution Press.

Rohter, Larry. 1994. "Brazilian Leader Introduces Program to End Slave Labor," *New York Times*, March 13.

———. 2002. "Ford Motor Is Linked to Argentina's 'Dirty War'," *New York Times*, November 27.

Romany, C. 1994. "State Responsibility Goes Private." Pp. 85–115 in *Human Rights of Women*, ed. Rebecca Cook. Philadelphia: University of Pennsylvania Press .

Roosevelt, Margot. 2000. "How Green Is Your Money?," *Time*, 156 (October 16), 79.

Rose, Nikolas. 1999. *Powers of Freedom*. Cambridge, UK: Cambridge University Press.

Rosen, Barry N., Dennis M. Sandler, and David Shani. 1991. "Social Issues and Socially Responsible Investment Behavior: A Preliminary Empirical Investigation," *Journal of Consumer Affairs*, 25 (2), 221–234.

Rothman, D. 1997. "Body Shop," *Sciences*, 37 (6), 17–22.

Rothman, D. J., E. Rose, T. Awaya, B. Cohen, A. Daar, S. L. Dzemeshkevich, C. J. Lee, R. Munro, H. Reyes, S. M. Rothman, K. F. Schoen, N. Scheper-Hughes, Z. Shapira, and H. Smit. 1997. "The Bellagio Task Force Report on Transplantation, Bodily Integrity, and the International Traffic in Organs," *Transplantation Proceedings*, 29, 2739–2745.

Ruggie, John. 1998. "What Makes the World Hang Together? Neo-utilitarianism and the Social Constructivist Challenge," *International Organization*, 52 (Autumn), 855–885.

Samber, Sharon. 2001. "A Priceless Effort," *The Jerusalem Post*, January 5.

Samson, Kurt. 2001a. "Drug Companies Withdraw AIDS Lawsuit," United Press International, April 18.

———. 2001b. "Prisoners' Organs Sold in China," United Press International, June 27.

Sandholtz, Wayne. 1999. "Globalization and the Evolution of Rules." In *Globalization and Governance*, ed. Aseem Prakash and Jeffrey A. Hart. pp. 77–102, London: Routledge.

Sassen, Saskia. 1996. *Losing Control? Sovereignty in an Age of Globalization*. New York: Columbia University Press.

———. 1998. *Globalization and Its Discontents*. New York: New Press.

Sauser, David A. 1997. "The Impact of Social-Responsibility Screens on Investment," *Review of Financial Economics*, 6 (Spring), 137–150.

Schabas, William A. 2003. "Punishment of Non-State Actors in Non-International Armed Conflict," *Fordham International Law Journal*, 26 (4), April.

Scheper-Hughes, Nancy. 1998a. "Truth and Rumor on the Organ Trail," *Natural History*, 107 (October), 48.

———. 1998b. "Organ Trade: The New Cannibalism," *New Internationalist*, 300 (April), 14–17.

———. 2000. "The Global Traffic of Human Organs," *Current Anthropology*, 41 (2), 191–224.

Schmitt, Eric. 2001. "INS Both Jailer and Parent to Child Without a Nation," *New York Times*, June 24.

———. 2002. "Child-Smuggling Ring Broken Up by the U.S. Immigration Agency," *New York Times*, August 13.

Schmitz, Hans Peter, and Kathryn Sikkink. 2002. "International Relations Theory and Human Rights." In *Handbook of International Relations*, ed. Thomas Risse and Beth Simmons. Thousand Oaks, CA: Sage.

Schoenberg, Karl. 2000. *Levi's Children: Coming to Terms with Human Rights in the Global Marketplace.* Boston: Atlantic Monthly Press.

Scholte, Jan Aart. 2000. *Globalization: A Critical Introduction.* New York: St. Martin's Press.

Schrage, Elliot, and Anthony Ewing. 1999. "Engaging the Private Sector," *Forum for Applied Research and Public Policy,* 14 (Spring), 44(8).

Sell, Susan K. 2000. "Structures, Agents and Institutions: Private Corporate Power and the Globalization of Intellectual Property Rights." Pp. 91–106 in *Non-State Actors and Authority in the Global System,* ed. Richard A. Higgott, Geoffrey R. P. Underhill, and Andreas Bieler. New York: Routledge Press.

Sen, Amartya. 1999. "Millions of Women Are Missing," *New York Review of Books,* December 20.

Sengupta, Somini. 2002. "Child Traffickers Prey on Bangladesh," *New York Times,* April 29.

Sharp, R. R., and M. W. Foster. 2000 "Involving Study Populations in Genetic Research," *Journal of Law and Medical Ethics,* 28, 41–51.

Shenon, Philip. 2002. "Claims Panel for Holocaust Is Struggling over Finances," *New York Times,* January 24.

"Shift of Care for Immigrant Children Alone," *New York Times,* November 27, 2002.

Shiva, Vandana. 2001. *Protect or Plunder? Understanding Intellectual Property Rights.* London: Zed Books.

Sikkink, Kathryn. 1986. "Codes of Conduct for Transnational Corporations: The Case of the WHO/UNICEF Code," *International Organization,* 40 (Autumn), 815–40.

_____. 1998. "Transnational Politics, International Relations Theory, and Human Rights," *PS: Political Science and Politics,* XXXI (3), September.

Silverman, Arnold R., and Dorothy E. Weitzman. 1986. "Nonrelative Adoption in the United States; a Brief Survey." Pp. 1–22 in *Adoption in Worldwide Perspective: A Review of Programs, Policies and Legislation in 14 Countries,* ed. R. A. C. Hoksbergen. Lisse: Swets and Zeitlinger.

Simon, Bernard. 2001. "Oil Company Defends Role in Sudan," *New York Times,* October 17.

Simon, Rita J., and Howard Altstein. 1991. "Intercountry Adoptions: Experiences of Families in the United States." Pp. 23–54 in *Intercountry Adoption: A Multinational Perspective,* ed. Howard Altstein and Rita J. Simon. New York: Praeger.

_____ and Howard Altstein. 2000. *Adoption Across Borders: Serving the Children in Transracial and Intercountry Adoptions.* Lanham, MD: Rowman and Littlefield.

Simons, Marlise. 1997. "Swiss Freeze the Assets of Four Argentines Accused in Spain," *New York Times,* July 4, A4.

_____. 2002. "Trial Centers on Role of Press During Rwanda Massacre," *New York Times,* March 3.

_____. 2003. "Sister Nicole Fights the Good Fight as Financier," *New York Times,* April 14.

Singer, Peter W. 2003. *Corporate Warriors: The Rise of the Privatized Military Industry.* Ithaca, NY: Cornell University Press.

_____. 2004a. "The Dogs of War Go Corporate," *The London News Review,* March 19.

_____. 2004b. "War, Profits, and the Vacuum of Law: Privatized Military Firms and International Law," *Columbia Journal of Transnational Law,* 42 (Spring).

Singh, Kavaljit. 2000. *Taming Global Financial Flows: A Citizen's Guide.* New York: St. Martin's Press.

Skene, Loane. 2001. "DNA Data Banks: Iceland and Tonga," *Genetics and Privacy,* Melbourne, Australia.

Smith, Craig. 2001. "Quandary in U.S. over Use of Organs of Chinese Inmates," *New York Times,* November 8.

Smith, Jackie, Charles Chatfield, and Ron Pagnucco (eds.). 1997. *Transnational Social Movements and Global Politics: Solidarity Beyond the State.* Syracuse, NY: Syracuse University Press.

Smith, Lucy. 1993. "Children, Parents and the European Human Rights Convention." Pp. 447–461 in *Parenthood in Modern Society,* ed. J. Eekelaar and P. Sarcevic. Dordrecht, The Netherlands: Martinus Nijhoff Publishers.

Smith, Timothy. 1992. "Pressure from Above," *Business and Society Review,* 81 (Spring), 36.

Snow and Benford. 1988. "Ideology, Frame Resonance and Participant Mobilization." In B. Klandemans, H. P. Knesi, and S. Tarrow (eds.), *From Structure to Action.* Greenwich, CT: JAI Press.

Snow, David and Robert D. Benford. 1992. "Master Frames and Cycles of Protest." In *Frontiers in Social Movement Theory,* ed. Aldon D. Morris and Carol McClurg Mueller. New Haven, CT: Yale University Press.

"Social Investing Roundtable," *Business Ethics*, July/August 1999.

Solomon, Alisa. 2002. "The Gatekeeper: Watch on the INS—Kids in Captivity," *The Village Voice*, week of February 27–March 5.

South Africa. 2000. Hearings on HIV/AIDS Treatment Access at the South African Parliament, May 9 and 10, www.pmg.org.za.

Spiro, Peter. 2004. "International Law and Citizenship. " In *People Out of Place: Rethinking Globalization and the Citizenship Gap*, ed. Alison Brysk and Gershon Shafir. New York: Routledge Press.

"States Act on Jewish Assets in Swiss Banks," *State legislatures*, 23 (7), July-August.

Stavenhagen, Rodolfo. 1996. "Indigenous Rights: Some Conceptual Problems." In *Constructing Democracy: Human Rights, Citizenship, and Society in Latin America*, ed. Elizabeth Jelin and Eric Herschberg. Boulder, CO: Westview Press.

Steiner, Henry, and Philip Alston (eds.). 1986. *International Human Rights in Context*. Oxford: Clarendon Press.

Stephens, Sharon (ed.). 1995. *Children and the Politics of Culture*. Princeton, NJ: Princeton University Press.

Strange, Susan. 1998. *Mad Money*. Manchester, UK: Manchester University Press.

Strom, Stephanie, and Matt Fleischer-Black. 2003. "Company's Pledge to Donate a Drug Is Falling Short," *New York Times*, June 5.

Stumberg, Robert, and William Waren. 1999. "The Boston Tea Party Revisited: Massachusetts Boycotts Burma," *State Legislatures*, 25 (May), 26.

Sullivan, Donna. 1995. "The Public/Private Distinction in International Human Rights Law." In *Women's Rights Human Rights: International Feminist perspectives*, ed. Julie Peters and Andrea Wolper. New York: Routledge Press.

Swarms, Rachel L. 2004. "Ashcroft Considers Granting of Asylum to Abused Women," *New York Times*, March 11.

"Swiss Freeze Assets of Milosevic and Defendants Indicted for War Crimes," *International Enforcement Law Reporter*, August 1999, 15 (8).

Symonides, Janusz (ed.). 1998. *Human Rights: New Dimensions and Challenges*. Paris/Burlington, VT: UNESCO/Ashgate.

Tahk, Youn-Taek. 1986. "Intercountry Adoption Program in Korea; Policy, Law and Services." Pp. 79–92 in *Adoption in Worldwide Perspective: A Review of Programs, Policies and Legislation in 14 Countries*, ed. R. A. C. Hoksbergen. Lisse: Swets and Zeitlinger.

Tamm, Ingrid. 2002. *Diamonds in Peace and War*. Cambridge, MA: World Peace Foundation.

Tarrow, Sidney. 2001. "Transnational Politics: Contention and Institutions in International Politics," *Annual Review of Political Science*, 4.

———. 2002. "From Lumping to Splitting: Specifying Globalization and Resistance." In *Globalization and Resistance: Transnational Dimensions of Social Movements*, ed. Jackie Smith and Hank Johnston. Lanham, MD: Rowman and Littlefield.

Taylor, Marisa. 2002. "Trapped in Security Net," *San Diego Union-Tribune*, August 15.

Textor, Martin R. 1991. "International Adoption in West Germany: A Private Affair." Pp. 109–126 in *Intercountry Adoption: A Multinational Perspective*, ed. Howard Altstein and Rita J. Simon. New York: Praeger.

"The Dilemmas of Experimenting on People," *MIT's Technology Review*, 100 (July), 31.

"The Disgrace: Not Just Noriega's," *New York Times*, November 20, 1990, A20.

"The Search Is On … ," *The Economist*, 342 (January 11).

Thompson, Elizabeth. 2001. "Feds Target Funding for Terrorism," *The Gazette (Montreal)*, October 3, A10.

Thompson, Ginger. 2003. "Littlest Immigrants, Left in Hands of Smugglers," *New York Times*, November 3.

Tickner, Ann. 2001. *Gendering World Politics*. New York: Columbia University Press.

Timmons, Heather. 2003. "Shell to Avoid Oil Drilling at Sites Listed by Unesco," *New York Times*, August 31.

Toebes, Brigit C. A. 1999. *The Right to Health as a Human Rights in International Law*. Antwerp: INTERSENTIA.

Torpey, John (ed.). 2003. *Politics and the Past: On Repairing Historical Injustices*. Lanham, MD: Rowman and Littlefield.

Treaster, Joseph B. 2002. "Court Favors Families in Suits over Holocaust-Era Insurance," *New York Times*, September 30.

_____. 2003a. "Holocaust Survivors' Insurance Ordeal," *New York Times*, April 8.

_____. 2003b. "Holocaust Insurance Effort Is Costing More Than It Wins," *New York Times*, September 17.

Uehling, Mark. 2003. "Decoding Estonia," *Bio-IT World*, February 10.

United Nations. 2001. Security Council, 4358th Meeting. SC/7158, September 28.

United Nations Children's Fund. 1998. *Newsline—Summarizing the Progress of Nations 1998*, July 8, www.unicef.org.

_____. 1999. *State of the World's Children*.

_____. 2001a. *A Decade of Transition*. November 30.

_____. 2001b. *Beyond Child Labour, Affirming Rights*.

_____. 2001c. *Profiting From Abuse*.

_____. 2001d. *Progress Since the World Summit*.

_____. 2002. *State of the World's Children*.

_____. 2003. *State of the World's Children*.

United Nations High Commission on Refugees. 2000. *The State of the World's Refugees 2000*. New York: Oxford University Press.

United Nations High Commission on Refugees. 2001. *Trends in Unaccompanied and Separated Children Seeking Asylum in Europe, 2000*. Geneva: UNHCR.

U.S. Congress. 1995. Senate Foreign Relations Committee. "Human Organ Trade in China," Washington, May 4.

_____. 1997. Senate, Committee on Banking, Housing, and Urban Affairs, Swiss banks and Attempts to Recover Assets Belonging to the Victims of the Holocaust: Hearing Before the Committee on Banking, Housing, and Urban Affairs, United States Senate, 105th Congress, 1st Session. Washington, DC: Government Printing Office.

_____. 1998. House of Representatives, Joint Hearings Before the Committee on Government Reform and Oversight and the Committee on International Relations, "The Sale of Body Parts By the People's Republic of China," 105th Congress, 2nd Session, June 4 and 16.

_____. 2001a. "Hearings on the Adminstration's 'National Money Laundering Strategy for 2001,'" Washington, September 26.

_____. 2001b. House of Representatives, House International Relations Committee, Subcommittee on International Operations and Human Rights, "Sale of Human Organs in China," June 27.

U.S. Department of Justice. (n.d.) *Immigration of Adopted and Prospective Adoptive Children*, M–249.

U.S. Department of State. 2000a. Office of Holocaust Assets Issues, Fact Sheet, August 18.

_____. 2000b. Ambassador J.D. Bindenagel, "Remembrance, Responsibility and the Future: Fulfilling the Promise of Justice through Dignified Payments," September 22.

_____. 2003. *Trafficking in Persons Report*, www.state.gov.

Vargas Llosa, Mario. 2001. "Crossing the Moral Boundary," *New York Times*, January 7.

Vayrynen, Raimo. 1999. "Norms, Compliance, and Enforcement in Global Governance." In *Globalization and Global Governance*, ed Raimo Vayrynen. Lanham, MD: Rowman and Littlefield.

Verschoor, C. 1998. "A Study of the Link Between a Corporation's Financial Performance and Its Commitment to Ethics," *Journal of Business Ethics*, October.

Vincent, Isabel. 1997. *Hitler's Silent Partners*. New York: William Morrow.

Vonk, M. Elizabeth, Peggy J. Sims, and Larry Nackerud. 1999. "Political and Personal Aspects of Intercountry Adoption of Chinese Children in the United States," *Families in Society: The Journal of Contemporary Human Services*, 80 (September), 496.

Wade, Nicholas. 2003. "Unusual Use of DNA Aided in Serial Killer Search," *New York Times*, June 5.

Wapner, Paul. 2000. "The Normative Promise of Nonstate Actors." In Wapner and Lester Edwin Ruiz (eds.), *Principled World Politics*. Lanham, MD: Rowman and Littlefield. pp. 261–274.

Weber, Max. 1964. *Theory of Social and Economic Organization*. Glencoe, IL: Free Press.

Weijer, C., G. Goldsand, and E. J. Emanuel. 1999. "Protecting Communities in Research," *Nature Genetics*, 23, 275–280.

Weiner, Tim. 2003. "U.S. Youths Rebel at Harsh School in Costa Rica and Many Head for Home," *New York Times*, May 27.

Weissbrodt, David. 2002. "Human Rights and Responsibility of Individual and Non-state Entities." Pp. 239–262 in *Justice Pending: Indigenous Peoples and Other Good Causes*, ed. Gudmundur Alfredsson and Maria Stavropolou. The Hague: Martinus Nijhoff.

Werlau, Maria. 1997. "Foreign Investment in Cuba: The Limits of Commercial Engagement," *World Affairs*, 160 (2), 51.

Whitaker, Barbara. 2001. "Judge Hearing Custody Fight Would Keep Thai Boy in U.S.," *New York Times*, June 5.

_____. 2001. "Ashcroft Wants Thai Boy Used by Smugglers to Stay in U.S.," *New York Times*, July 24, 2001.

Wilson, David, Paul Cawthorne, Nathan Ford, and Saree Aongsonwang. 1999. "Global Trade and Access to Medicines: AIDS Treatments in Thailand," *The Lancet*, 354 (November 27), 1893.

Wines, Michael. 2003a. "14 Arrested in the Sale of Organs for Transplant," *New York Times*, December 8.

_____. 2003b. "AIDS Blamed for Legions of Orphans in Africa," *New York Times*, November 27.

_____. 2003c. "Pact Expands Generic Drugs in South Africa to Fight AIDS," *New York Times*, December 11.

Winston, Morton Emmanuel. 2000. *Indivisibility and Interdependence of Human Rights*. University of Nebraska, International Human Rights and Human Diversity Initiative Monograph Series, Volume 2, Number 1, text of public lecture presented September 3, 1999.

Winters, Jeffrey. 1999. "It Pays to Think Big: History Favors Dictators Who Take Billions, Not Millions," *Time International*, 153 (May 24), 26.

Wintersberger, Helmut. 2000. "Family Citizenship or Citizenship for Children? Childhood Perspectives and Policies." Pp. 174–188 in *The New Citizenship of the Family*, ed. Henry Cavanna. Aldershot: Ashgate.

World Health Organization. 1994. *Legislative Responses to Organ Transplantation*. Amsterdam: Martinus Nijhoff/Kluwer.

Wright, Robin. 2000. "In Ecuador, a Coalition of Savvy Children," *Los Angeles Times*, January 31.

Yamey, Gavin. 2001. "US Trade Action Threatens Brazilian AIDS Programme," *British Medical Journal*, 322 (February 17), 383.

Zakaria, Fareed. 2003. *The Future of Freedom: Illiberal Democracy at Home and Abroad*. New York: W. W. Norton.

Zhao, Yilu. 2002. "Immersed in 2 Worlds, New and Old," *New York Times*, April 9.

Index

A

advocacy groups, 8
AIDS pharmaceuticals
    Brazil and, 97
    Doctors Without Borders, 95
    science and globalization, 94–100
    South Africa, 95–96
    Thailand and, 97
asset control, international finance, 79–85

B

bin Laden, Osama, 83
Brazil, AIDS pharmaceuticals and, 97
Burma, 78

C

Calvert funds, 73, 75
changes, private authority, 117–121
Child Citizenship Act of 2000, 56
child sex trafficking, 45
children across borders, 29–58
    children's rights regime, 36–40
        global adovacy groups, 39
        globalization of personhood, 36–40
        international norms for, 38
        issues networked, 39
    dependent rights, 46–49
        United Nations HIgh Commission
            on Refugees, 46–47
    displaced workers, 40–42
    exploitative enforcement, 44–46
    families as private authority, 31–35
    family reunification, 41

    globalization, 35–36
    identity rights, 49–58
        China, 55
        international adoption regime,
            53–54
        Korea, 54
    illegal parents, 41
    migration, 35–36
    patriarchy, 58–59
    patrimony and, 34
    personhood, 58–59
    refugee minors, 46–49
        dependent rights, 48–49
    rights, 35–36
    trafficking, 42–44
    transnational adoption, 49–58
children's migration, 10–11
children's rights regime
    children across borders, 36–40
    global adovacy groups, 39
    globalization of personhood, 36–40
    international norms for, 38
    issues networked, 39
China
    identity rights, 55
    transplant trafficking, 102
citizenship, 32
civil society, norm change in, 15–21
    feminist theory and, 18
Clinton, Bill, 83
coalitions, 30
Cold War, 6, 82
constructing norms, 21–28
constructing norms in global civil society,
    21–24

contesting private authority global civil society, 24–27
Convention on the Rights of the Child, 37
Cuban Family Code, 49

D

DeBeers, 79
dependent rights, children across borders, 46–49
diamond industry, 78–79
dictatorships, 8
displaced workers, children across borders, 40–42
Doctors Without Borders, 8
    AIDS pharmaceuticals, 95

E

Eli Lilly Company, 99
enforcement
    children across borders, 44–46
Europe international adoption, 51
expanding rights, 21–28
    norm change in global civil society, 21–24
exploitative enforcement, children across borders, 44–46

F

families as private authority, 31–35
Feinstein, Dianne, 46
feminist theory, global civil society and, 18

G

genetic research, science and medicine globalization, 106–115
Germany
    international finance, 63
    reparations, 64–72
global adovacy groups, children's rights regime, 39
global civil society, 16
    international political economy and, 18–19
global governance and private authority, 117–128
globalization, 1–14
    branches, 8–10
    children across borders, 35–36
    global perspective, 10–12
    human rights struggle, 12–14

roots and responses, 4–8
Gonzalez, Elian, 10, 48–49
Green Century, 73
guardianship, 58

H

habeas corpus, science and medicine globalization, 115–116
Hague Convention Conference, 40
Holocaust, 4–6
    international finance, 63–64
    international response to, 6
    medicine during, 5
    refugees, 5–6
human rights
    private wrongs, 12–14
    science and medicine globalization, 90–94
Human Rights Watch, 8

I

identity rights
    children across borders, 49–58
    China, 55
    India, 58
    international adoption regime, 53–54
    Korea, 54
    Sweden, 57
Immigration and Naturalization Service (INS), 27
India identity rights, 58
information politics, 26, 62
institutionalization, private authority, 120–121
Inter-country Adoption Act of 2000, 56
intercountry adoptions since World War II, 50
international adoption
    Europe, 51
    identity rights, 53–54
International Concerns Committee, 52–53
international finance
    about, 61–62
    asset control, 79–85
    Germany, 63
    global finance norms, 63–64
    global governance from below, 72–79
    Holocaust, 63–64
    human rights versus business as usual, 63–64
    information politics, 62
    profits and principles, 85–87

reparations, 64–72
    oil companies, 64–72
    socially responsible investment, 72–79
    state sanctions, 79–85
international norms for children's rights regime, 38
international political economy, global civil society and, 18–19
international response to Holocaust, 6
internationalism, 7
Iraq transplant trafficking, 101

K

Kindertransport, 6
Korea identity rights, 54
Krupp, Alfred, 5

L

League of Nations, 37
leverage, 30

M

medical globalization, 89–116
medicine and globalization, 89–116
    about, 89–90
    AIDS pharmaceuticals, 94–100
    genetic research, 106–115
    habeas corpus, 115–116
    during Holocaust, 5
    human rights and, 90–94
    scientific research and, 12
    transplant trafficking, 100–106
migration, children across borders, 35–36
moral induction, 59

N

Nader, Ralph, 73
Nestle, 11
New Africa Fund, Calvert, 73
nonstate authority, in global civil society, 15–21
norm change in global civil society, 15–28
    civil society and nonstate authority, 15–21
    constructing norms, expanding rights, 21–24
    contesting private authority, 24–27
Novartis, 99

O

oil companies reparations, 64–72
Organization for Economic Cooperation and Development (OECD), 47
orphans, 51

P

patriarchy, children across borders, 58–59
patrimony, children across borders and, 34
personhood, children across borders, 58–59
Pioneer Fund, 73
principles, international finance, 85–87
private authority
    changes, 117–121
    families as, 31–35
    global governance and, 117–128
    institutionalization, 120–121
    needs, 121–125
    symbolic politics, 119
private wrongs, 1–14
    branches, 8–10
    global perspective, 10–12
    globalization and, 1–14
    Holocaust, 4–6
    human rights struggle, 12–14
    roots and responses, 4–8
profits, international finance, 85–87
Puhl, Emil, 5

Q

Quakers, 73

R

Rasche, Karl, 5
refugees, Holocaust, 5–6
reparations, international finance, 64–72
rights
    children across borders, 35–36
    expansion, 21–28
        norm change in global civil society, 21–24
Russia transplant trafficking, 101

S

science and globalization, 89–116
    about, 89–90
    AIDS pharmaceuticals, 94–100
    genetic research, 106–115

habeas corpus, 115–116
human rights and, 90–94
transplant trafficking, 100–106
scientific research and medicine, 12
September 11, 2001 attacks, 83
Seuss, Dr., 29
Shell, 11
Sierra Leone, 81
Social Investment Forum, 73
South Africa, AIDS pharmaceuticals, 95–96
state sanctions, international finance, 79–85
Sudan, 81
Sweden identity rights, 57
symbolic politics, private authority, 119

T

Thailand
    AIDS pharmaceuticals, 97
    transplant trafficking, 101
trafficking
    child sex, 45
    children across borders, 42–44
    transplant, 100–106
        China, 102
        Iraq, 101
        Russia, 101
        Thailand, 101
        Turkey, 101
transnational adoption, children across borders, 49–58
transnational issue-networks, 7
transplant trafficking
    China, 102
    Iraq, 101
    Russia, 101
    science and medicine globalization, 100–106
    Thailand, 101
    Turkey, 101
Turkey transplant trafficking, 101

U

UN Convention on the Rights of the Child, 30–31, 53
United Nations Development Programme (UNDP), 33
United Nations HIgh Commission on Refugees, 46–47
Universal Declaration of Human Rights, 9

W

World Trade Organization (WTO), 27
World War II, intercountry adoptions since, 50

Y

Yugoslavia, 85